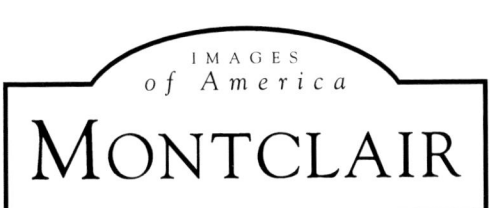

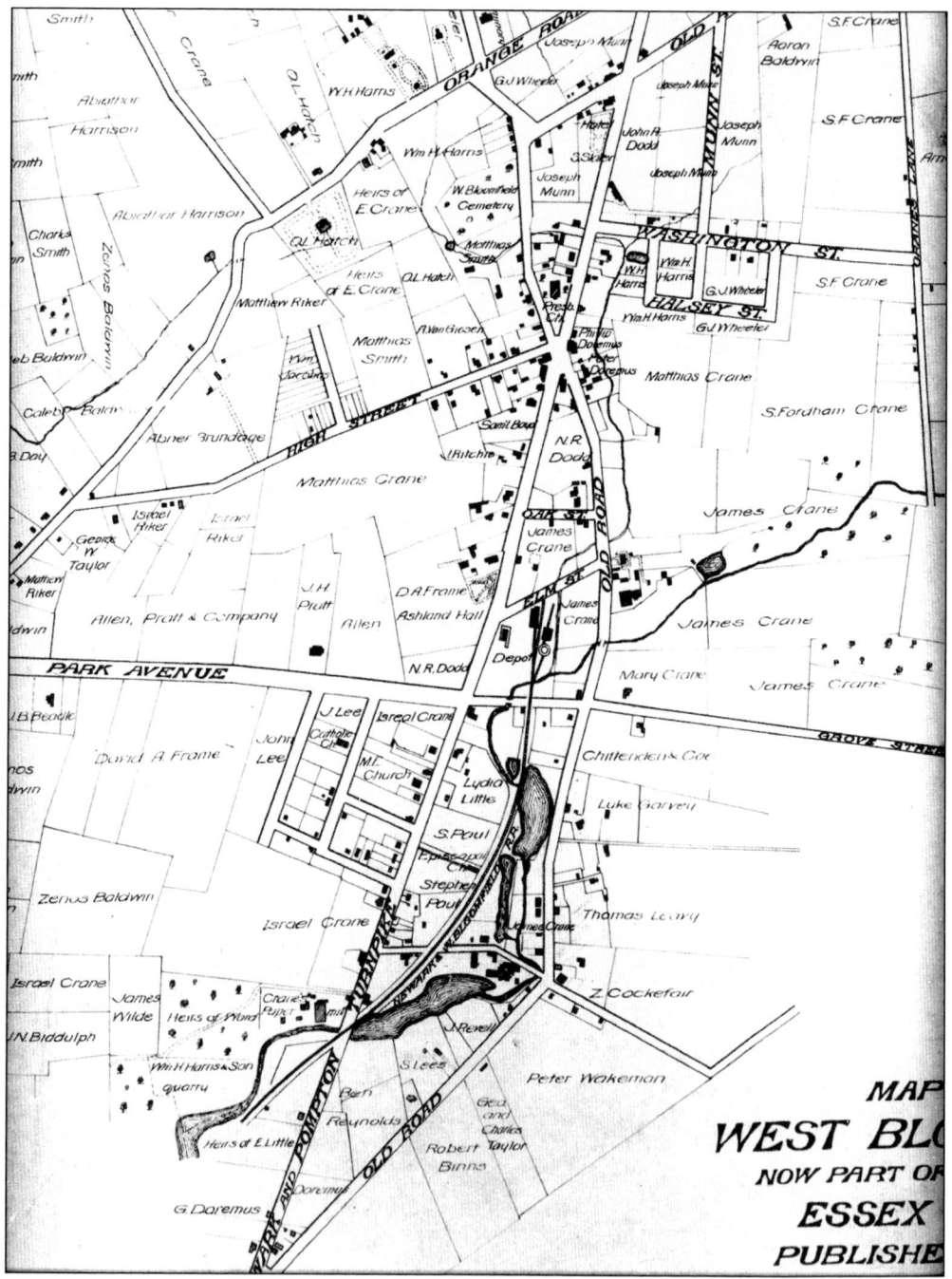

WEST BLOOMFIELD, 1857. This is the center of the community that in three years will become known as Montclair. The depot for the new railroad is in place. The name J.H. Pratt, on Park Avenue, indicates that the first commuters have arrived. Park Avenue will become Elm Street after Pratt plants trees there. The Newark and Pompton Turnpike (now, Bloomfield Avenue) provides a straight alternative to what was known as the old road, which wound through town. Four churches, a hotel, and several schools are in evidence. Just beyond this section of the map lies Mountain Avenue (now, South Mountain Avenue) awaiting its mansions.

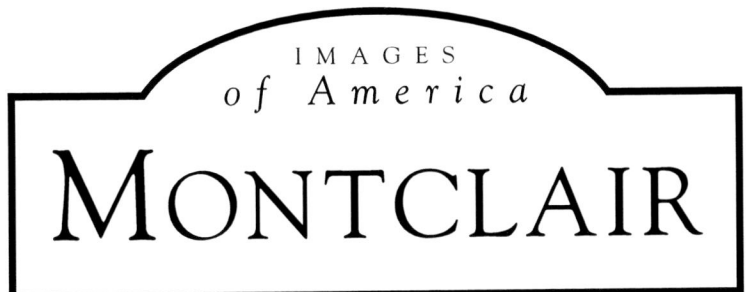

Elizabeth Shepard and Royal F. Shepard Jr.

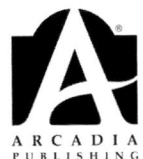

Copyright © 2003 by Elizabeth Shepard and Royal F. Shepard Jr.
ISBN 978-0-7385-1349-2

Published by Arcadia Publishing
Charleston, South Carolina

Printed in the United States of America

Library of Congress Catalog Card Number: 2003110753

For all general information contact Arcadia Publishing at:
Telephone 843-853-2070
Fax 843-853-0044
E-mail sales@arcadiapublishing.com
For customer service and orders:
Toll-Free 1-888-313-2665

Visit us on the Internet at www.arcadiapublishing.com

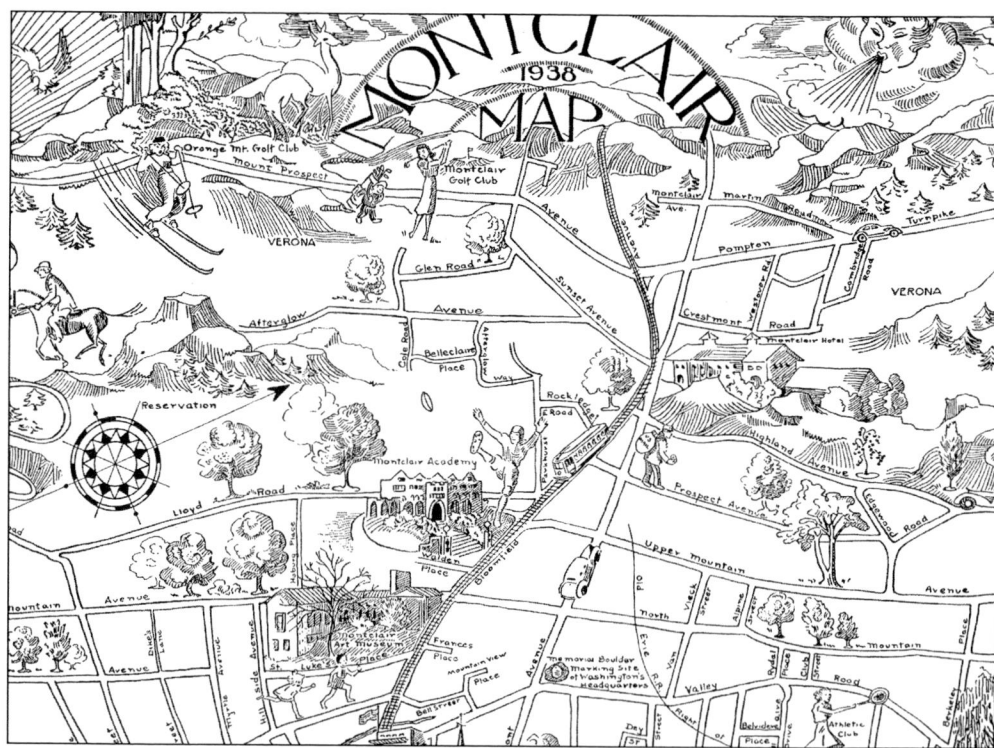

A LIVELY LANDSCAPE. Montclair's mountain receives imaginative treatment in this 1938 pictorial map. Really in Verona, the Montclair Golf Club appears to be located in the High Sierra. The Montclair Hotel is still there but is about to give way to the Rockcliff Apartments. Farther down the slope, the Washington Boulder is in place to remind us that George Washington slept here. Montclair Academy and the Montclair Art Museum loom large. (Map copyright © 1938 Committee for the Maternal Health Center of Montclair.)

CONTENTS

Acknowledgments		6
Introduction		7
1.	Pioneers	9
2.	New Pioneers	19
3.	Multicultural Heritage	31
4.	Arts	43
5.	Education	55
6.	Religious Life	69
7.	Government	81
8.	Commerce	89
9.	Organizations	103
10.	Montclair Views	117

ACKNOWLEDGMENTS

Our thanks are extended especially to the Montclair Public Library, the source of the great majority of images in this book, for allowing us to scan its materials and more generally for providing access to the library's extensive local history collection. More particularly, our thanks are due to William T. Fischer, who is in charge of the collection. We are also grateful to the Montclair Historical Society and director Alicia Schattemann for access to the society's collection and for sharing news of our project through the society newsletter. We appreciate the assistance of Mark Porter, editor of the *Montclair Times*, in clearing the way for the use of photographs that appeared in that newspaper.

Individuals and organizations that provided us with photographs to scan have been credited in connection with particular images. In addition, we wish to thank Dr. Joel Schwartz of Montclair State University for pointing our way to useful materials and to Donato DiGeronimo and Marisa S. Trubiano, assistant professor of Spanish and Italian at Montclair State University, for sharing photographs that are part of the Italians of Montclair research project. Rose Shaw of the Evangelical Covenant Church and members of the Franciose family were among those who helped us obtain information.

Finally, we appreciate the advice and encouragement of John Chance, former Montclair township historian, and of Philip Jaeger, who suggested that we undertake this book and whose own book, *Montclair: A Postcard History of Its Past*, has proven a source both of information and inspiration.

INTRODUCTION

For many centuries the Lenape, or "original people," hunted in the area that is now Montclair and made trails as they passed through on their trips to and from the seashore. A more settled population arrived when people from Connecticut founded Newark on the banks of the Passaic River in 1666. First to settle in the area that became Montclair were Azariah Crane, his wife, Mary, and their son, Nathaniel. The Cranes built a home near the present intersection of Myrtle Avenue and Orange Road c. 1694. The name Cranetown came to be used for the hamlet that rose around these pioneers. Within a few years, people of Dutch descent settled to the north and gave their neighborhood the name Speertown. Both settlements remained part of Newark until 1812, when they were included in the new township of Bloomfield. West Bloomfield was the name applied to the former Cranetown area until some residents persuaded the post office and the railroad to adopt the name Montclair in 1860. It was not until 1868 that Montclair became a separate municipality.

Yet over the previous century and a half, the area had been nurturing its own distinct heritage. During the Revolutionary War, the mountain provided lookout points for observing the movements of the British troops to the east. A strong tradition holds that General Washington himself stayed at a home at the present corner of Valley Road and Claremont Avenue and that he looked out from the cliffs above with his spyglass in October 1780. In 1796, Israel Crane built a large home on present-day Glenridge Avenue and soon opened nearby the first general store. Crane was also instrumental in building the town's main street and in establishing its first manufacturing concern. Meanwhile, the farms became known for their apples and the production of cider.

Well into the 19th century, Montclair remained a farming community with the people in its northern parts still speaking Dutch and only a few small business establishments in its central area. This rural setting ended with the coming of the railroads. The history prepared by Col. Frederick Harris for a celebration of the national centennial in 1876 declared, "These railways have completely changed the character of our town, from a sparsely settled agricultural region to a community of elegant suburban homes." Although many of the newcomers had lived in New York and made their fortunes there, most were themselves the products of small towns. They shared with the natives a preference for a quiet, neighborly community of private homes linked by the railroads to the resources of the metropolis. Many were New Englanders who brought with them a "city on the hill" vision of creating a model community. Not all the commuters were rich, and those who were tended to avoid ostentation. Accounts of the town stressed that Montclair was a place where people were valued not for their wealth but for their character and talent. Among the talented were artists from a colony who began to make their homes here *c.* 1870 and whose leading figure was landscape painter George Inness. By the mid-20th century, Montclair could boast as many as a 150 names in *Who's Who in America*.

Montclair was never composed of just one sort of people. To the descendants of the British and Dutch were added Germans, Irish, Scandinavians, Italians, and large numbers of African Americans from the South. The town also grew increasingly diverse with respect to occupations and income levels. Hundreds of residents performed the services and ran the businesses that made it possible for the commuters to live here. Such diversity was not achieved without stress and expressions of social prejudice. However, Montclair has gained a reputation over the years as a place where people work hard at realizing the American dream of an inclusive society. A special effort has been made in this book to depict the rich human mix that has gone into the shaping of the community.

Despite its nearness to Newark and New York, Montclair quickly developed its own distinctive cultural institutions. Its schools, religious organizations, art museum, libraries, theatrical groups, and musical programs drew people from a wide area. Montclair is unusual, too, in its strong sense of ongoing identity. Unlike many residential suburbs that rose up in later times, Montclair was not laid out almost overnight from open fields where no community had existed earlier. It is a seasoned place whose sense of continuity combines with a shared focus on contemporary issues. The presence of the same local newspaper since 1877 has enhanced the town's self-awareness.

The images shown here reflect earlier eras in Montclair's story. In later years Montclair has continued to change. At the end of World War II, the town still lay near the outer rim of the metropolitan area. Now the rim stretches far beyond. The aim of keeping a community mostly of single-family homes with spacious gardens and a canopy of trees has contended with ceaseless pressure toward increased density and urbanization. Still, Montclair retains its beauty and the character of a family-centered place. Harry Trippett, who served as town clerk for 50 years, set the standard for us: "Montclair . . . is primarily a residential center . . . where brains and good manners, not bank balances, give rating to her citizens; where the exchange of thoughts are considered of more value than the exchange of commodities. She is essentially a home town."

One
PIONEERS

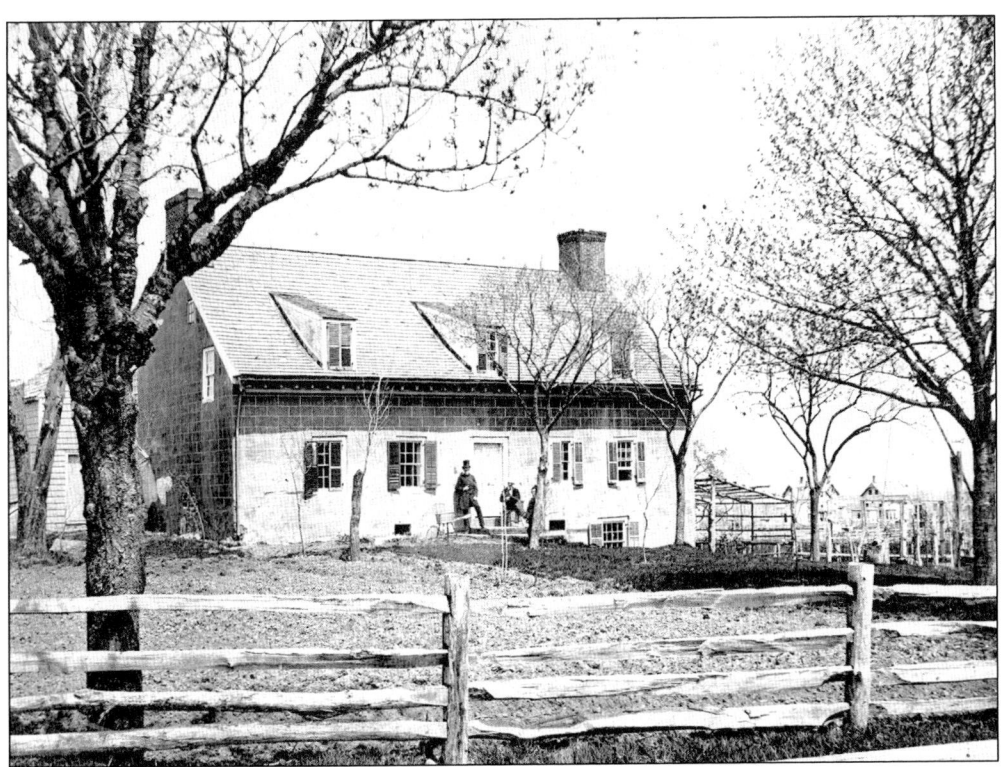

WASHINGTON'S HEADQUARTERS. Built c. 1740, this was the home of William and Mercy Crane when George Washington is said to have lodged here in October 1780. While Lafayette attempted to raid a British supply depot on Staten Island, Washington sent troops to guard Crane's Gap on First Mountain and posted lookouts atop the cliffs. Located at what is now the northwest corner of Claremont Avenue and Valley Road, the house was torn down c. 1900.

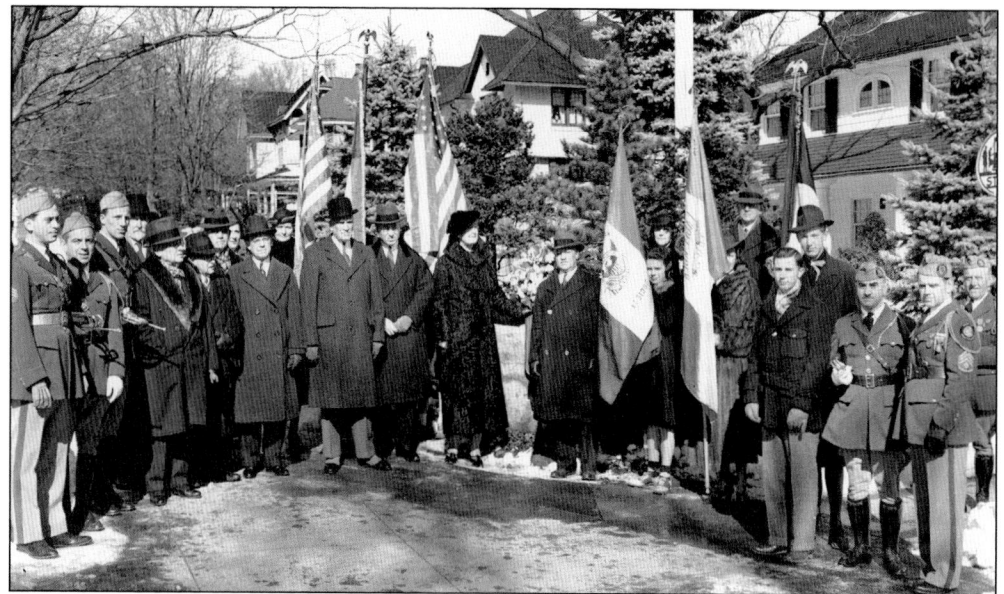

THE DEDICATION OF THE WASHINGTON BOULDER. By 1922, the home of town physician Dr. Maurice Cohen stood on the site of the old Crane homestead. However, George Washington's presence here was not forgotten. The local chapters of the Sons and Daughters of the American Revolution arranged for a suitable memorial on a small parcel of land donated by William Cohen. A commemorative plaque was attached to a boulder that lay on the property. The memorial remains.

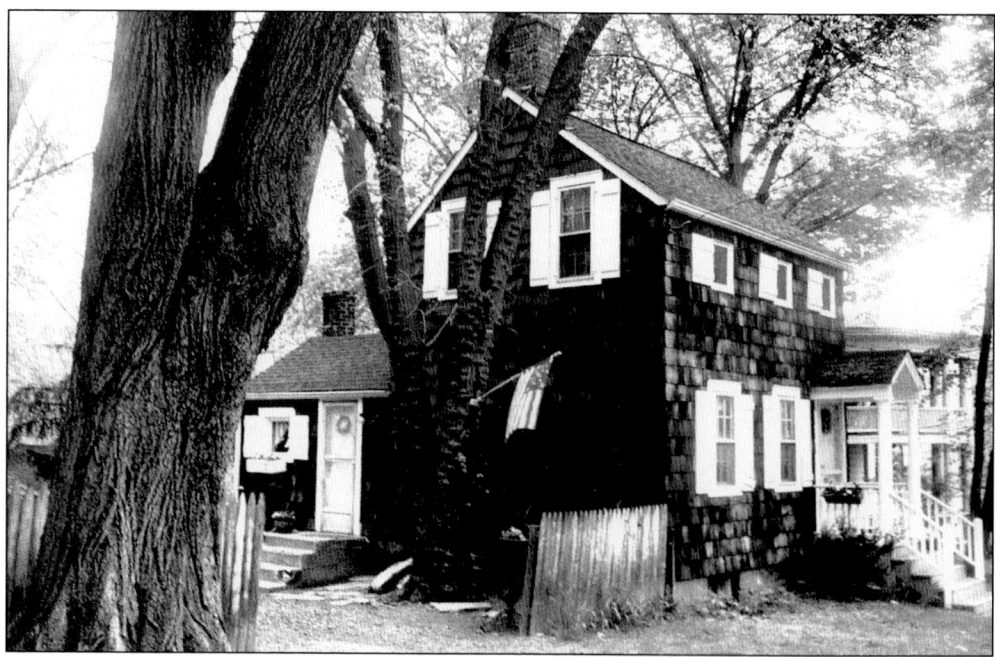

THE JAMES HOWE HOUSE. In 1831, "Major" Nathaniel Crane bequeathed a house and six acres to "James How, a colored man, late a slave, whom I manumitted." Now more than two centuries old, the house stands at 369 Claremont Avenue. It is probably the first house owned by an African American in Montclair.

ISRAEL CRANE. The grandson of William and Mercy Crane, Israel Crane became known as "King Crane" for his many enterprises. He opened a general merchandise store c. 1800 on what is now Glenridge Avenue. The construction of the Newark–Pompton turnpike and a cotton mill on Toney's Brook were among his other interests.

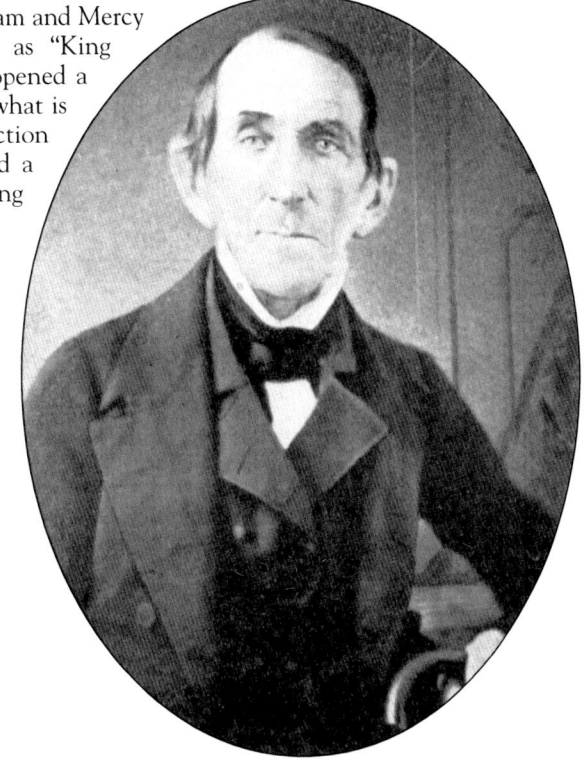

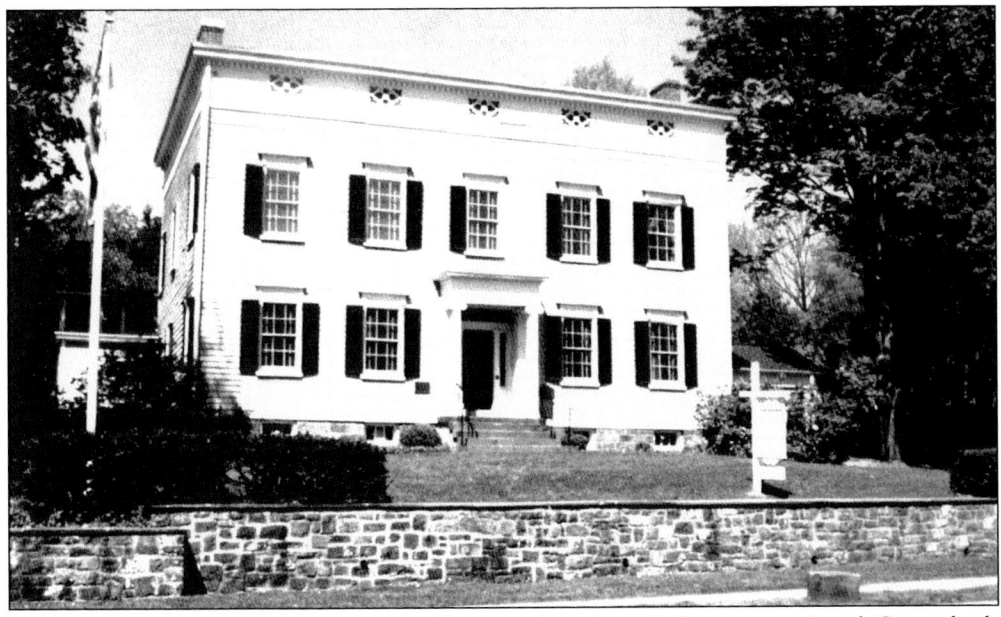

THE ISRAEL CRANE HOUSE. His neighbors predicted ruin when young Israel Crane built the largest house c. 1796. But his business acumen outstripped their prophecy. Later home to the YWCA, the house was scheduled for demolition when it was rescued and moved from Glenridge Avenue to Orange Road. Since then it has served as a museum maintained by the Montclair Historical Society.

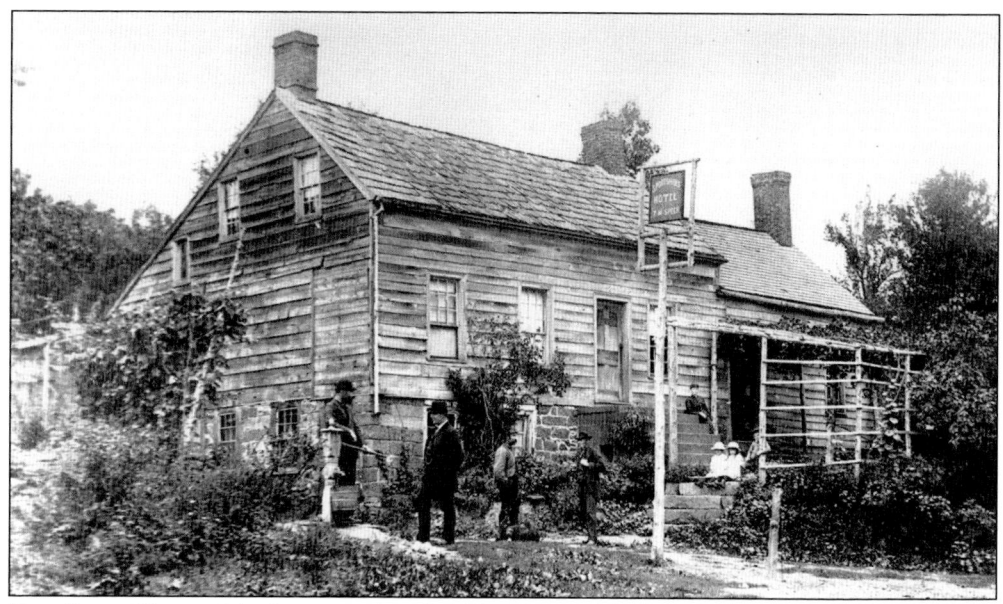

THE SPEER HOUSE. The homestead at 612 Upper Mountain Avenue was probably built about the time Rynier Speer married Maria Jacobusse in 1788. Although the house stands just inside Little Falls, members of the Speer family owned much of Upper Montclair, which was known as Speertown into the 1870s. This home came to serve as both residence and tavern, as is attested by the Sportsman's Hotel sign in this 19th-century photograph.

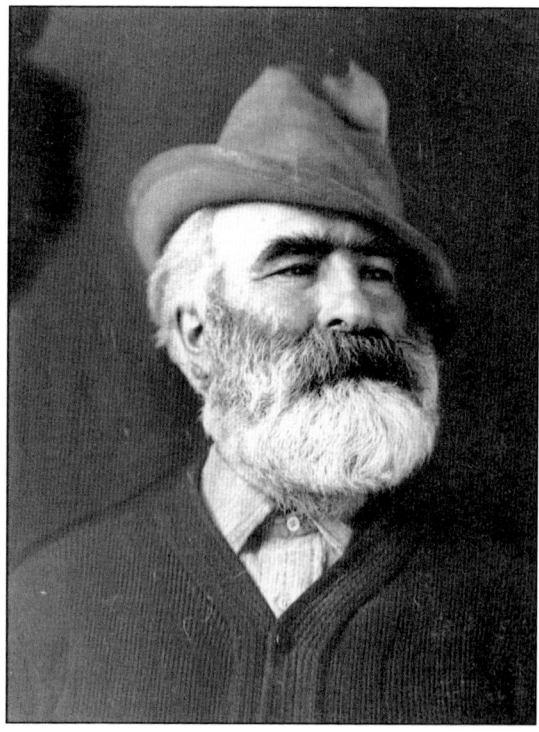

PETER GARRETT SPEER. Here and in other pictures, Pete Speer brings to mind a figure in a Frans Hals portrait. Fond of shooting crows behind his home, he bestowed on his daughter, Caroline, and her husband, Thomas Van Reyper, the land on which they built the Italian Villa now housing offices of Montclair State University at 848 Valley Road.

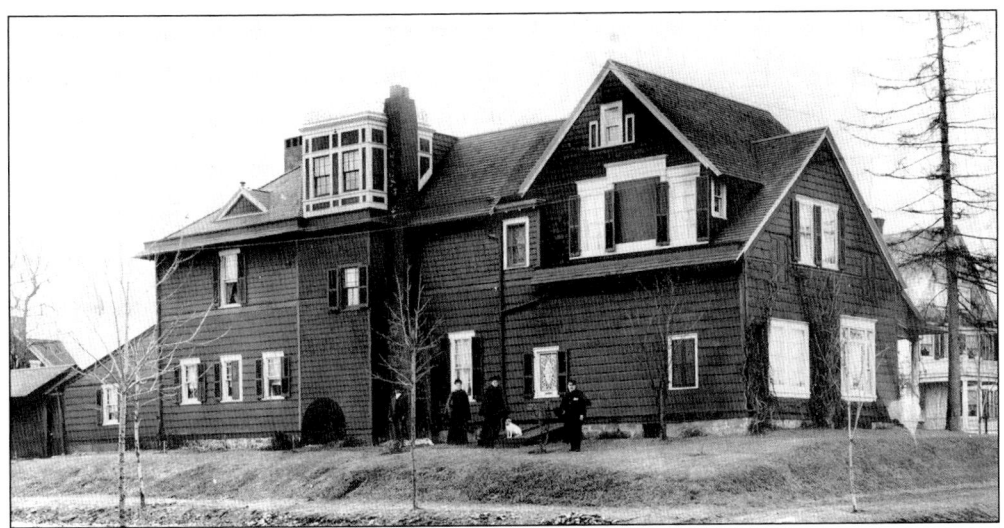

THE VAN WINKLE HOME. Johannes Van Winkle built his home here c. 1740. In this photograph, the Van Winkle house at 771 Valley Road was greatly changed and was owned by the Da Cunha family. Viewed from the rear, the original stone foundation can be seen. Also visible are the Valley Road trolley tracks. Running to the left, Alexander Avenue appears to be a narrow dirt road.

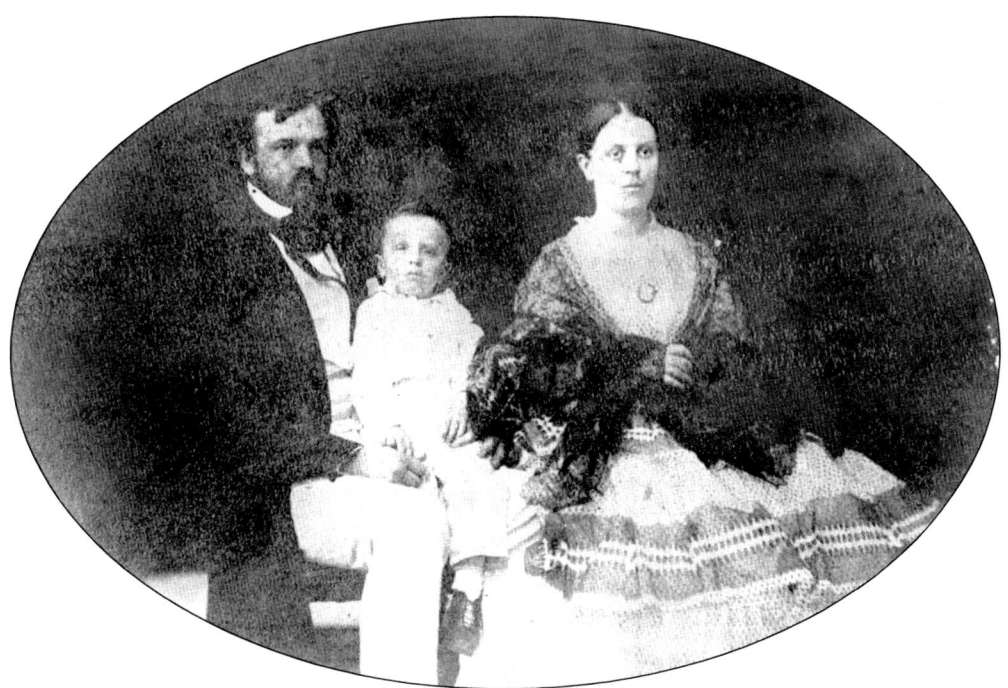

THE AMOS BROADNAX FAMILY. When Montclair became a separate township in 1868, Amos Broadnax was chosen chairman of the Township Committee. Thus, he is often called Montclair's first mayor. He and his family also lived in the house at 771 Valley Road.

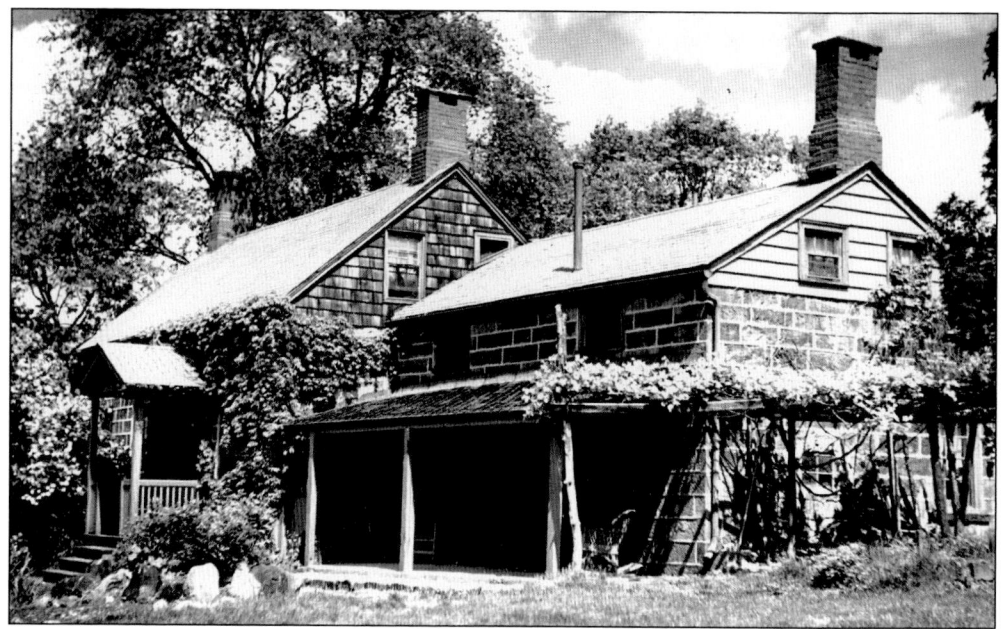

THE DANIEL SIGLER HOME. Most early Dutch homes faced south or east. Facing south, this one at 471 Valley Road was built c. 1785 as the home of Daniel and Jane Sigler. Much later, it was the home of the DeForest family. Lee DeForest pioneered the development of radio. The dwelling remains as one of Montclair's better preserved pioneer homes.

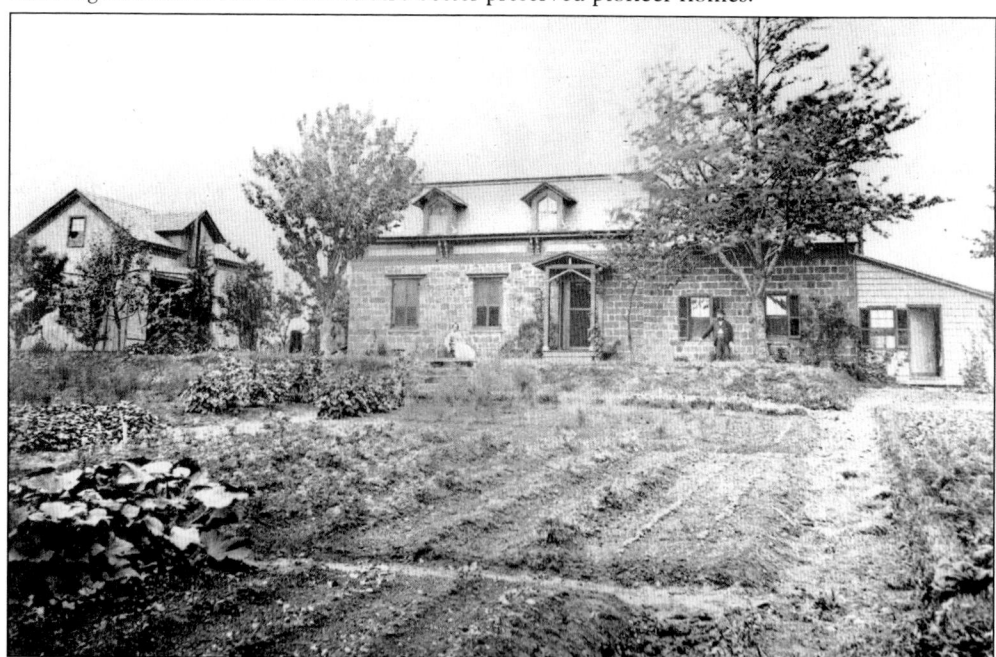

THE GARRABRANDT HOUSE. Perpendicular to the avenue and facing east is this very early home at 149 Watchung Avenue. Its first residents were Nicholas and Mary Garrabrandt. At the time of this photograph in 1865, the house belonged to Abraham Zeek, whose garden lies in the foreground. Local historian Mary Arny, who lived here for many years with her husband, Robert, wrote a book about their home called *Seasoned with Salt*.

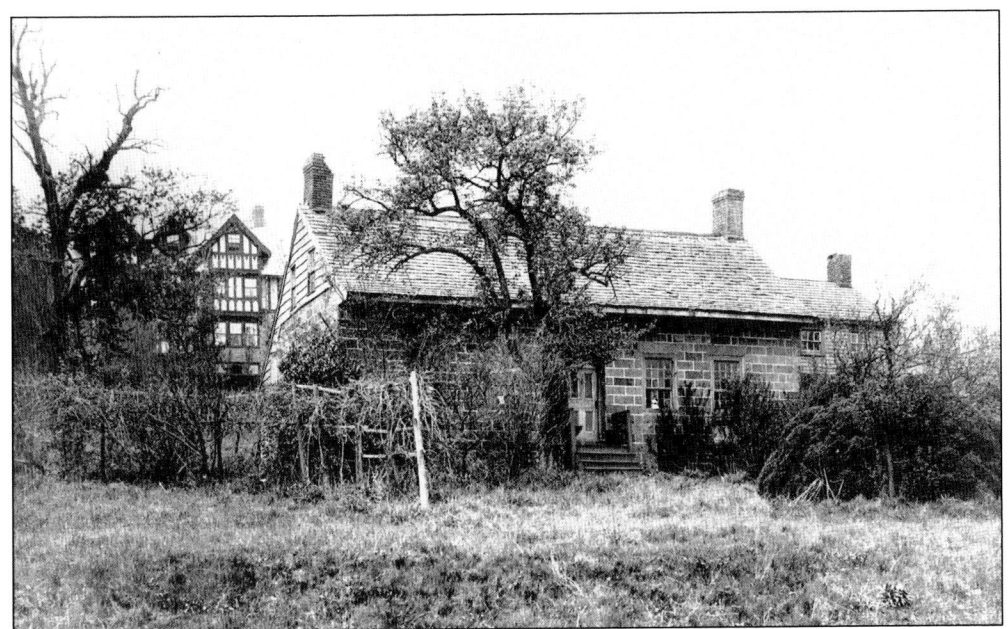

THE EGBERT HOUSE, AN EARLY VIEW. In Colonial times the Egberts owned much land south of Watchung Avenue and west of Midland Avenue. This red sandstone home was built by Walling Egbert in 1786. It is pictured early in the 20th century, when the property had fallen into neglect. The boxwood bush to the right was planted in 1833 and flourishes today several times as large.

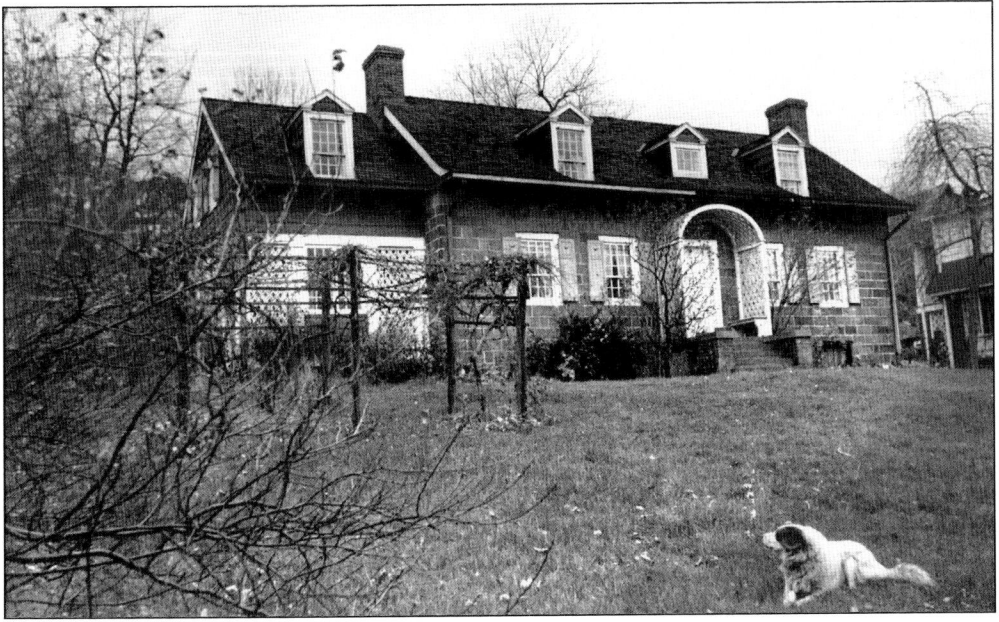

THE EGBERT HOUSE, A LATER VIEW. In 1910, architect A.F. Norris presided over the restoration and enlargement of the Egbert House. His work was described in *American Homes and Gardens*, and the house received mention in *The Federal Writers Guide to New Jersey* and *Collier's Encyclopedia*. The dog overseeing the property in this 1943 photograph is named Stag. The house stands at 128 North Mountain Avenue.

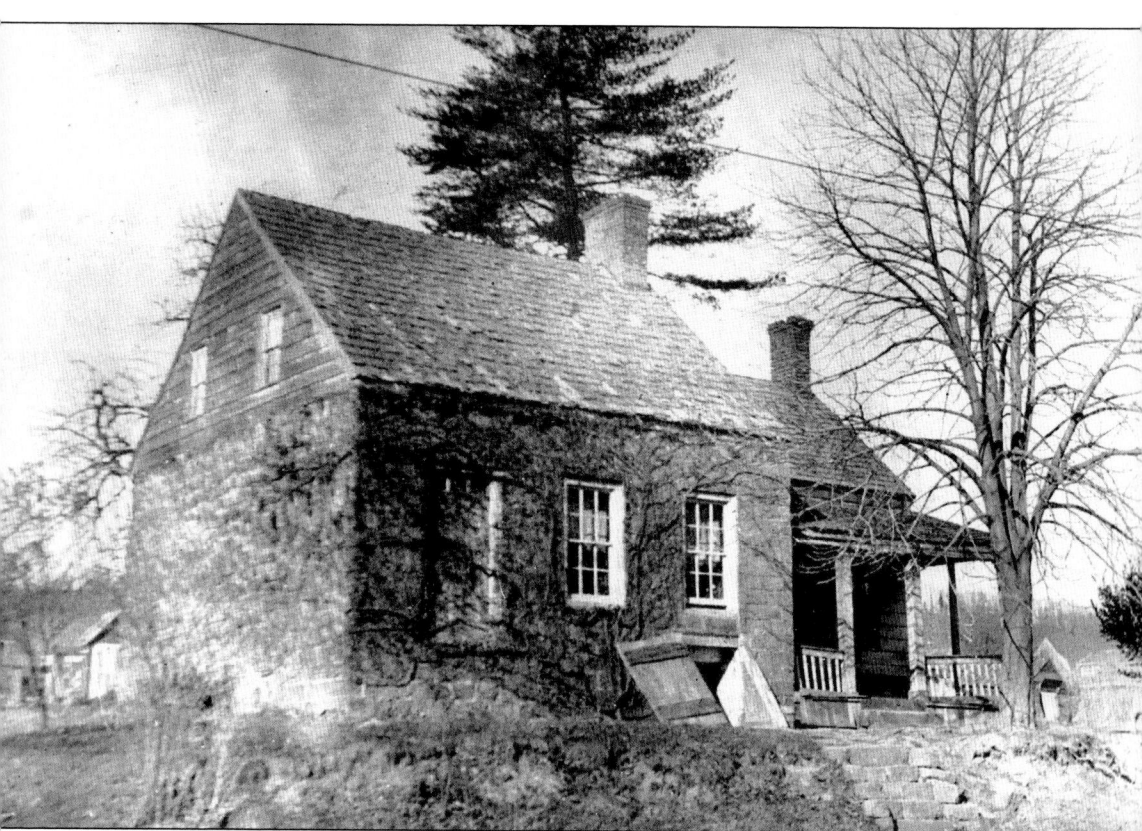

THE JEROME SIGLER HOME. Nearly a century ago, someone wrote these lines about a house that once stood near the site of King's supermarket: "An old house stands on Valley Road, so forlorn and tumbled down, It must be quite a century old so weather stained and brown." In her "Decade Files," Gladys Segar notes that this house was built by Daniel Sigler in 1802. The last Sigler to live here was Jerome, who gave his name to Jerome Place.

LUCY STONE. Founder of the American Suffrage Association, Lucy Stone was described by Edith Cady Stanton as "the first person by whom the heart of the American public was deeply stirred on the woman question." In 1857, she refused to pay her real estate tax in neighboring Orange on the grounds that "women suffer taxation yet have no representation." In 1858, she moved with her husband, Henry Blackwell, and their infant daughter to what is now 118 North Mountain Avenue.

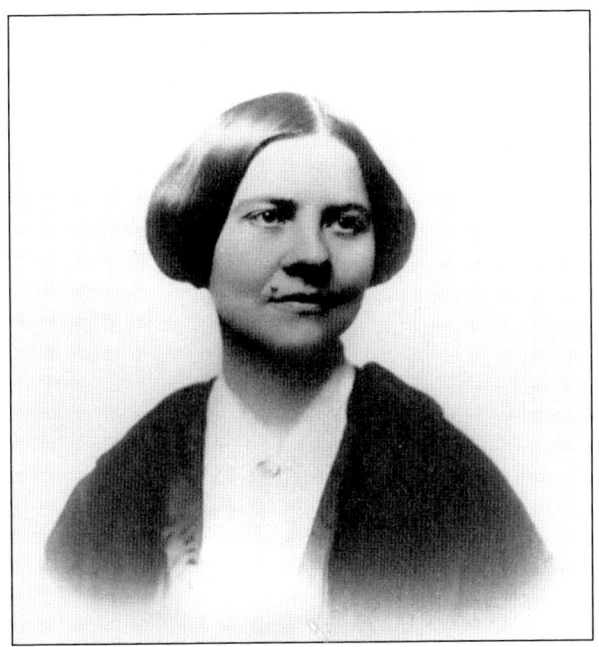

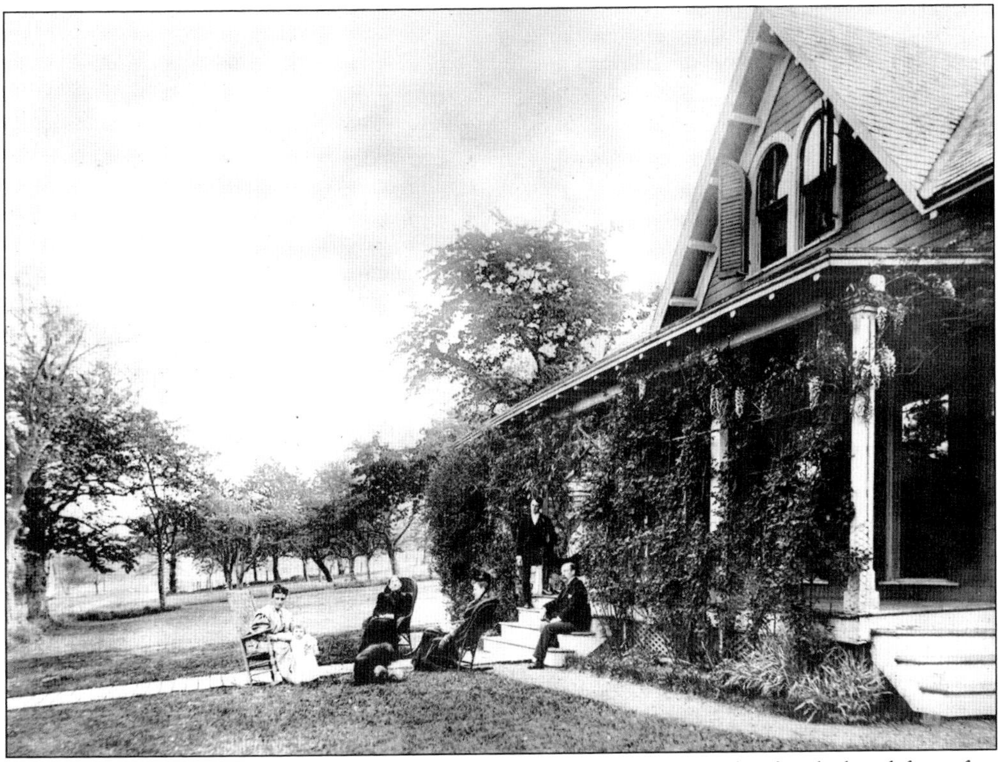

THE LUCY STONE HOUSE. Lucy Stone's daughter, Alice, wrote, "The family lived for a few years in West Bloomfield (now Montclair) and enjoyed the beautiful scenery of the Orange Mountains. . . . Sometimes Horace Greeley dropped in for a chat and gave advice about the garden and orchard." The original house, built by Garret Egbert before 1788, had been remodeled by the time Stone and her family arrived.

MOSES HARRISON. Born c. 1758, Moses Harrison served in the Essex Militia during the Revolution and in old age entertained his neighbors with accounts of his war experiences. He came from Orange in 1802 and purchased 60 acres from the Egberts along the Speertown (Valley) Road.

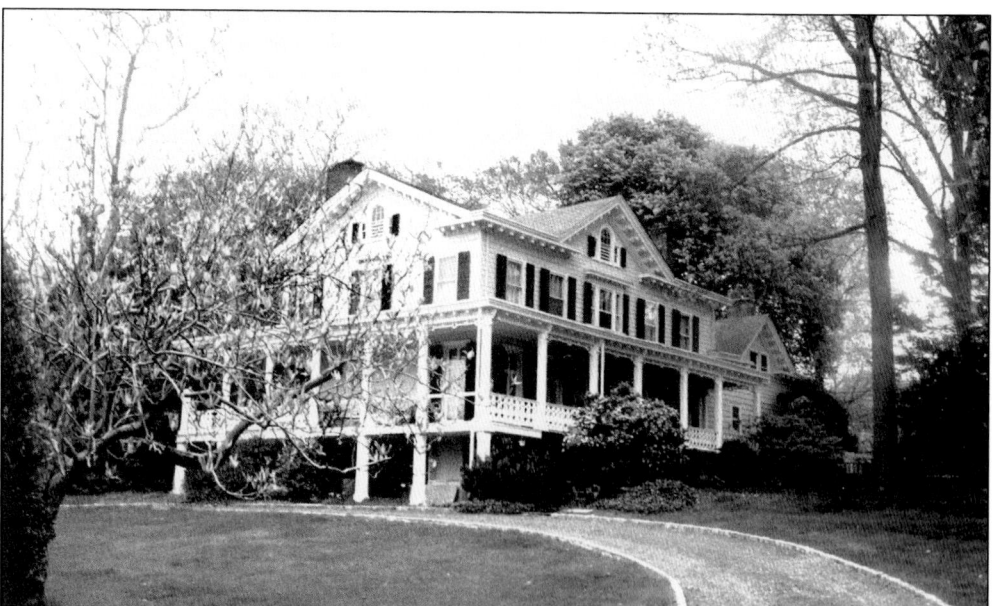

THE HARRISON HOUSE. Moses Harrison's son Jared Erwin Harrison built this house in 1840. He married Catherine Egbert, raised apples, and made cider. Dr. Samuel Watkins wrote of visits here on New Year's Day, "I always remember with great pleasure the wonderful doughnuts and cider which Mrs. Erwin Harrison provided." Today, the enlarged house stands opposite Edgemont Park and is surrounded by the Erwin Park neighborhood, both developed from the Harrison farm.

Two
NEW PIONEERS

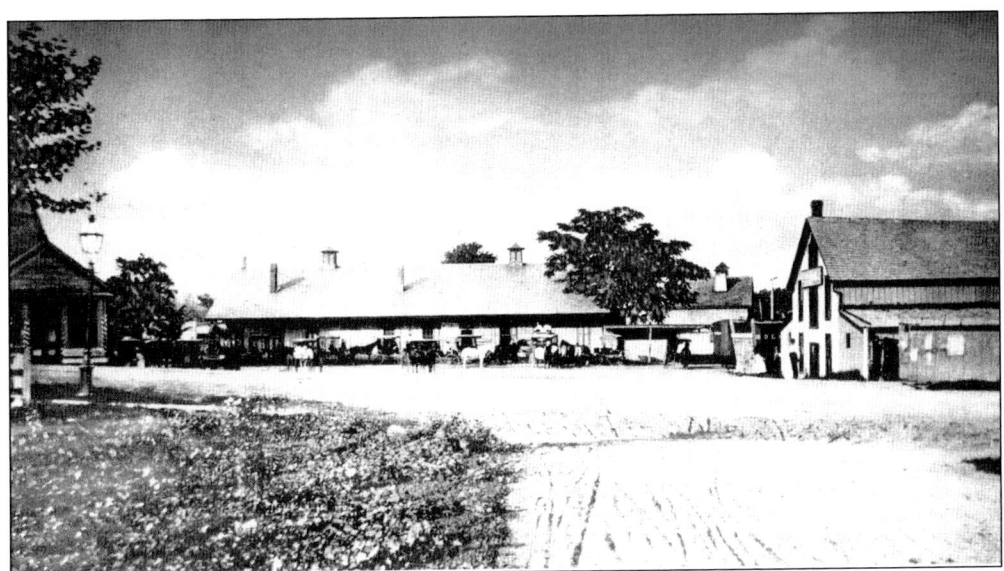

THE EARLY TRAIN STATION. The trains changed the small farming community of West Bloomfield into the densely populated commuter town of Montclair. That transformation called for the leadership of a later generation of pioneers. The first train station, built in 1856, was described by Dr. Samuel Watkins as "what you would expect to see in a new mining town which had been built overnight." He reports that the one pictured here appeared c. 1878.

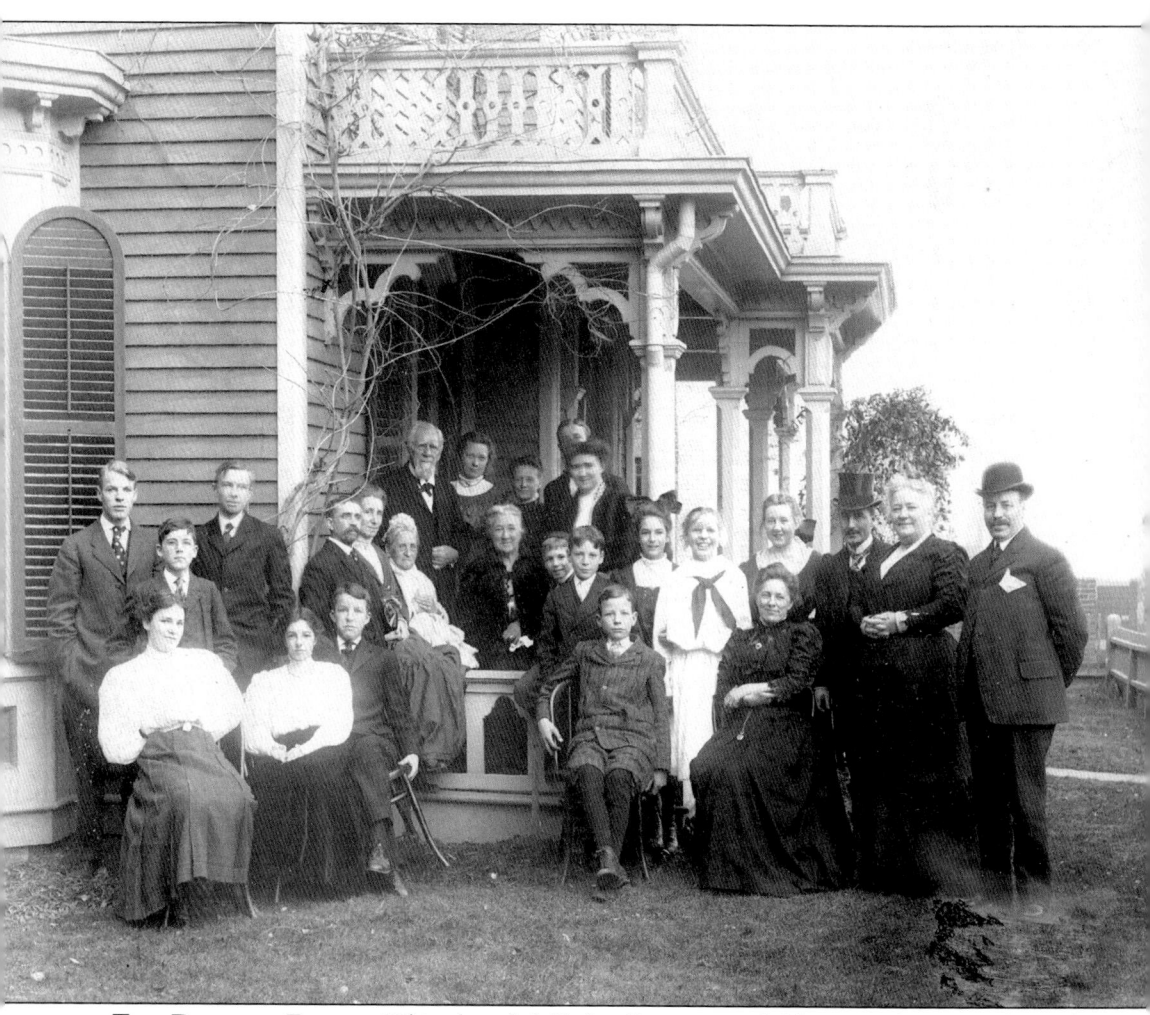

THE DOREMUS FAMILY. White-bearded Philip Doremus, a lifelong resident, stands on his porch at 223 Glenridge Avenue surrounded by his descendants and their spouses. Doremus was a leading merchant, Presbyterian churchman, and the first president of the Montclair Savings Bank. Lawyer and historian Edwin Goodell, husband of Annette Doremus, sits on the porch rail with his back against the house.

DR. JOHN J.H. LOVE. In his book *Montclair: The Evolution of a Suburban Town* (1934), Edwin Goodell names a trio of influential men "who did most to shape the life of Montclair during all its formative years." First to arrive was Dr. John J.H. Love, who in 1855 became Montclair's first resident physician. A large, imposing man, he chaired both the school and library boards. He served in the Union army as a division surgeon.

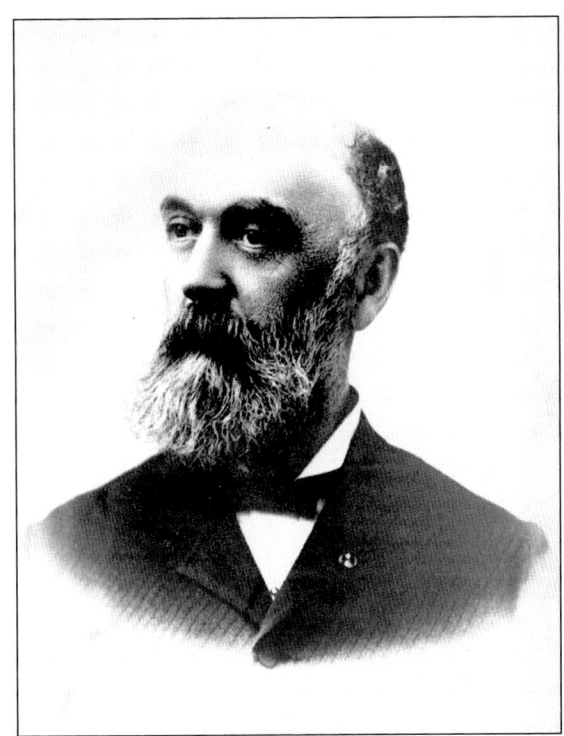

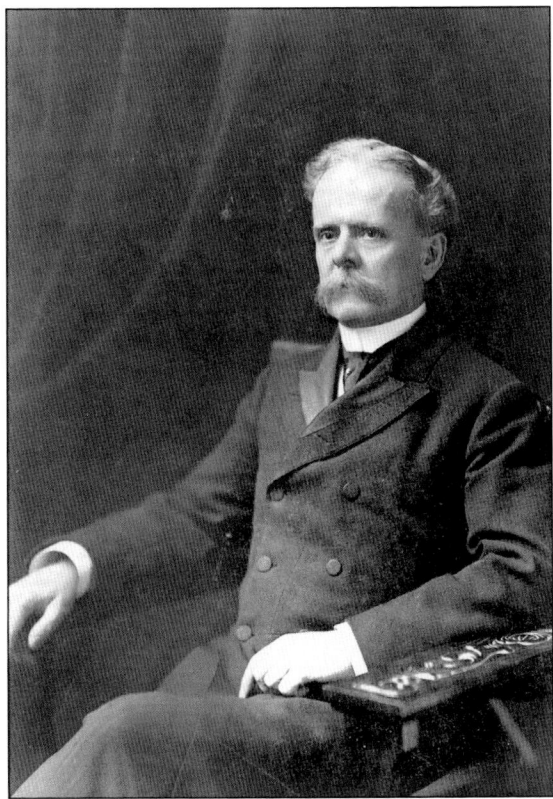

REV. AMORY HOWE BRADFORD, D.D. The second of author Edwin Goodell's central figures, Rev. Amory Howe Bradford, arrived fresh out of theological school in 1870 to serve as the first pastor of the First Congregational Church, a post he held for 40 years. He was a guiding spirit behind nearly every important community enterprise. At his death, the mayor proclaimed a day of mourning and an editorial called him "the first citizen of Montclair."

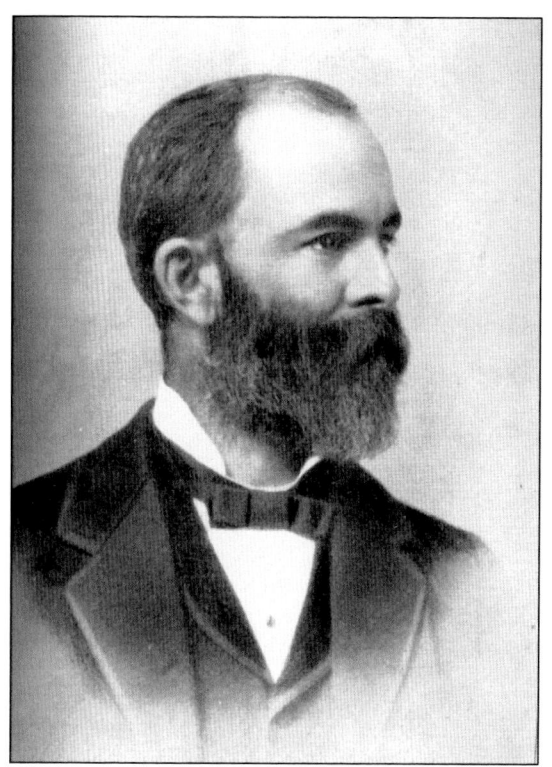

RANDALL SPAULDING. The third leading figure in what author Edwin Goodell calls "Montclair's romantic age" arrived in 1874 to become principal of the high school. Randall Spaulding, a graduate of Yale who also studied in Germany, was made superintendent of schools when a unified district was established. He is credited with laying the foundation of a school system regarded as one of the finest in the nation.

SARAH J. CHURCHILL. Arriving in 1870 to teach singing in the schools, Sarah J. Churchill was one of those who responded to Rev. Dr. Amory Howe Bradford's plea that something be done to aid "the fresh air children" of New York. The resulting Children's Home became in time a shelter for the orphaned and homeless. Sarah Churchill was also a founder of the New Jersey Commission for the Blind.

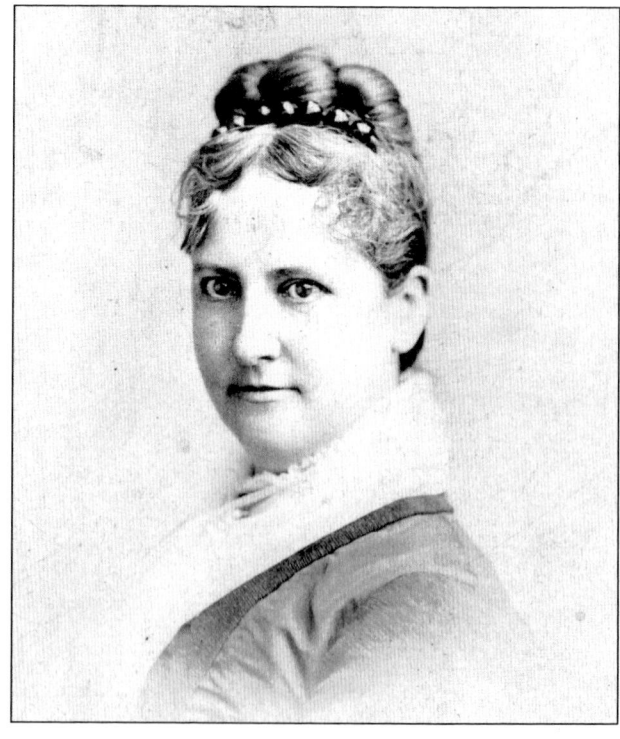

COL. FREDERICK H. HARRIS. Born in Newark in 1830, Frederick H. Harris moved to Montclair in 1853. Answering to President Lincoln's call for volunteers, he raised a company and entered the Union army. The sword shown here was "presented to Captain Fred. H. Harris by his friends, Montclair, NJ, August 21, 1862." Mustered out a lieutenant colonel, Harris became president of the American Insurance Company and wrote the first printed sketch of Montclair's history in 1876.

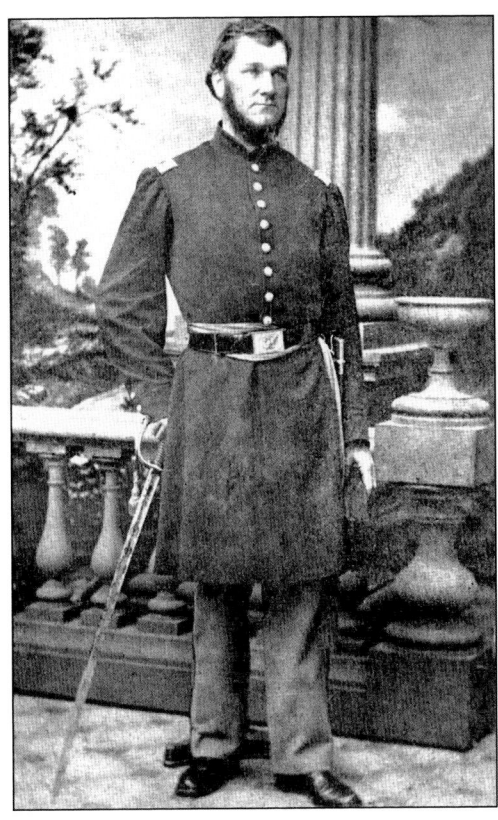

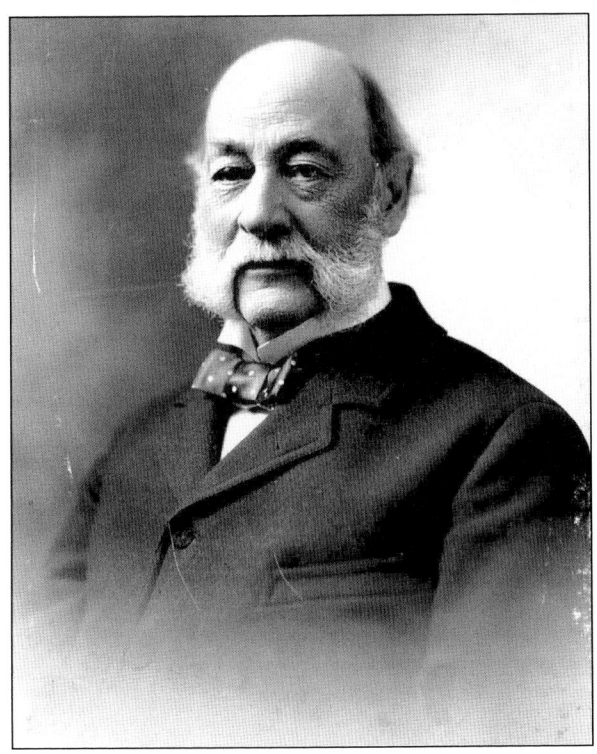

JULIUS H. PRATT. It was Julius H. Pratt who gave the speech at Col. Frederick H. Harris's sword presentation. A native of Meriden, Connecticut, Pratt started commuting from Montclair to New York in 1857. He named his new home Apple Grove (now Martin's Funeral Home). Contemporary reports support the tradition that it was Pratt who suggested the name Montclair for the town at a meeting held in 1860.

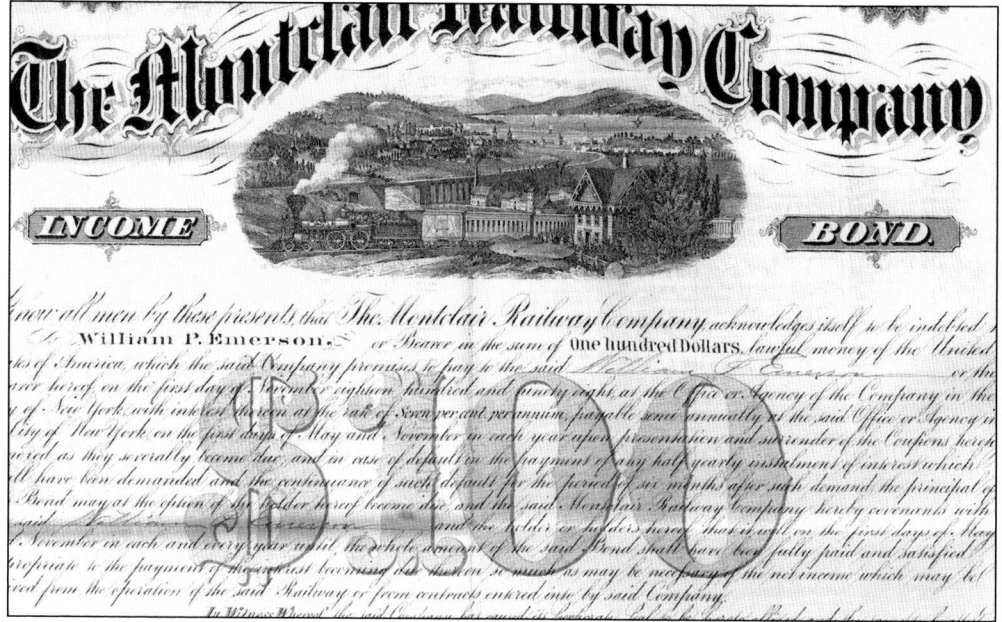

THE MONTCLAIR RAILWAY BOND. Dissatisfied with the services of the first railroad, Julius H. Pratt led the movement to build a second line and toward that end to have Montclair set off from Bloomfield in 1868. Support of the new railway led to Montclair's defaulting on its debt in the panic year of 1873, the same year the trains began running. A new township committee composed of wealthy and savvy businessmen came to the rescue. (Courtesy the Montclair Historical Society.)

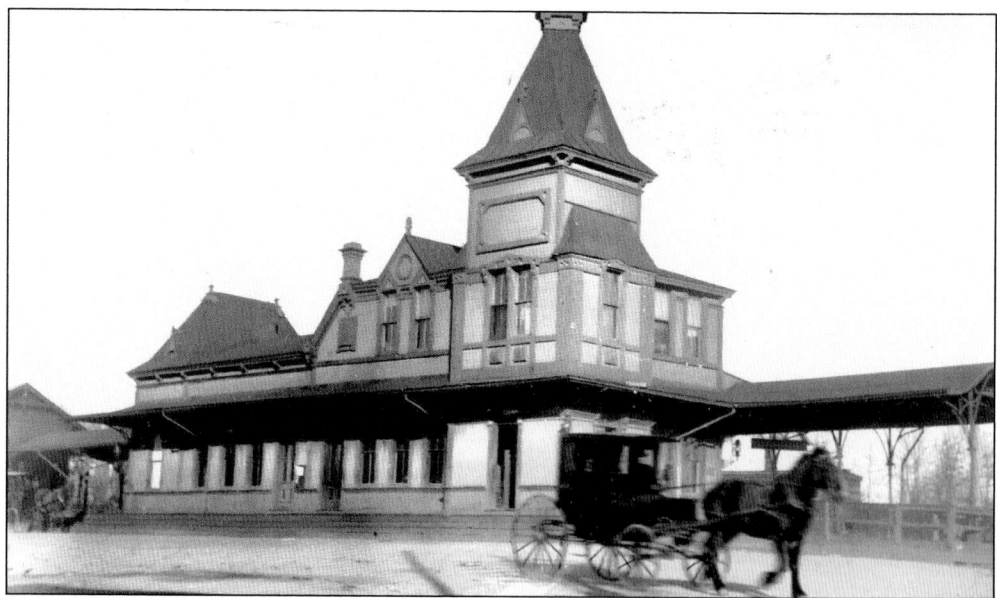

THE OLD WALNUT STREET STATION. Known originally as the Montclair Station of the New York and Greenwood Lake Line, this flamboyant structure later became the Erie Railroad's first stop in Montclair. It carried commuters directly to the ferries in Jersey City and immediately stimulated growth in the northern half of town. The year 2002 brought the joining of the two rail lines, with some trains running directly to Penn Station in New York.

ADELINE BARNES PRATT. In 1886, many in Montclair grieved at the death of Julius Pratt's "dear and lovely companion." Of Adeline Barnes Pratt, Rev. Dr. Amory Howe Bradford said, "She had a mysterious way of bearing the griefs and sharing the anxieties of almost all the homes in the village."

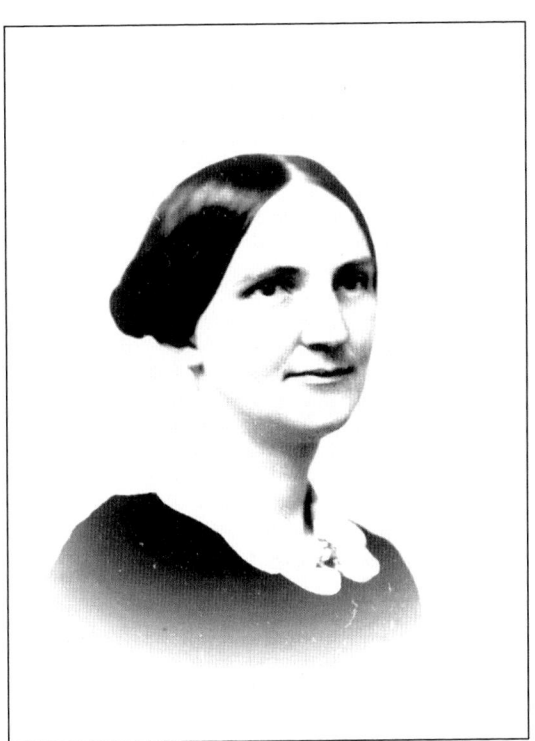

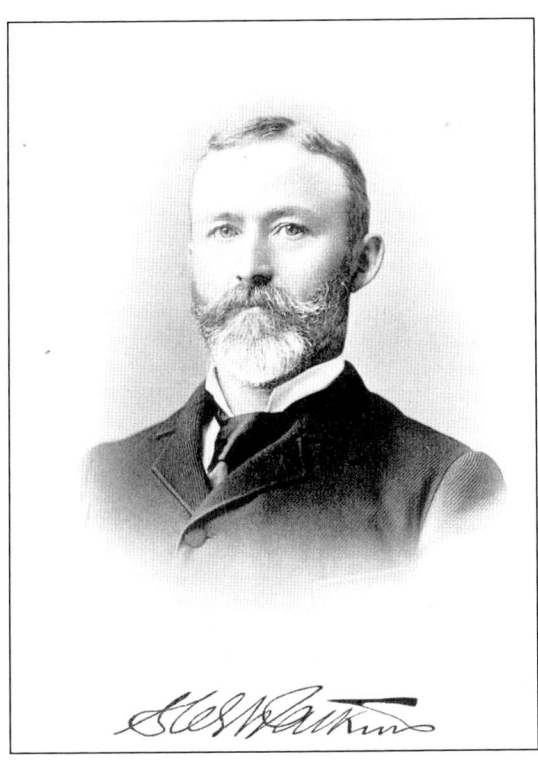

DR. SAMUEL C.G. WATKINS. A native of Canada, Dr. Samuel C.G. Watkins became Montclair's first resident dentist in 1876. He married Philip Doremus's daughter, Mary, and soon made the acquaintance of nearly everyone. As late as the 1930s, he was a familiar presence at public meetings. His *Recollections of Montclair* (1929) is packed with lively anecdotes about people and places.

DR. ELIZABETH BLACKWELL. The first woman to graduate from an American medical school and to be licensed as a physician was Dr. Elizabeth Blackwell. She and her sister, Emily, founded the New York Infirmary for Women and Children. Aided by a gift from a French countess, these women built on Upper Mountain Avenue a retreat intended as a convalescent home. During the New York draft riots of 1863, some African American families are believed to have been given refuge there.

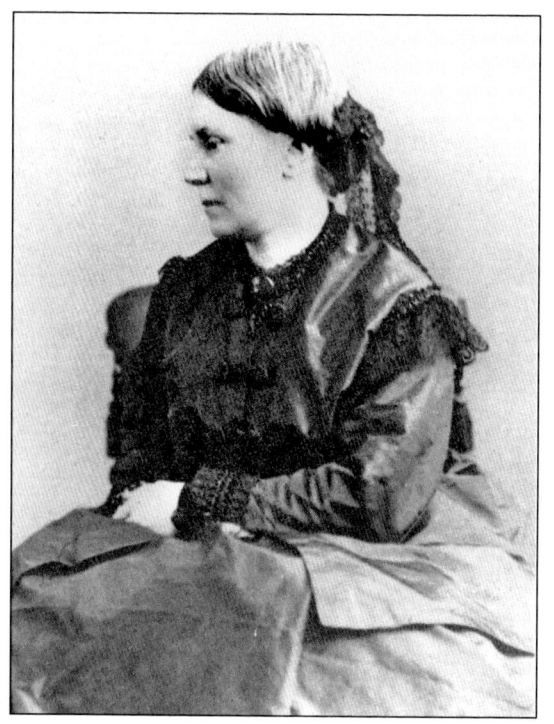

DR. EMILY BLACKWELL. After 1900, Dr. Emily Blackwell shared a home at 17 Plymouth Street with her colleagues Drs. Elizabeth Cushier and Elizabeth Mercelis. The latter was Cushier's niece and, as treasurer of a Montclair group that lent support to author Edith Wharton's relief work among displaced women and children in France during World War I, she corresponded with the famed novelist.

Augustus C. Studer. In the winter of 1876, a young Newark man of Swiss and German parentage got off the train in Montclair and trudged through the snow to canvass community leaders on the chances of a newspaper succeeding here. Opinions were mixed, but in May of the following year, Studer began publishing the *Montclair Times*. The paper still comes out every week.

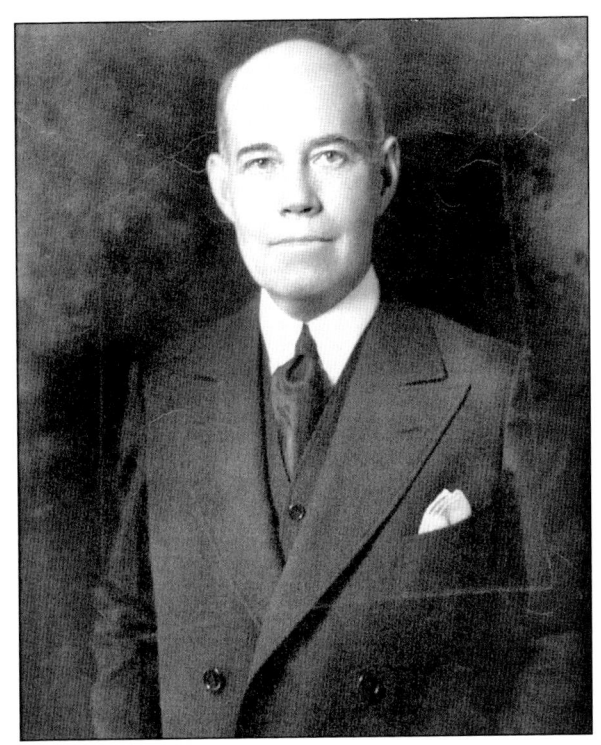

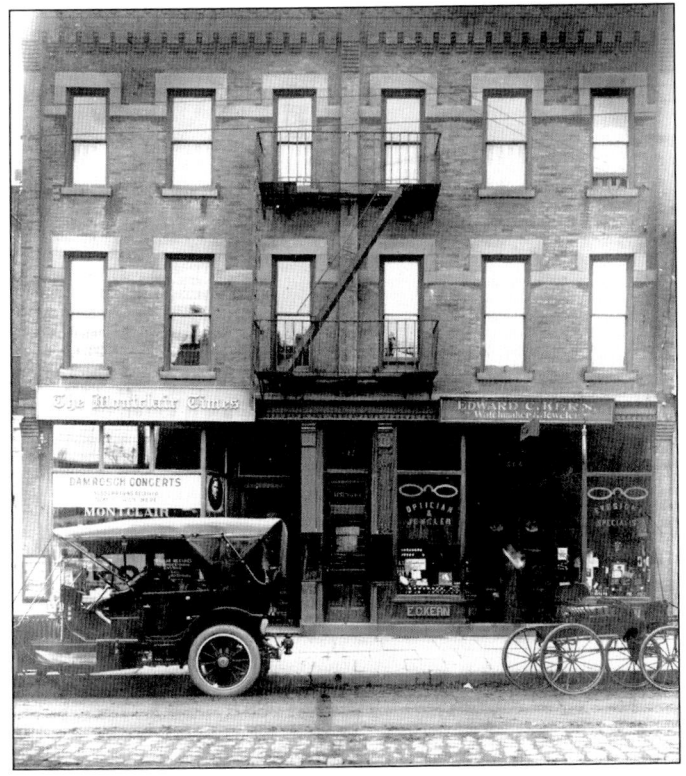

The *Times* Office. This building at 442 Bloomfield Avenue once housed not only the *Montclair Times* but also the ticket office for youth concerts conducted by the renowned Walter Damrosch and the premises of jeweler and optician Edward C. Kern. Although the newspaper was sheltered at various sites over the years, its ongoing identity has undergirded that of the town and contributed immeasurably to Montclair's strong sense of community.

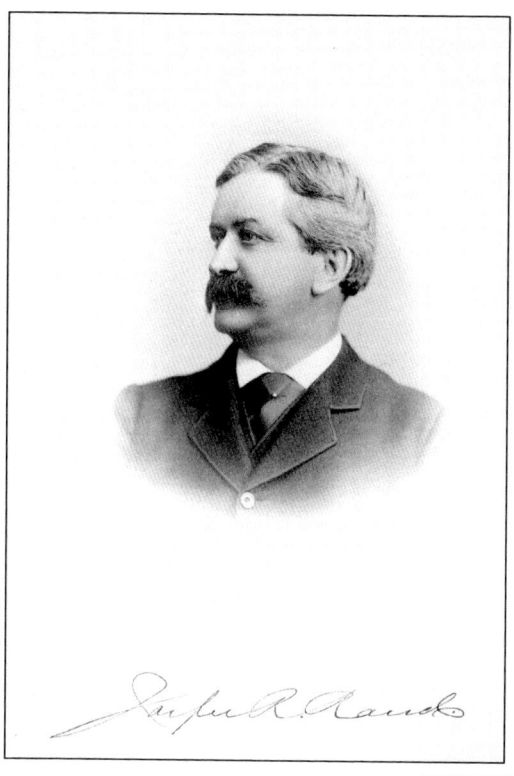

JASPER R. RAND. Like many of the "city men" who moved to Montclair, Jasper R. Rand was a small-town New Englander by birth. Moving here in 1873, he built a home on Hawthorne Place, where apartments stand today. President of the Rand Drilling Company (later, Ingersoll Rand), he quickly became a community leader. Elected to the township committee, he was the first president of the Montclair Club and was a founder and president of the Bank of Montclair.

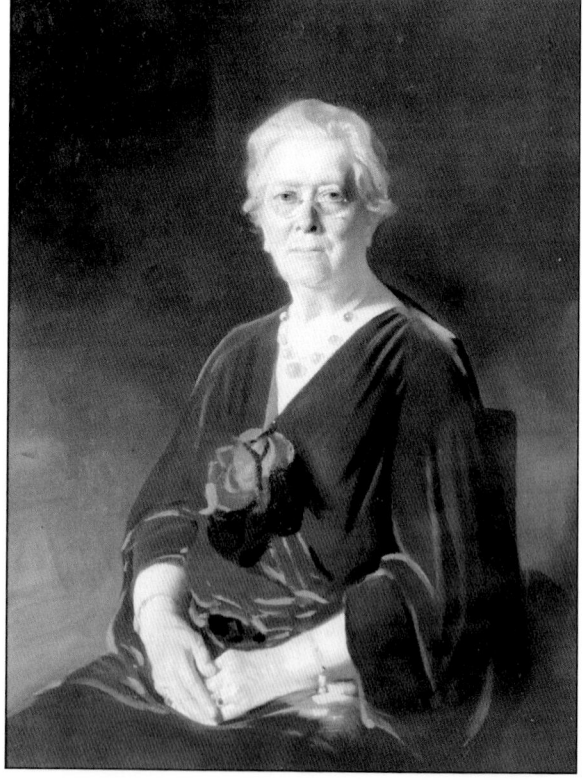

FLORENCE RAND LANG. The daughter of Jasper and Annie Rand, Florence Rand Lang continued her family's involvement in community affairs. Her generosity made possible the building and development of the Montclair Art Museum. The wife of Henry Lang, she is pictured in this portrait painted by Leopold Seyffert.

A Memorial. At the base of a tree west of the pond in Edgemont Park, this stone recognizes William B. Dickson's role in developing Montclair's park system. A laborer at the Homestead Steel Works at age 15, he rose to first vice president of U.S. Steel. He became an advocate for a shorter work week and spearheaded a workman's compensation law.

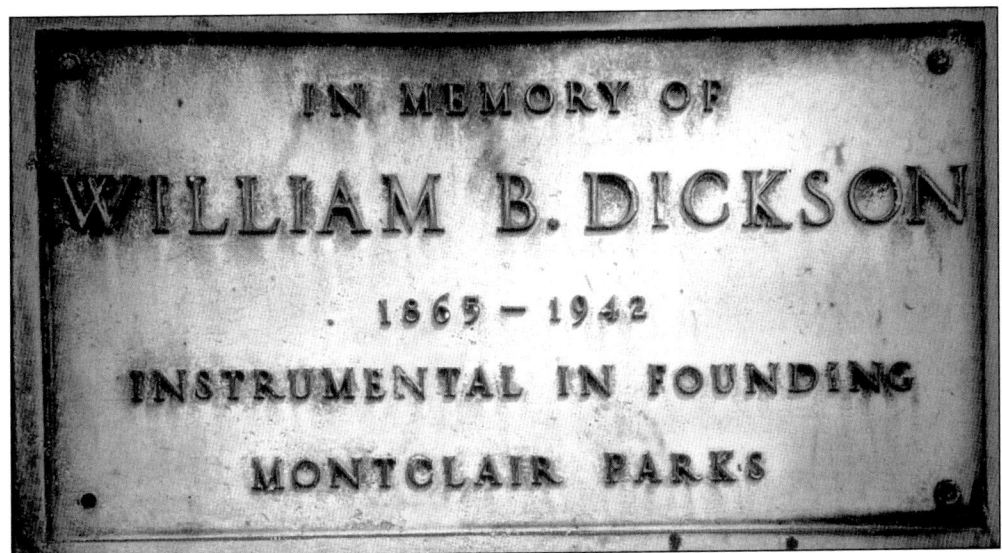

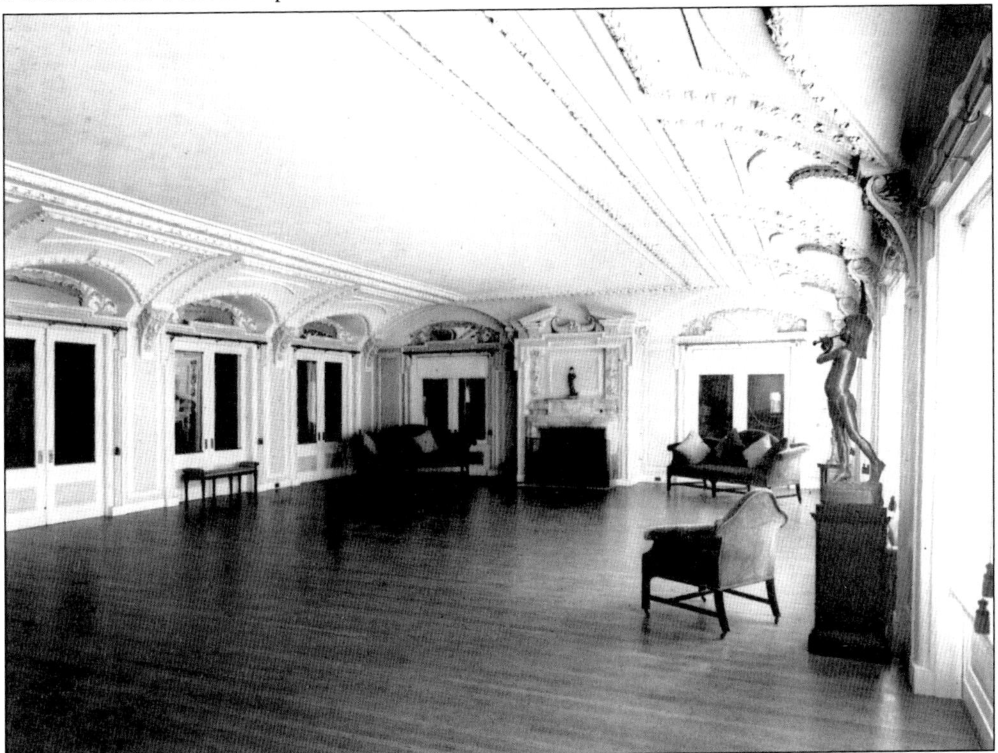

A Grand Ballroom. In 1903, William B. Dickson built a large home on Llewellyn Road above Eagle Rock Way. Not only balls but also musical performances by local talent were held here. The pedestaled figure is Montclair sculptor Jonathan Hartley's *Indian Boy*, now to be seen in the Montclair Art Museum.

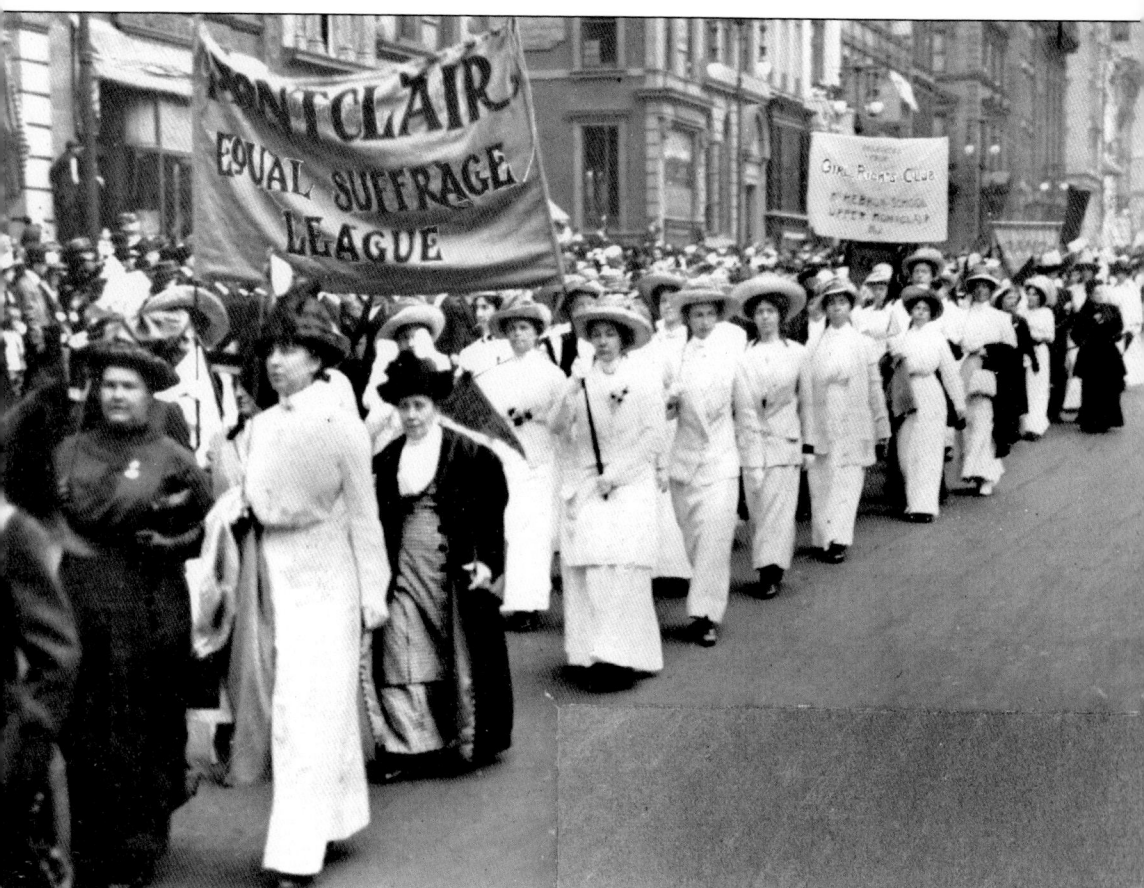

THE SUFFRAGE MARCH, FIFTH AVENUE, MAY 3, 1912. "We dressed in white with yellow sashes from shoulder to hip," wrote Florence Foster years later, "and we had a banner eight feet long with the name, Montclair Equal Suffrage League carried by two of our prettiest members." Behind the Montclair women can be seen a delegation of girls from the Mount Hebron School. Although the woman suffrage movement was active earlier in Montclair, the Equal Rights League was organized in 1910 in Florence Foster's home and included Florence Rand Lang among its membership. In 1920, when ratification of the woman suffrage amendment was certain, 100 women gathered at the Unitarian church for a victory celebration and organized the first chapter of the League of Women Voters in New Jersey.

Three
MULTICULTURAL HERITAGE

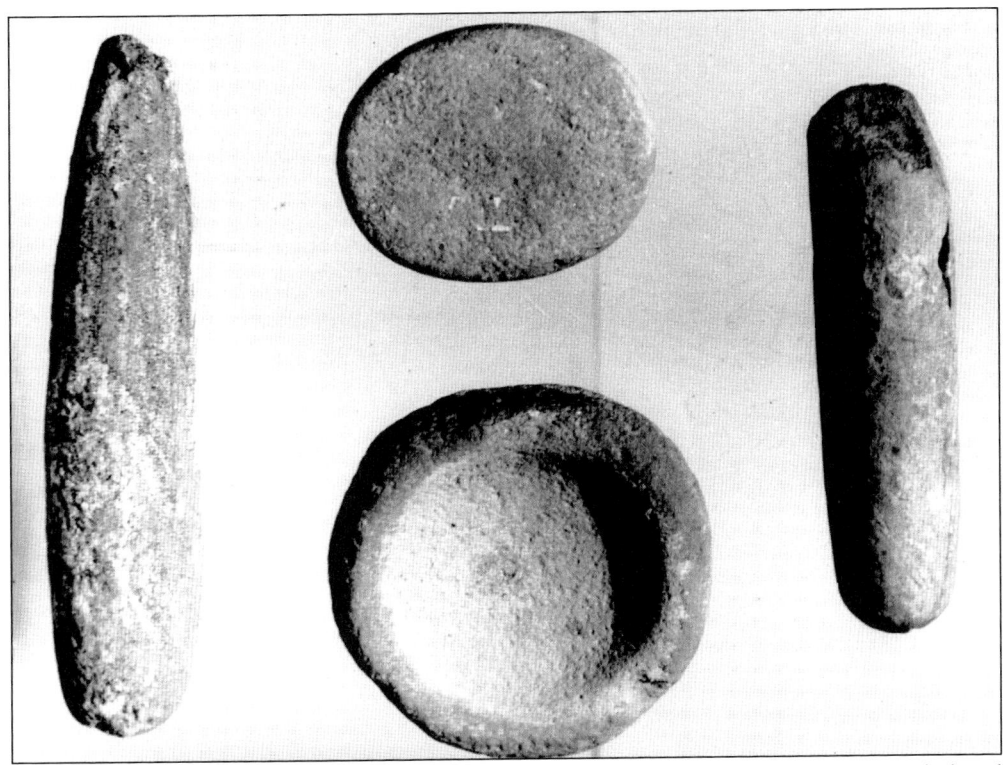

LENNI LENAPE ARTIFACTS. The Lenape Indians, members of the Delaware Nation, inhabited New Jersey. Several peaceful American Indian tribes lived in the Montclair area. The Lenape used stone tools and lived in longhouses. The Lenni Lenape, which means "original people," claimed to be descendants of ancient people.

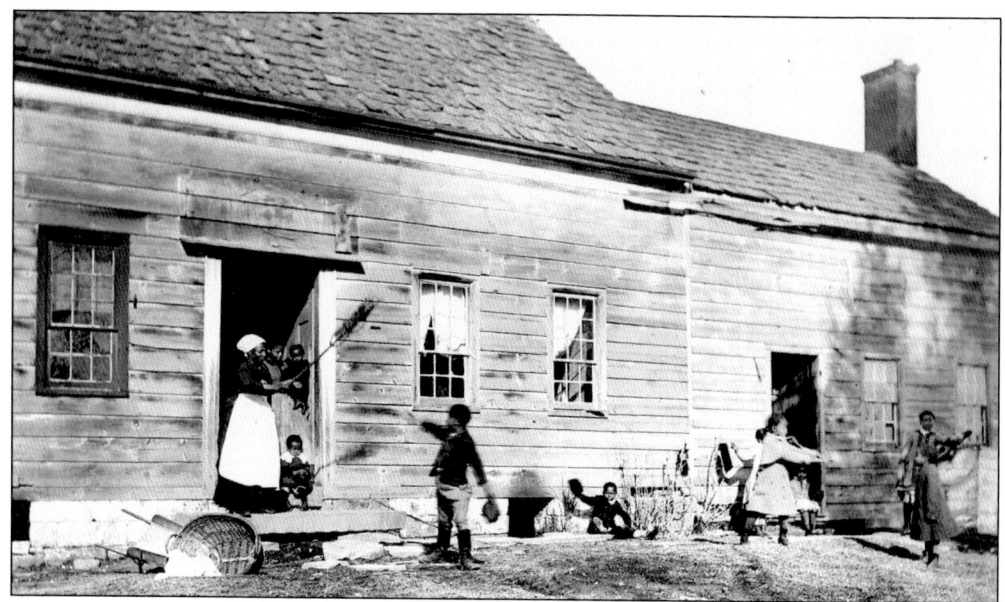

POLLY DAVIS. The first enslaved African Americans were brought to Montclair by the white settlers in the Colonial period. After the Civil War, former slave Polly Davis lived in a house built by Joseph Crane on Plymouth Street and Orange Road. She used a stick to chase off boys or sat in the doorway with her clay pipe. Traveling to President Lincoln's second inauguration, she later took up collections to attend other ceremonies in Washington. The house was demolished c. 1890.

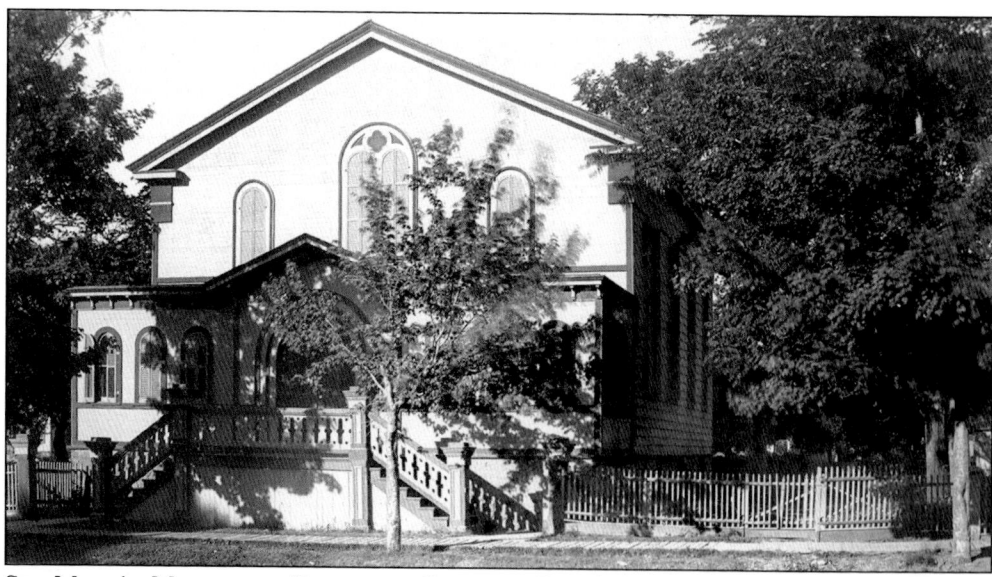

ST. MARK'S METHODIST EPISCOPAL CHURCH. Founded in 1880, St. Mark's is the first African American church in Montclair. The congregation first rented and later purchased the First Methodist Episcopal Church building at 194 Bloomfield Avenue. That structure, built in 1836—the oldest church building in Montclair—burned to the ground on Good Friday, April 1, 1947. On November 6, 1949, the current building was completed on Elm Street, on property that the congregation had bought back in 1926.

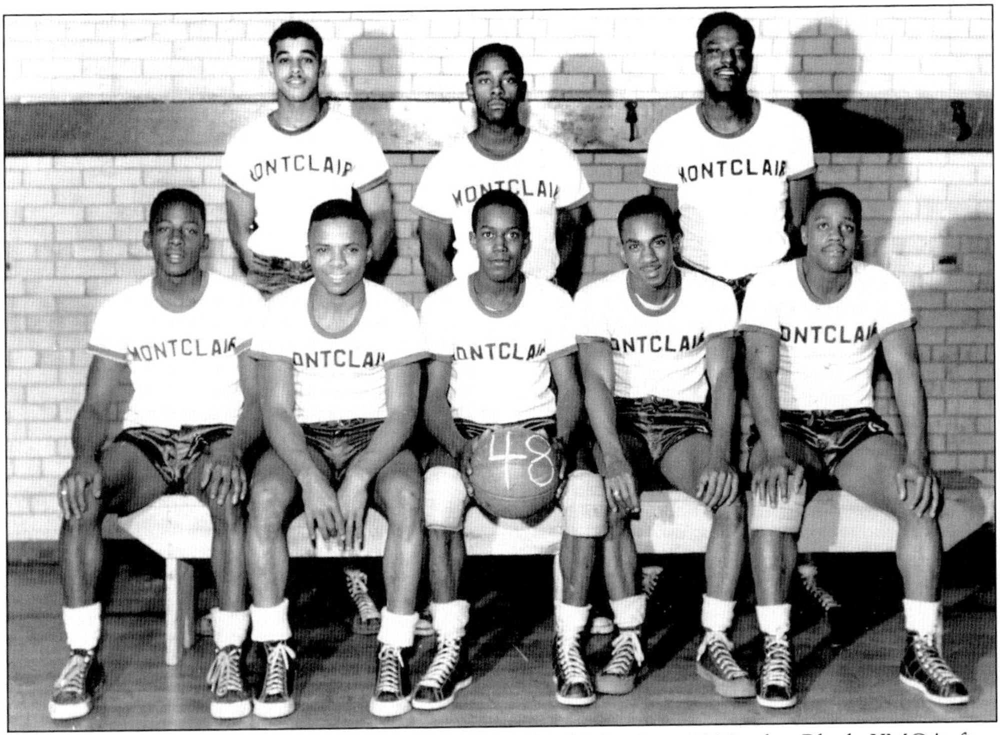

THE WASHINGTON STREET (BLACK) YMCA. Established in 1903, the Black YMCA first met at 381 Bloomfield Avenue. Later it moved above the Harrison Market at 469 Bloomfield Avenue and then to 522 Bloomfield Avenue. In 1916, Charles Bullock became the director. After the First Methodist Church donated the land, the Washington Street branch (below) was built in 1927. In November 1959, the Black YMCA integrated with the Park Street Y. Above is the 1948 basketball team. (Below photograph by James Boylan.)

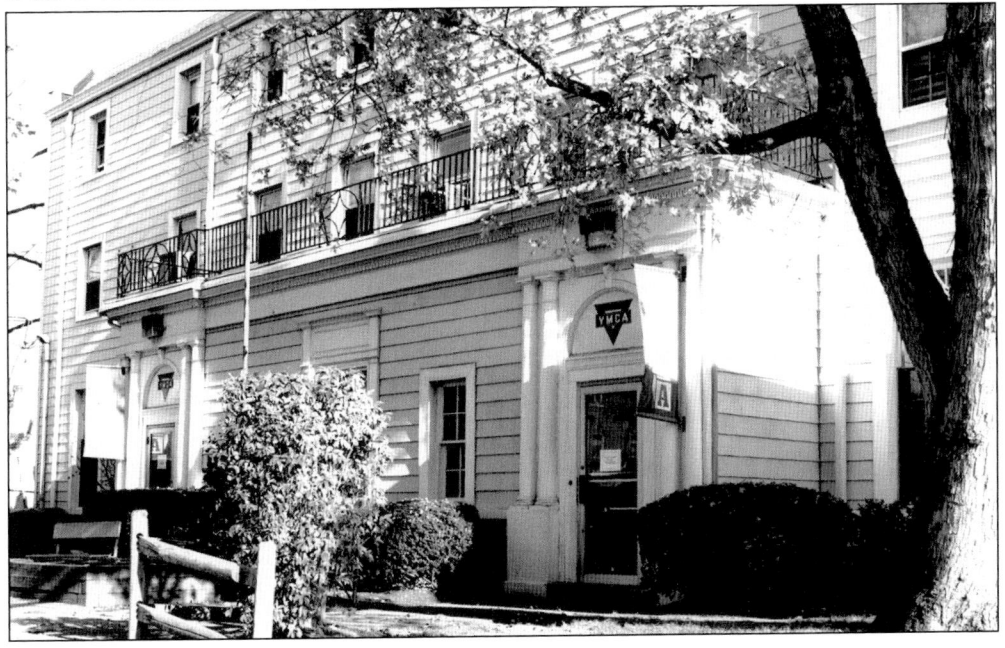

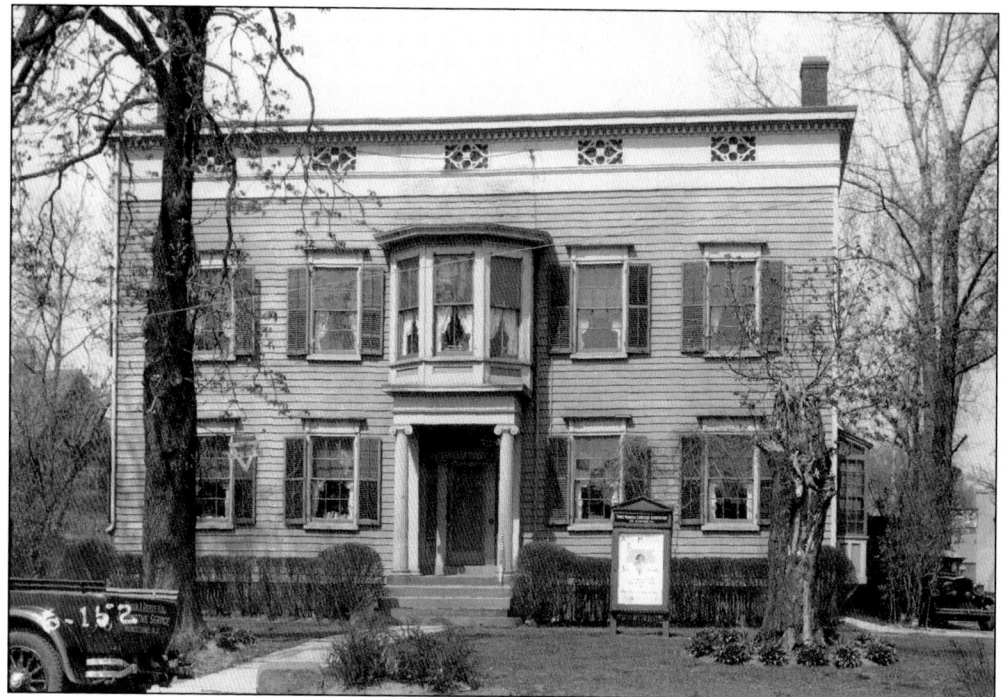

THE YWCA. The YWCA and (Black) YMCA were the social hubs of the African American community. Founded in 1912 at 89 Forest Street, the YWCA received the first charter in America given to African American women. In 1922, the YWCA moved into the Crane House (above) on Glenridge Avenue. In the 1950s, the YWCA became integrated. The groundbreaking (below) for a new building was held on August 15, 1965, and the dedication was held on September 29, 1968. (Above photograph by R. Lacey Merritt.)

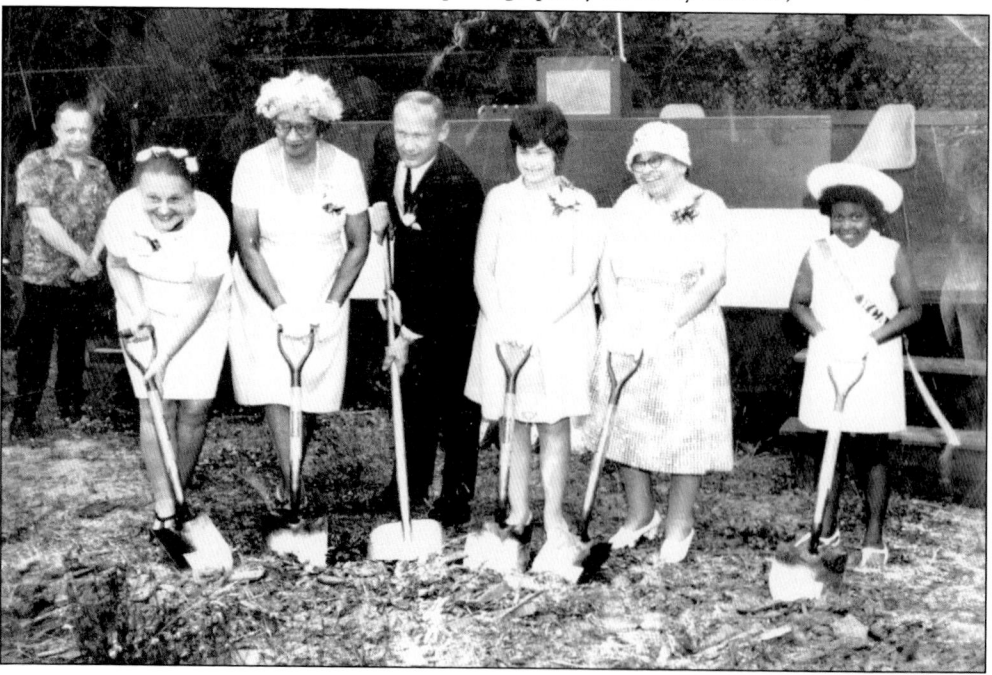

THE AMERICAN LEGION CRAWFORD CREWS POST 251. Incorporated in 1934, the African American post honored four Montclair African American citizens who died in World War I: Crawford Crews, Austin Barnes, Alzono Mills, and Benjamin Smith. Since African American regiments were not allowed to fight with the American soldiers, they fought under the French army. All four were awarded the highest French medals. The post bought the former Washington Hose Company building at 210 Bloomfield Avenue in 1944. (Courtesy John Garrett.)

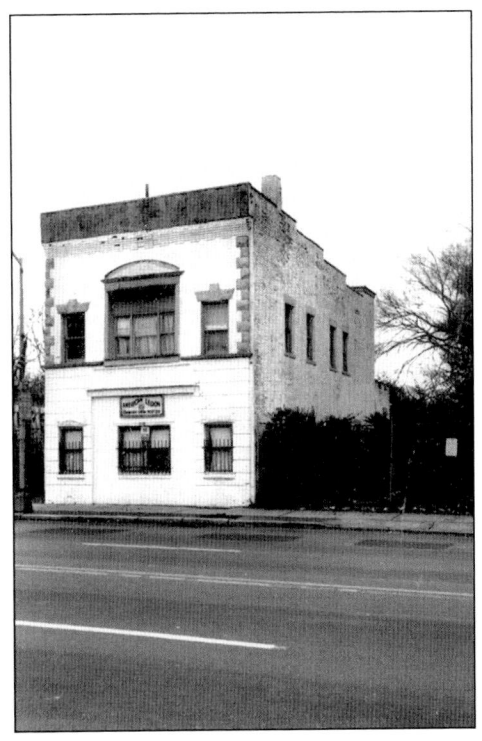

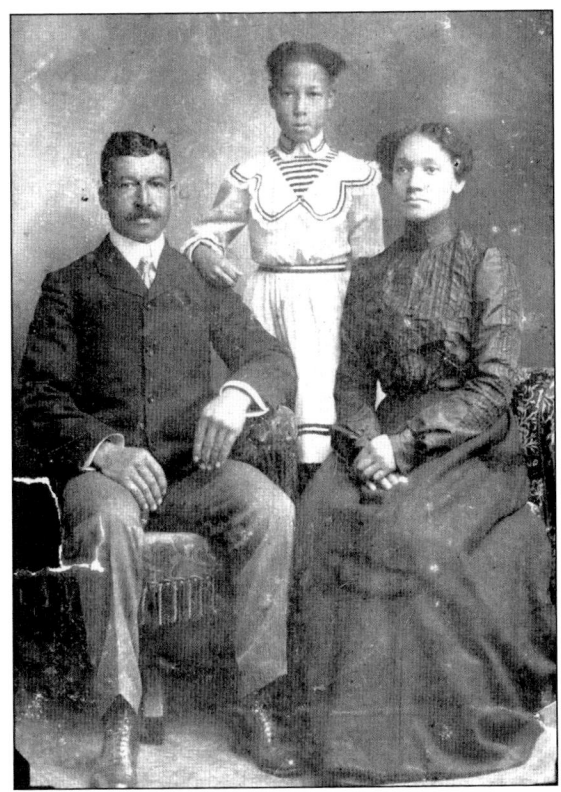

THE NICKENS FAMILY, C. 1899. Coming to Montclair from Virginia prior to 1890, William Nickens worked at a coal company, and his wife, Betty, worked in domestic service. William Nickens served as the first treasurer of St. Mark's Methodist Episcopal Church. The Nickenses' daughter, Arrie Nickens Douglas, was the mother of Dr. Frederick Douglas, the first African American attending physician at Mountainside Hospital. (Courtesy Daisy Douglas.)

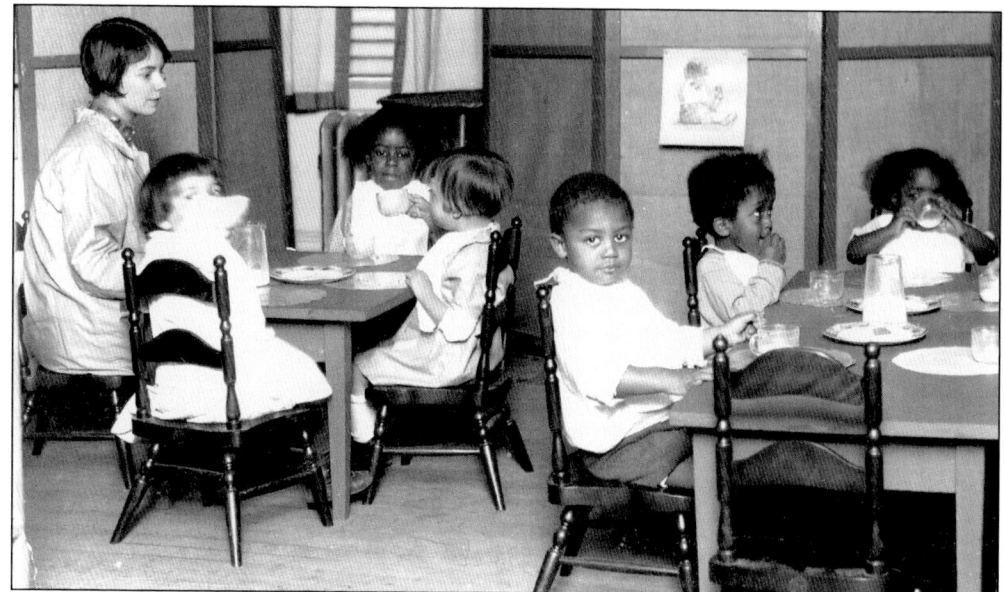

THE JUNIOR LEAGUE NEIGHBORHOOD COMMUNITY HOUSE, 1927. In 1926, the Junior League rented from an Italian family a house across the street from the Glenfield School on Maple Avenue. This house featured a small library, clubrooms, and a nursery school. In 1929, the Junior League purchased another house across from the school and built an addition, which included a large auditorium and nursery school facilities. The Junior League served the African American and Italian communities in the Fourth Ward. (Courtesy the Junior League.)

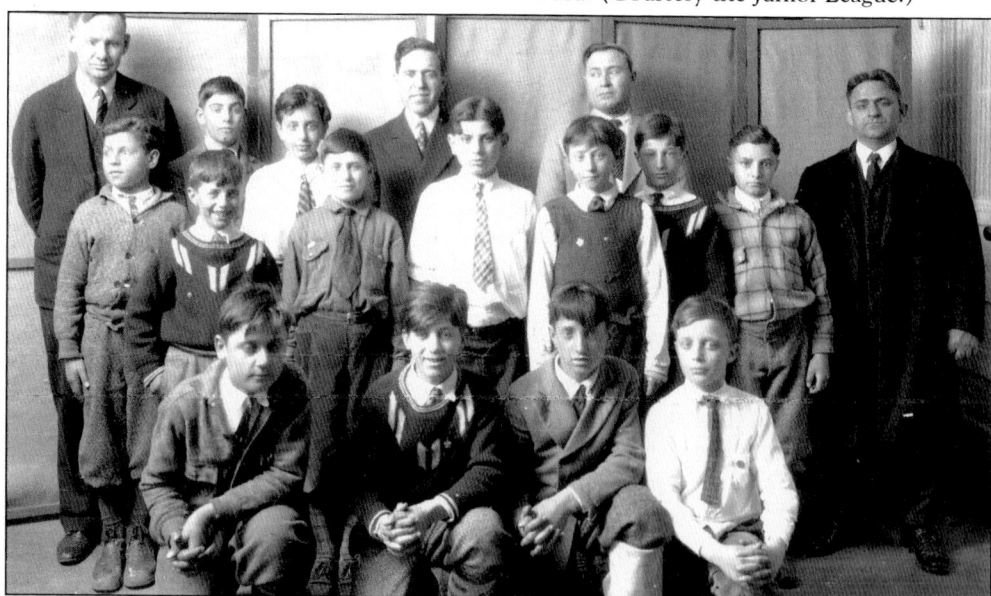

THE JUNIOR LEAGUE NEIGHBORHOOD COMMUNITY HOUSE, 1927. Programs for children and adults included Boy Scouts (shown here), Girl Scouts, English classes, sewing lessons, arts and crafts classes, Children's Theater, dancing, sports, the Civics Club, health clinics, the Montclair Social Economic Forum, and the Free Time Guild. In 1940, the Neighborhood Council was formed as an advisory group, and in November 1953, it purchased the property from the Junior League. It was renamed the Neighborhood Center. (Courtesy the Junior League.)

MINNIE LUCEY WITH ITALIAN CHILDREN. In 1915, social worker Minnie Lucey was hired by the principal of Baldwin Street School to work with foreign-born, mostly Italian students. Also interested in assisting immigrant mothers in caring for their children, she required that they bring a baby with them when they enrolled in her mothers classes. She was the founder of the Baldwin Street Community Center. She died in 1930 at the age of 45.

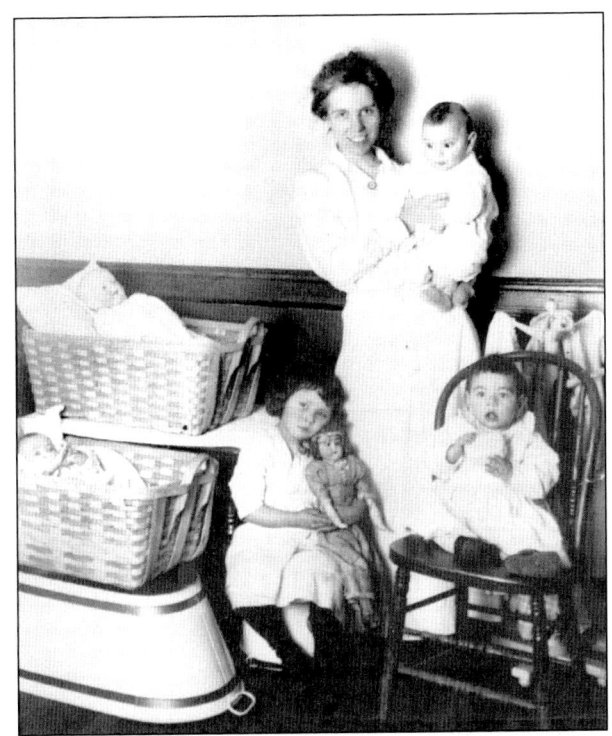

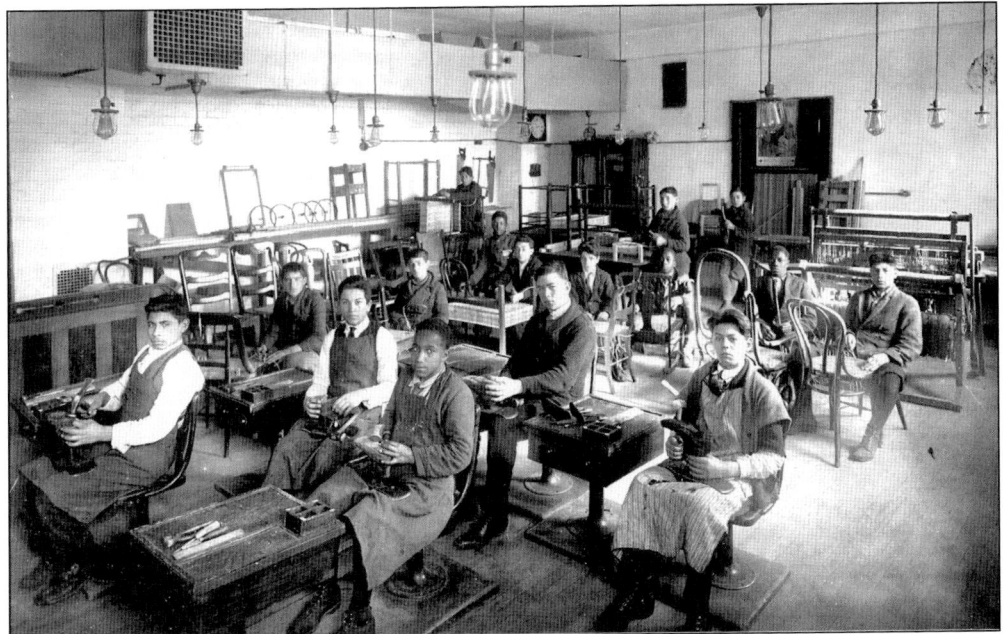

THE OPPORTUNITY CLASS, BALDWIN STREET COMMUNITY CENTER. In 1928, the Baldwin Street Community Center was erected and, in 1932, was renamed the Minnie Lucey Community House. The center assisted mostly Italian families, although African Americans also attended some of the programs, which included skills and English classes for youth and adults, and child care for younger children. Miss Agnes taught the opportunity class for Italian and African American boys.

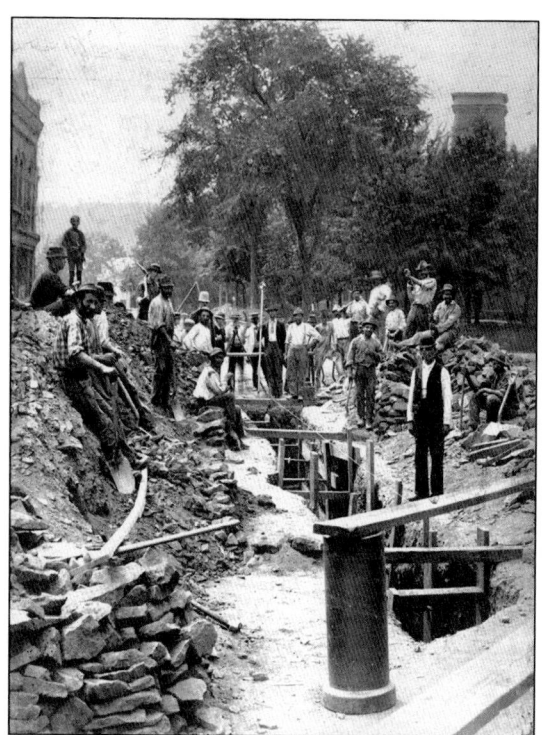

ITALIAN LABORERS LAYING SEWAGE PIPES, 1887. Italian immigrants came to Montclair to work as unskilled laborers. Early Italians in Montclair were employed to dig the water and sewer lines at Bloomfield and Church Streets. The immigrants lived in tents on a vacant lot on Midland Avenue and could be heard singing around the bonfires. Some stayed on in Montclair working as shoe shiners, gardeners, handymen, and railroad workers.

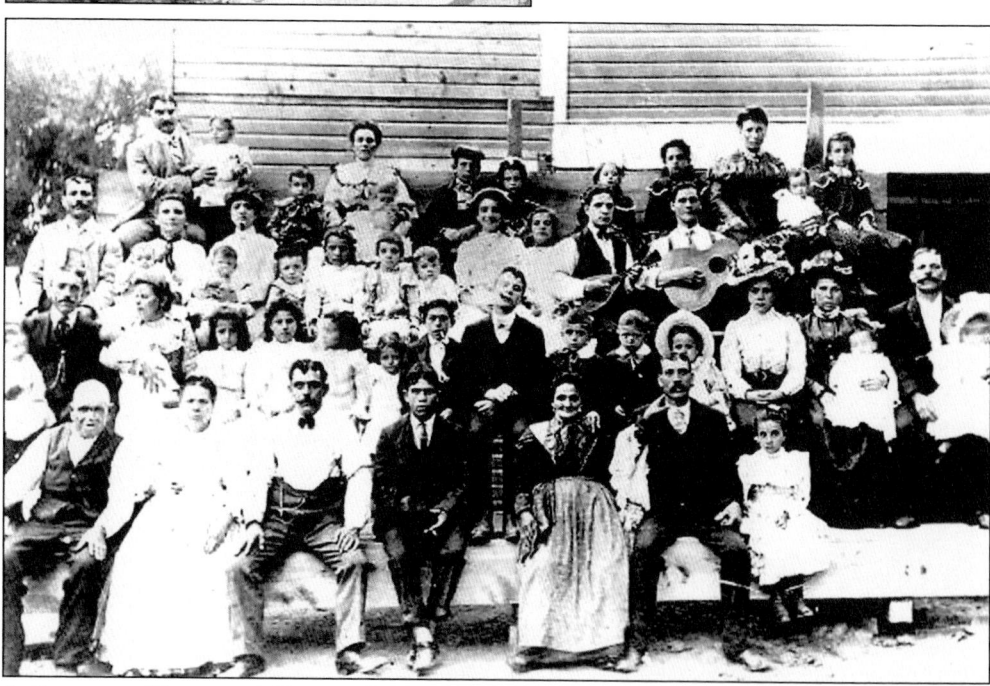

A SANDORA (SANTORO) FAMILY GATHERING, C. 1902. The Sandora family came from San Fele, in the province of Potenza in the Campania region of Italy, to Newark in 1888. The family moved to Cherry Street in Montclair c. 1902. The twin daughters married two DiGeronimo brothers, both having large families of 15 and 13 children. This picture was taken on the corner of Glenridge Avenue and Bay Street. (Courtesy Molly DeCarlo.)

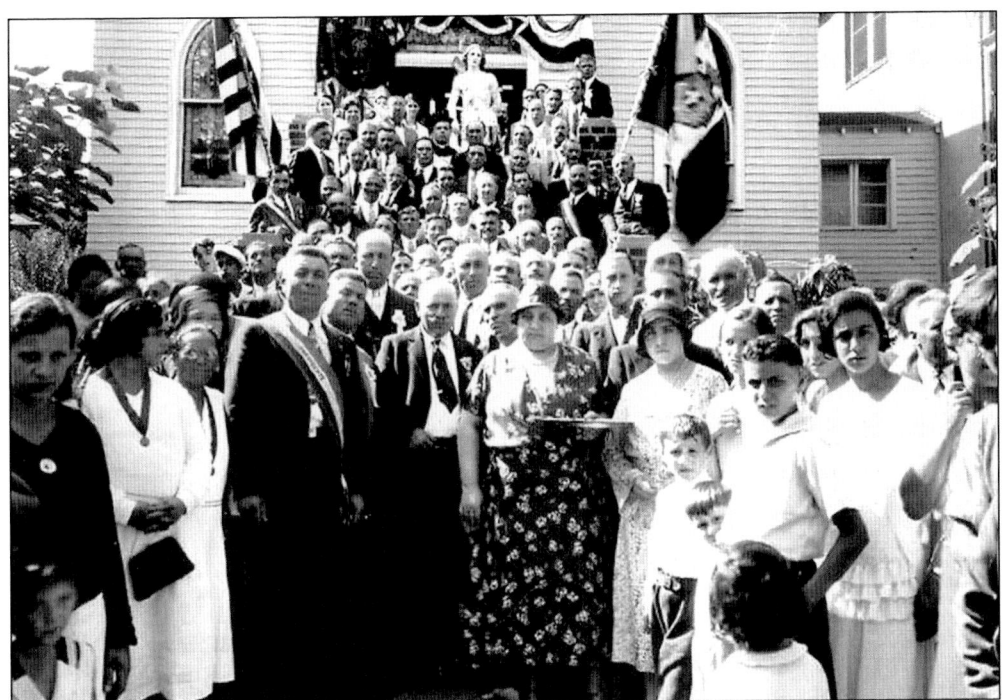

THE ST. SEBASTIAN FEAST, 1926. Built in 1907, the Our Lady of Mount Carmel Church served the Italian Catholic community. Starting in the 1920s, the Societa de Sebastiano sponsored the St. Sebastian Feast and the church sponsored a smaller Our Lady of Mount Carmel Feast. Pine Street was the scene of a street fair where homemade and religious goods were sold. After the High Mass for St. Sebastian, the statue of the saint was paraded through the streets. (Courtesy Paul Porcelli.)

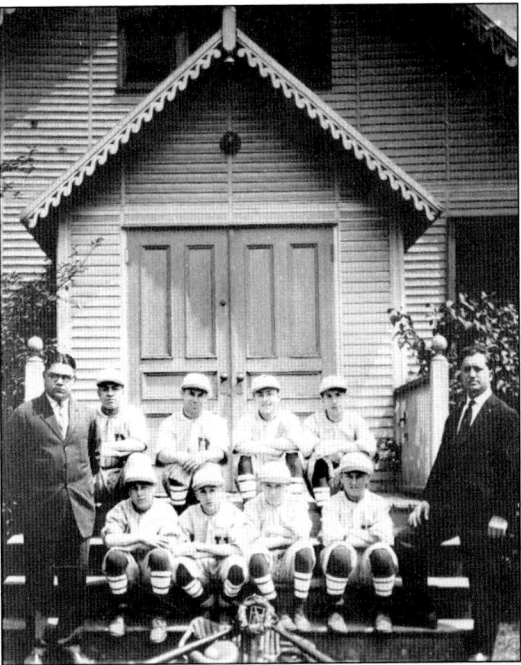

THE FIRST ITALIAN PRESBYTERIAN CHURCH BASEBALL TEAM. Members of First Presbyterian Church assisted the Protestant Italians in organizing the church in 1900. The church was erected at the corner of Grove Street and Glenridge Avenue and was dedicated in April 1906. Both English and Italian were spoken at the services. In 1922, the church met at the Central Presbyterian Church. The members called their church the Church of Our Savior.

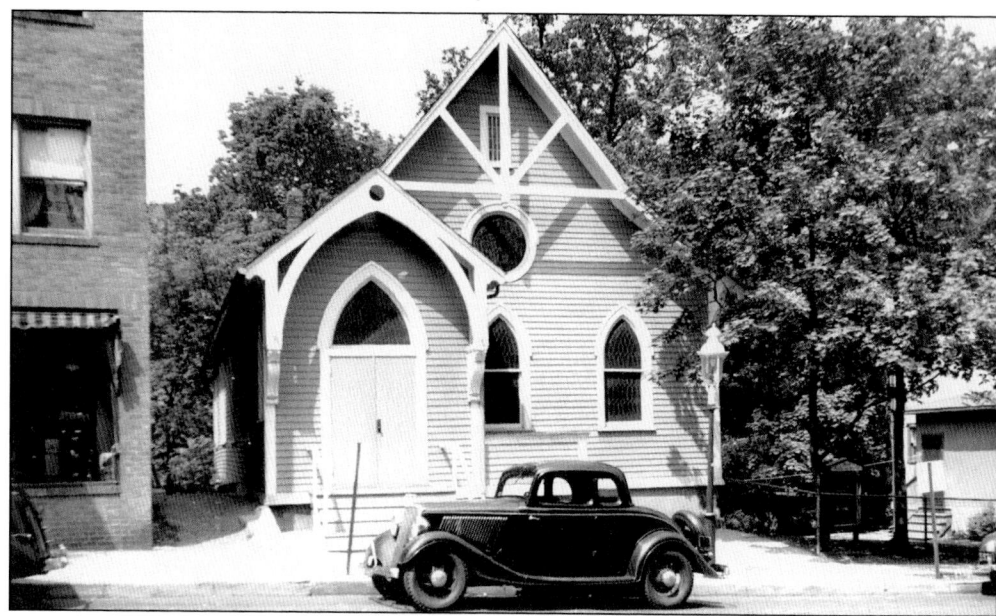

ST. ERIC'S EVANGELICAL LUTHERAN CHURCH. Built in 1896 by volunteer labor supervised by the Carlson Brothers, St. Eric's Church on Glenridge Avenue served the Swedish Lutheran population with the services originally conducted in Swedish. The church's name was changed to the First Evangelical Lutheran Church in 1929, and in 1960, a new church was built on Park Street. The original building is now used by St. Paul's Seventh-Day Christian Church. (Photograph by Frank Brown; courtesy the *Montclair Times*.)

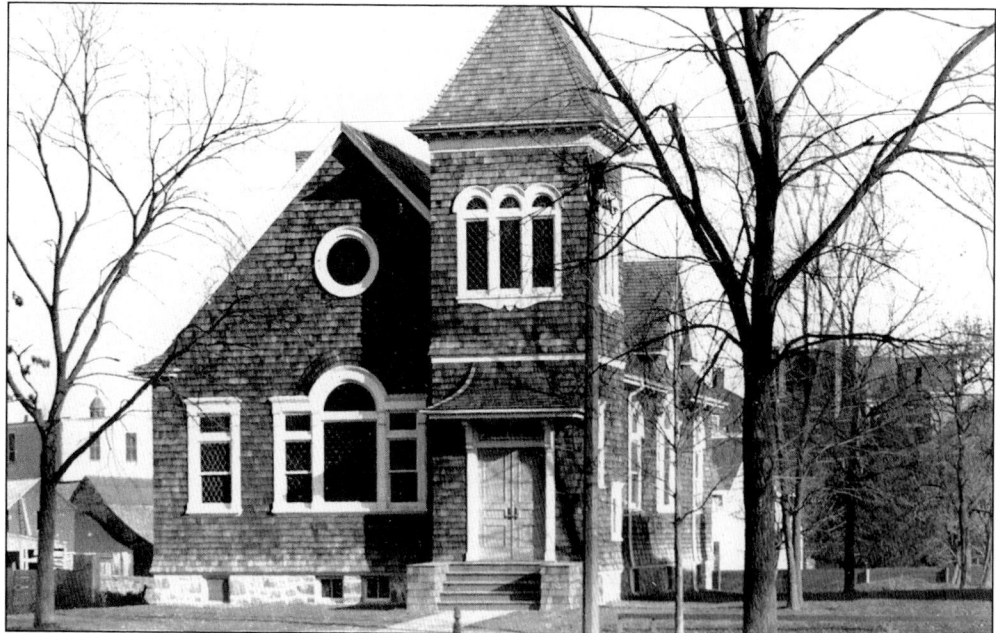

THE SWEDISH CONGREGATIONAL CHURCH. Founded in 1899, the church built by Swedish carpenters on Valley Road served a Swedish population. The name was changed to Valley Road Congregational Church *c.* 1947. After joining the Evangelical Covenant denomination *c.* 1957, the church changed its name to the Evangelical Covenant Church. (Courtesy Elaine Fiveland.)

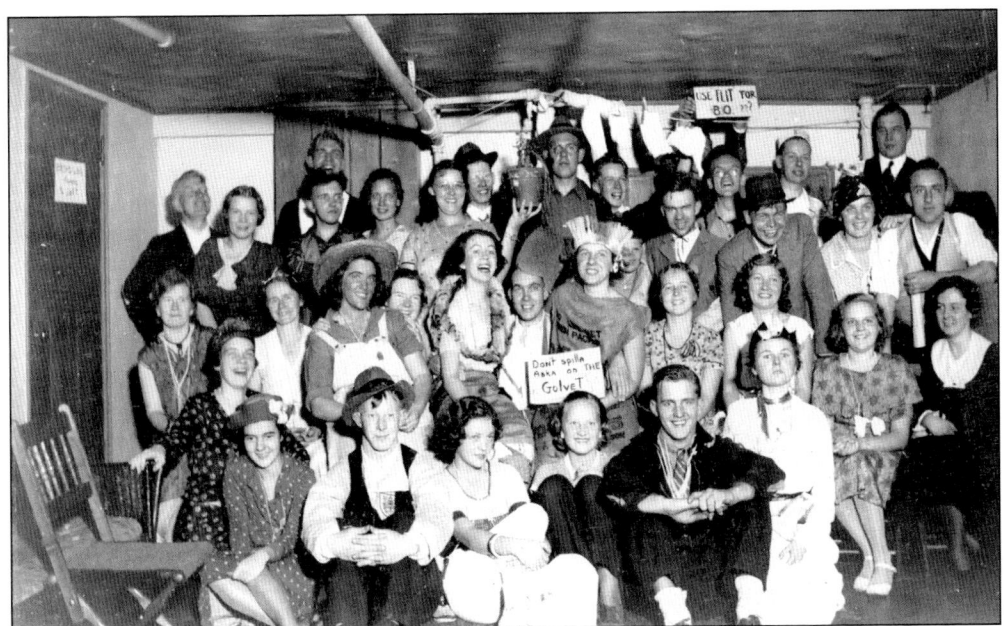

THE SWEDISH YOUNG ADULT GROUP. Swedish immigrants came to Montclair in the second half of the 19th century. Skilled in the building trades, they constructed many of Montclair's homes and public buildings. Many Swedes lived east of Park Street and north of Glenridge Avenue. This club for young adults was sponsored by the Swedish Congregational Church in the Depression era. (Courtesy Elaine Fiveland.)

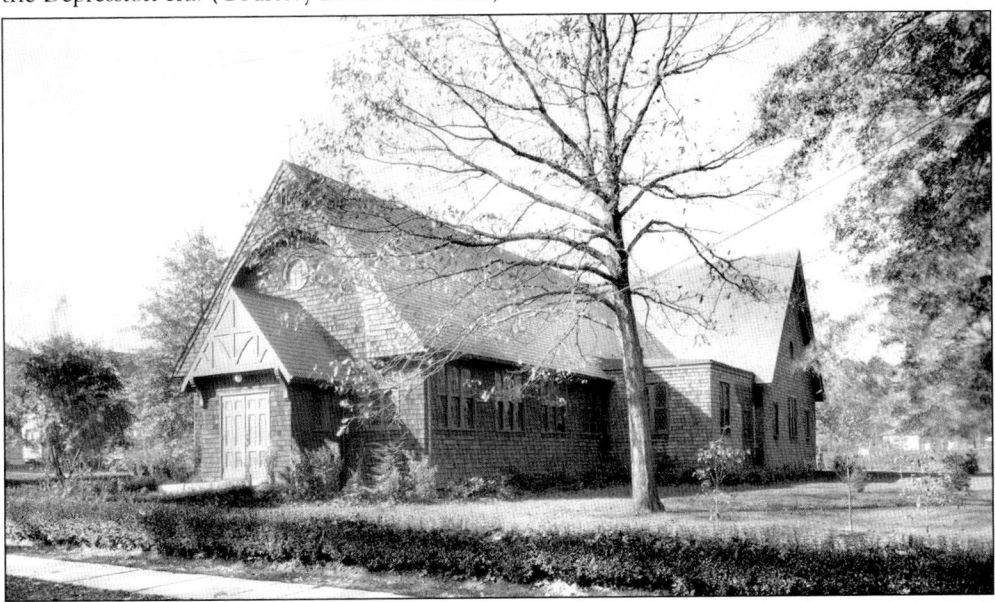

ST. CASSIAN'S ROMAN CATHOLIC CHURCH. Founded in 1895, the church served the Irish population on Norwood Avenue in Upper Montclair. Fleeing the potato famine, the Irish came to Montclair in the 1840s, working as domestics and laborers. The early Irish erected the Immaculate Conception Church in the Washington Street area then known as Irishtown. The early Irish grew to become prominent members of Montclair society; however, in 1890s, a small population of Irish women domestics still worked in Upper Montclair.

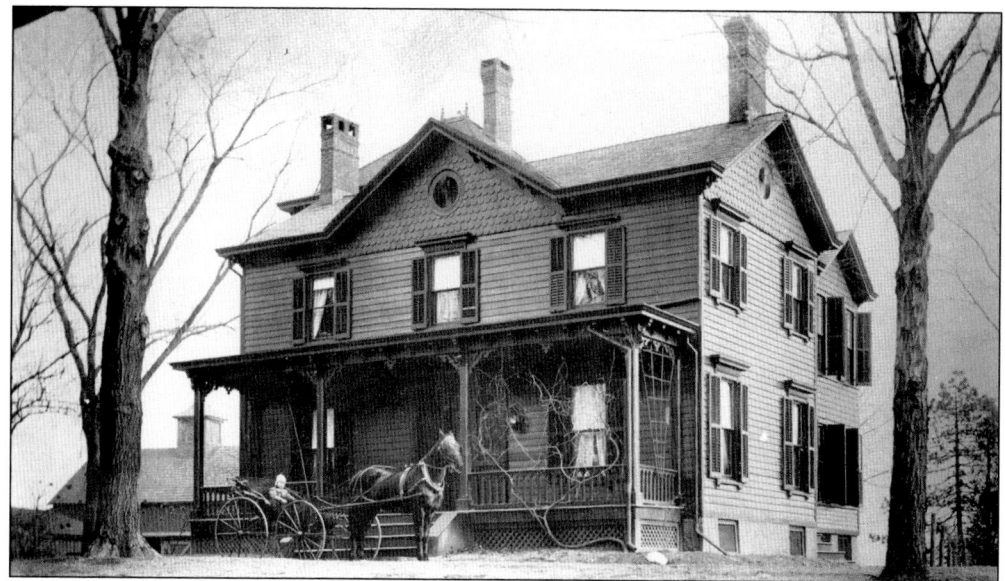

CHRISTOPHER HINCK'S RESIDENCE, GROVE STREET. Germans came to Montclair in the second half of the 19th century. One prominent German resident was Christopher Hinck, who purchased this house at 205 Grove Street in 1886. He bought up land around his house and with his daughter, Louise, was responsible for laying and building houses on the neighboring streets including Christopher Street, Cambridge, Ardsley, Tudor, and Tremont Roads. His son, Ernest Hinck, became a mayor. The boy in the carriage is named Christopher after his grandfather, who lived in the house.

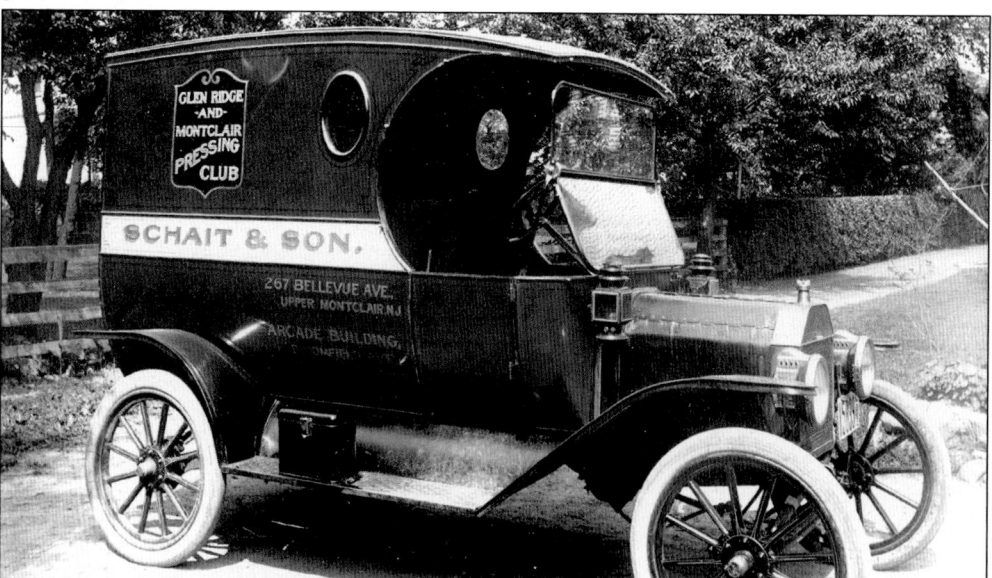

THE SCHAIT & SONS DELIVERY TRUCK. Another prominent German resident was Frank Schait. He opened a cleaning and pressing store at 267 Bellevue Avenue in Upper Montclair and, later, another store at the Arcade on Bloomfield Avenue. Before coming to Montclair, he had a shop on Fifth Avenue in New York. His wife, Grace, ran an employment agency at the Bellevue Avenue location. During the years following 1910, the Schaits had a Ford Model T delivery truck for returning clothes to their clients.

Four

ARTS

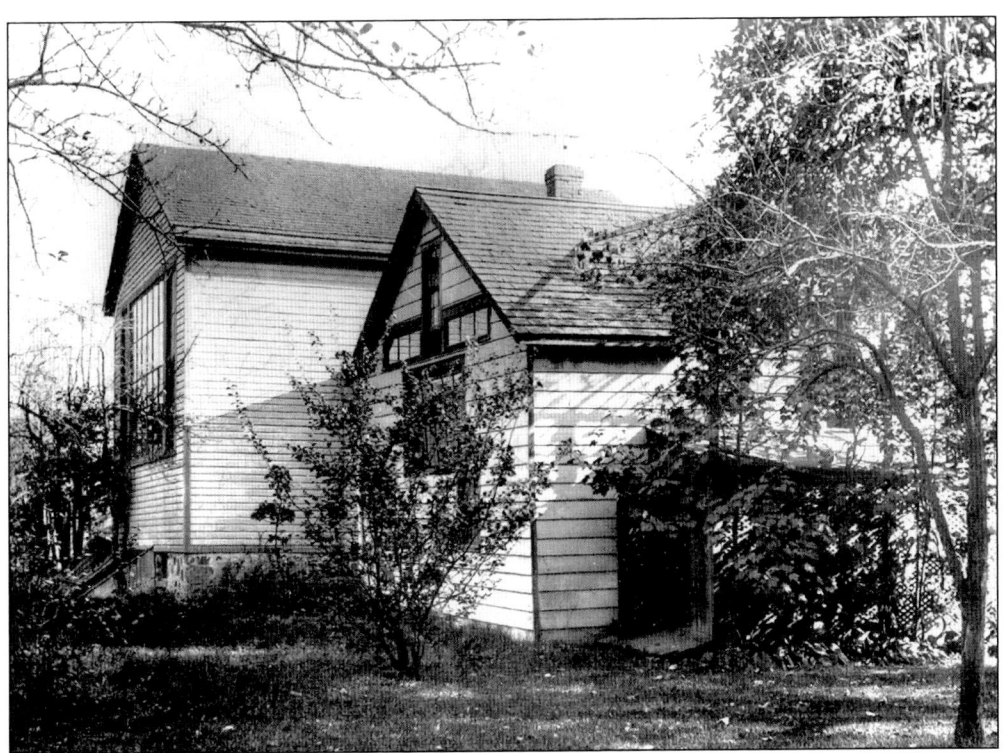

THE GEORGE INNESS SR. STUDIO. The Montclair Art Colony centered around George Inness Sr., who bought his Grove Street home, the Pines, in December 1884. His son-in-law, sculptor Jonathan Hartley, owned a house connected to the Inness home by a second-floor gallery walkway. The barn was made into a double studio for the two artists. The Montclair Art Colony was a group of 14 well-known artists who worked in Montclair from c. the 1860s to the 1920s.

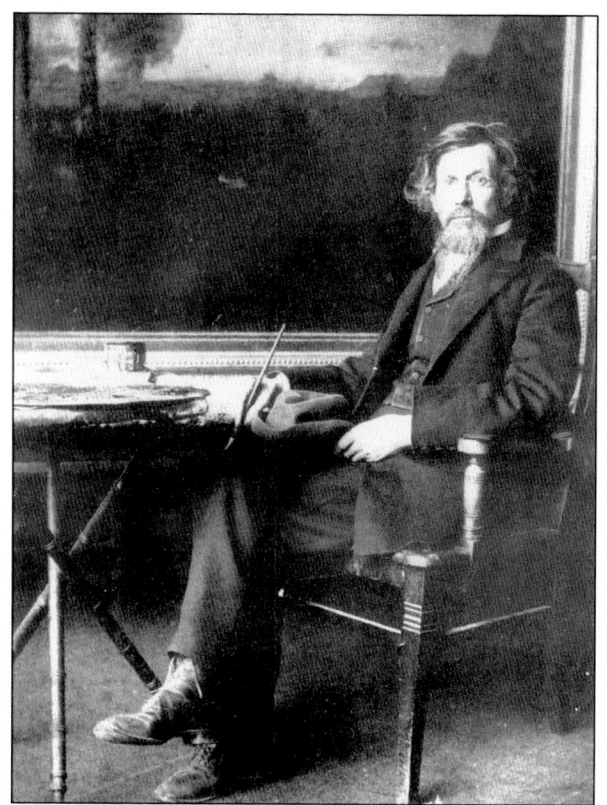

GEORGE INNESS SR. Landscape artist George Inness Sr. came to Montclair in the summer of 1878. He rented rooms at the Mansion House and various homes for several summers until he purchased his Grove Street home, the Pines. The internationally known artist was a major American landscape painter of his time. In 1894, he died in Scotland after viewing a sunset and exclaiming, "Oh how beautiful!" His son, George Inness Jr., also a Montclair Art Colony painter, lived in Montclair from 1881 to 1900.

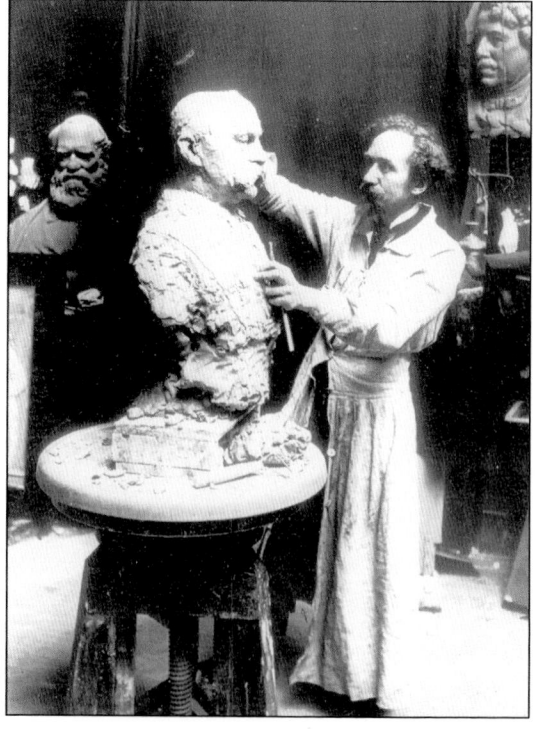

JONATHAN HARTLEY IN HIS STUDIO. Sculptor Jonathan Hartley followed his father-in-law to Montclair in 1885 to join the Montclair Art Colony. He married two Inness daughters: first, Rose Inness, and, later, Helen Inness. He was one of the founders of the Salmagundi Club and the Arts Student League in New York. He lived in Montclair until 1910 and died two years later. Other Montclair Art Colony sculptors were Thomas Ball and his son-in-law William Couper, who came to Montclair in 1897.

HARRY FENN. English-born illustrators Harry Fenn and Charles Parsons came to Montclair c. 1865 and were later part of the Montclair Art Colony. Fenn illustrated John Greenleaf Whittier's books *Snowbound* (1868) and *Ballads of New England* (1870). He is best known for his "Picturesque America" series, published in the *Appleton Journal*. He later painted watercolors. He died in 1911. This portrait was painted by Lawrence Earle, a Montclair Art Colony portrait painter who lived in Montclair from 1895 to 1908.

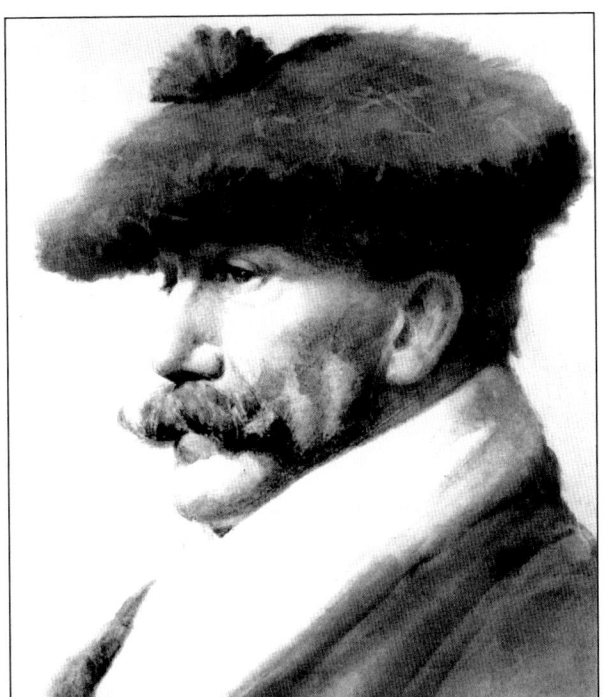

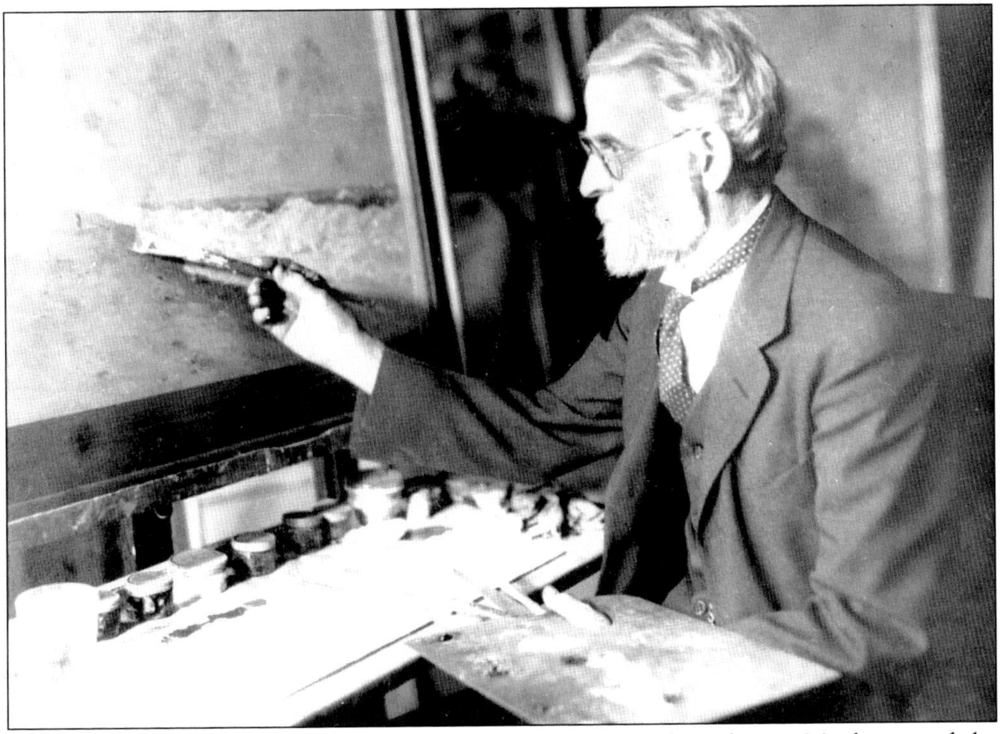

THOMAS MANLEY IN HIS STUDIO. Landscape painter and etcher Thomas Manley joined the Montclair Art Colony in 1893. He etched illustrations for magazines and newspapers, and also painted landscapes. His studio was in a rented carriage house on Dikes Lane. He was known for grinding his own pigments. He died in 1938.

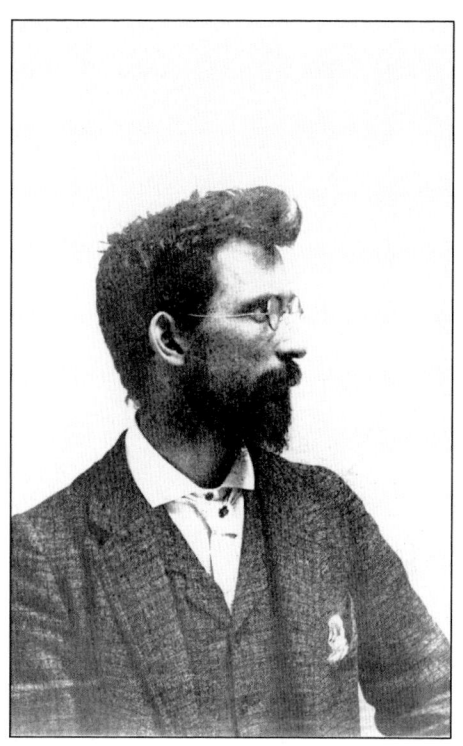

WALTER GREENOUGH. Emilie and Walter Greenough joined the Montclair Art Colony in 1890. They were stained-glass designers for the John La Forge Studio in New York. Emilie Greenough was also a portrait painter, and Walter Greenough designed book covers. Both staged plays and tableaux. He died in 1898, and Emilie in 1955. Their daughter, Emilie, married the actor Edgar Stehli. Other Montclair Art Colony artists were Joseph King, Henry Poore, Douglas Volk, and Frederick Waugh.

WILLIAM EVANS. Between 1880 and 1910, William Evans purchased 800 American paintings, thus creating the largest collection of American art at that time. Many of the Montclair Art Colony works were in his collection. In 1909, he offered to donate 26 of his paintings to the town if Montclair would build an art museum. The Montclair Art Association was organized to build and administer the museum, and Florence Rand Lang provided much of the financing.

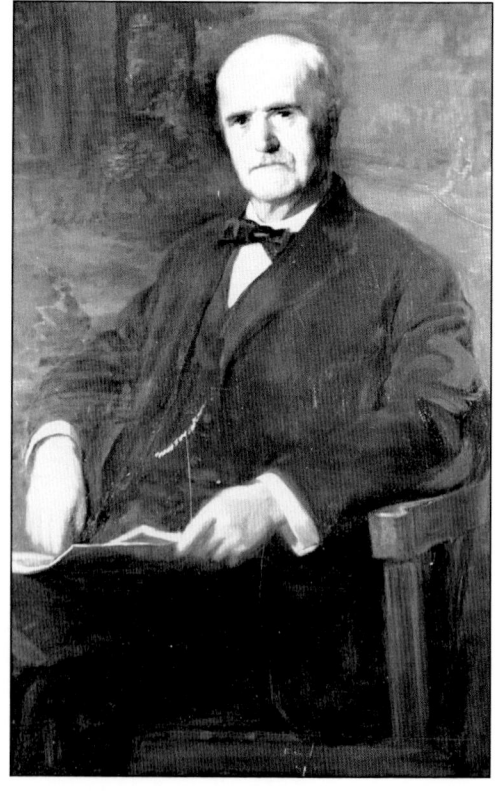

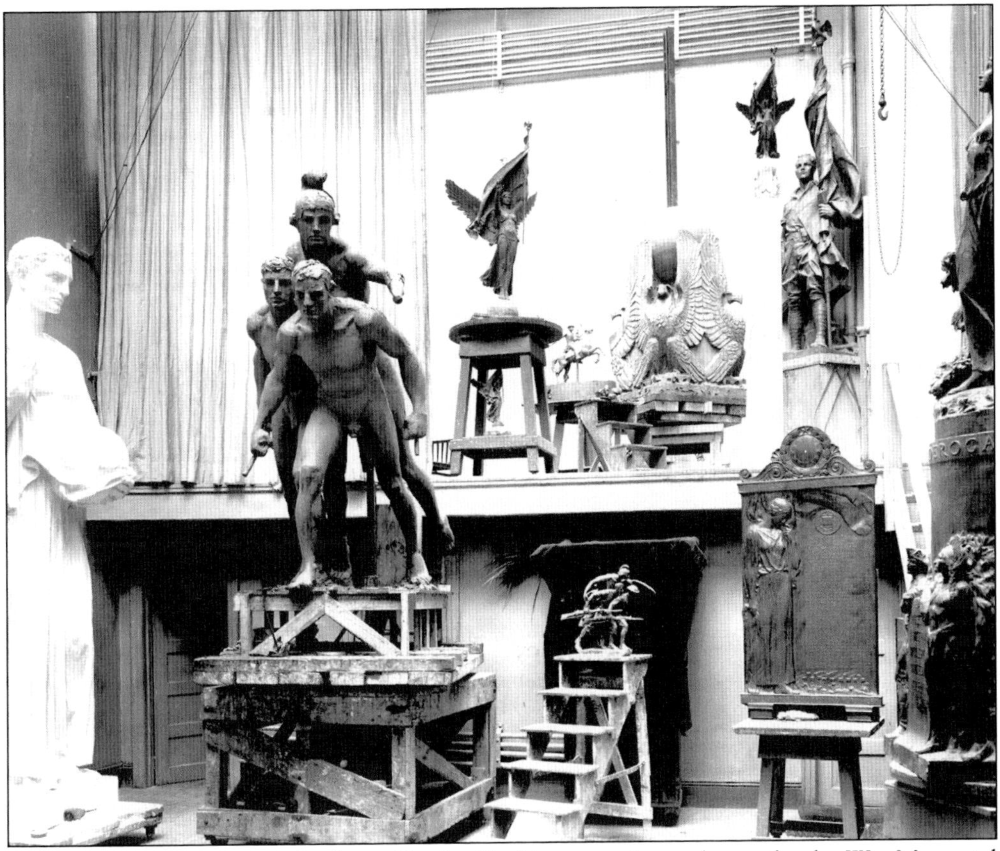

CHARLES KECK'S STUDIO. Sculptor Charles Keck's proposal was chosen for the War Memorial in Edgemont Park and was dedicated on Armistice Day 1925. Keck's work won the Medal of the Architectural League as the outstanding work of an American artist in 1925. Models for the memorial sculpture can be seen in this photograph of his New York studio. (Photograph by Louis Dryer.)

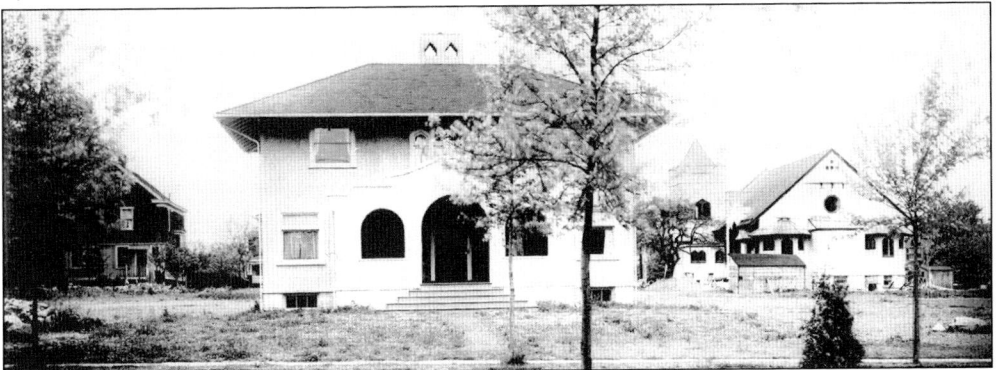

DUDLEY VAN ANTWERP, ARCHITECT. Dudley Van Antwerp was one of many esteemed architects working in Montclair. He came to Montclair as a child in 1880. He opened an office c. 1905 at 483 Bloomfield Avenue, where he designed Montclair Academy on Lloyd Road, the Monondock Inn in Caldwell, and 500 homes. He designed his own home (shown here), at 31 Fairfield Street. In the background is another of his designs: Watchung Congregational Church. His daughter married Harry Fenn.

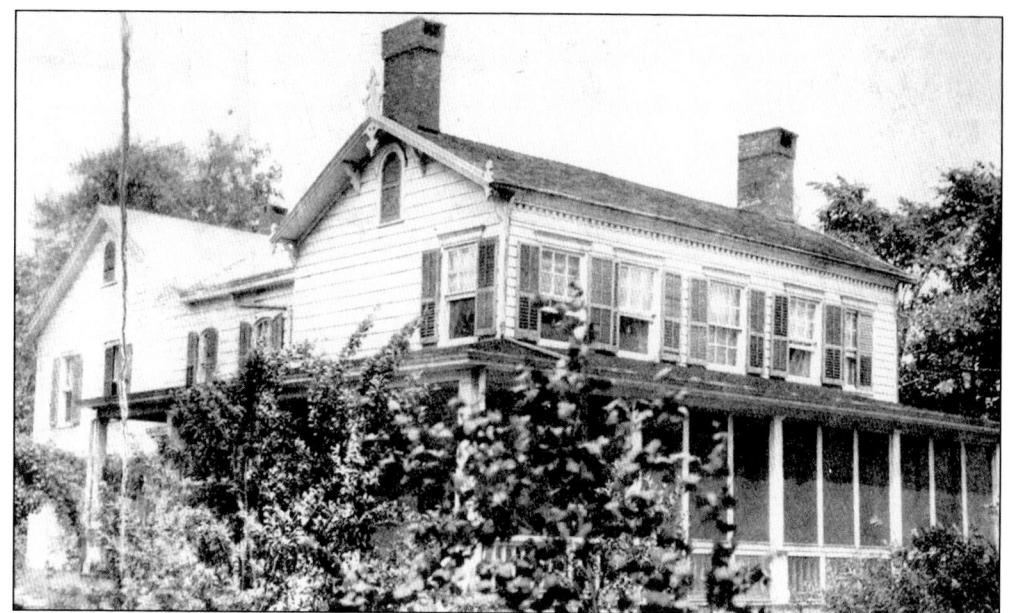

FREDERICK MELCHER'S HOUSE. Frederick Melcher, the president of R.R. Rowker and the editor-owner of *Publishers Weekly*, purchased the Green Farm at 228 Grove Street in 1918. He served on the Montclair Board of Education and Library Board and was president of the Unitarian Church and Montclair Art Museum. On a national level, he founded the Newberry Awards and organized the American Booksellers Association. His wife, Marguerite Fellows, was a playwright, poet, and short story author. Many famous writers gathered at his house.

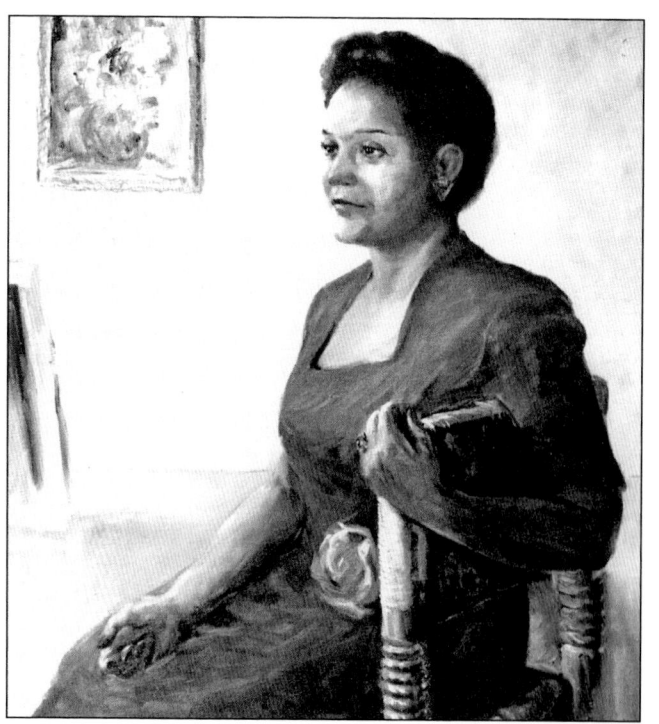

JESSIE FAUCET HARRIS. Author, editor, and poet Jessie Faucet Harris was one of the many esteemed writers in Montclair. Her best-known novel is *Chinaberry Tree*. She was the literary editor of *Crisis Magazine*, a publication of the National Association for the Advancement of Colored People (NAACP). Organized in 1916, the Montclair Branch of the NAACP is the second oldest branch in New Jersey.

RICHARD WILBUR. Richard Wilbur journeyed daily on foot and by trolley from his home in North Caldwell to attend Montclair High School. He is described under his self-illustrated yearbook photograph as "a first class scholar, a clever talker and cartoon drawer." He was appointed America's second poet laureate, and his name appears in the high school's entrance hall as a member of its hall of fame.

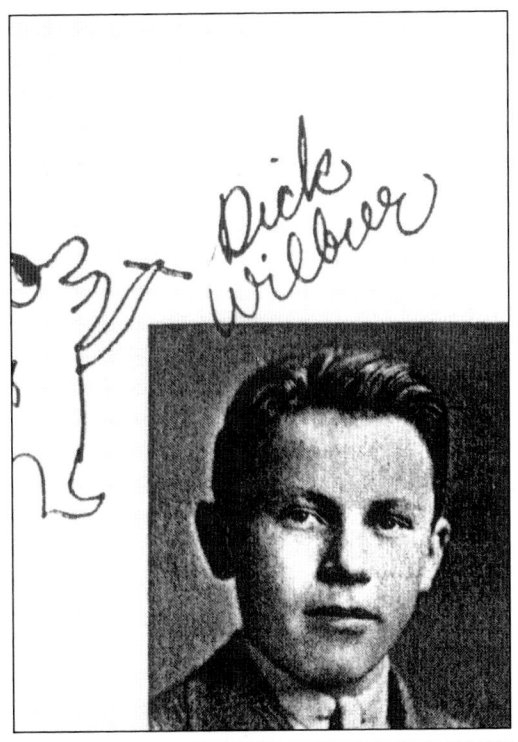

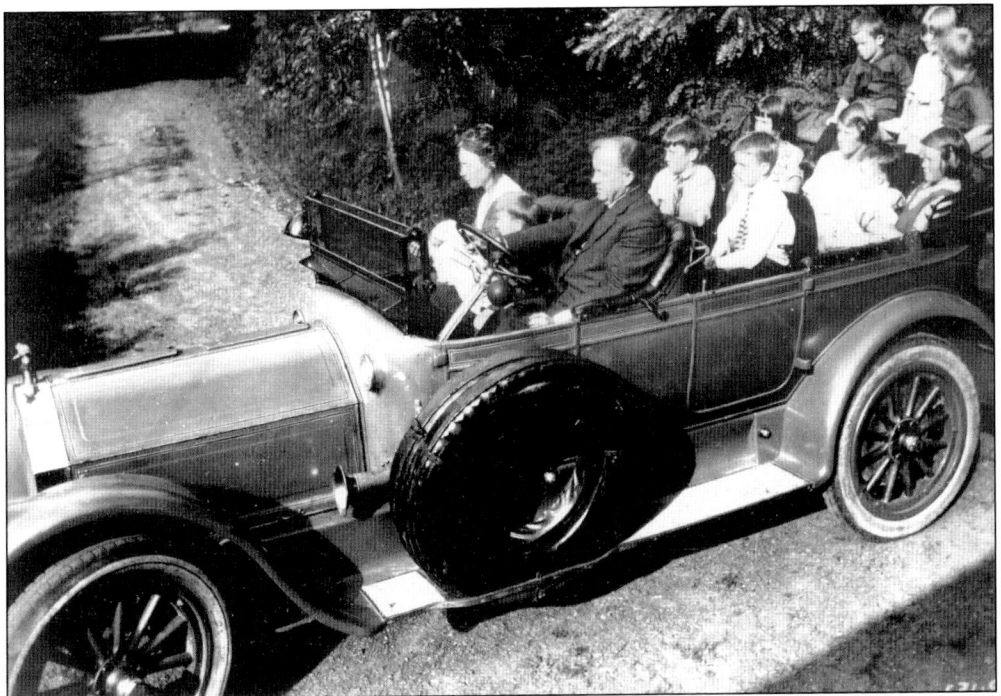

A GILBRETH FAMILY OUTING. Driving the Pierce Arrow is Frank Bunker Gilbreth Sr., who with his wife, Lillian Moller Gilbreth, pioneered the field of time-motion study. The story of the family's life in Montclair is told in books written by two of the 12 Gilbreth children, Frank Jr. and Ernestine: *Cheaper by the Dozen* and *Belles on Their Toes*.

Second Bach Festival Service

Sunday Afternoon
May 20, 1906
At Three O'Clock

Preceded by a Public
Rehearsal, Saturday
Evening, May 19th
At Eight O'Clock

✠

First Congregational Church

THE BACH FESTIVAL. Started in 1905 by Rev. Amory Bradford at the First Congregational Church, the Bach Festival was a major annual event for many years. Special trains from New York City to Lackawanna Station brought New Yorkers to the concerts.

UNITY CONCERTS. Founded in 1920 by Rev. Edgar Weirs of Unity (Unitarian) Church, Unity Institute provided cultural programs for Montclair. The first concert was held in October 1920. Top musicians including artists from the Metropolitan Opera Company were featured at this concert series, which became independent in 1982 and changed its name to Unity Concerts of New Jersey. Unity Institute also featured Unity travel, literary, science and drama courses, chamber music, the Symphony for Young People, children's matinees, Unity Forum, and Collegiate Pulpit.

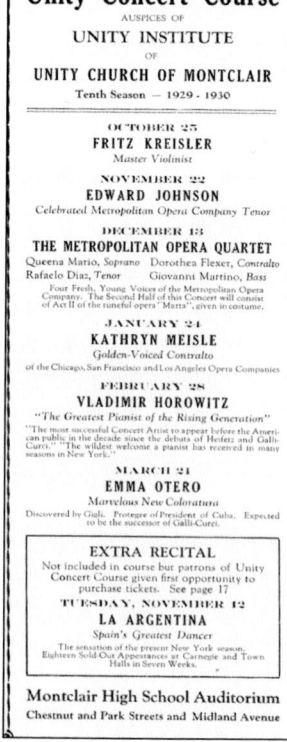

50

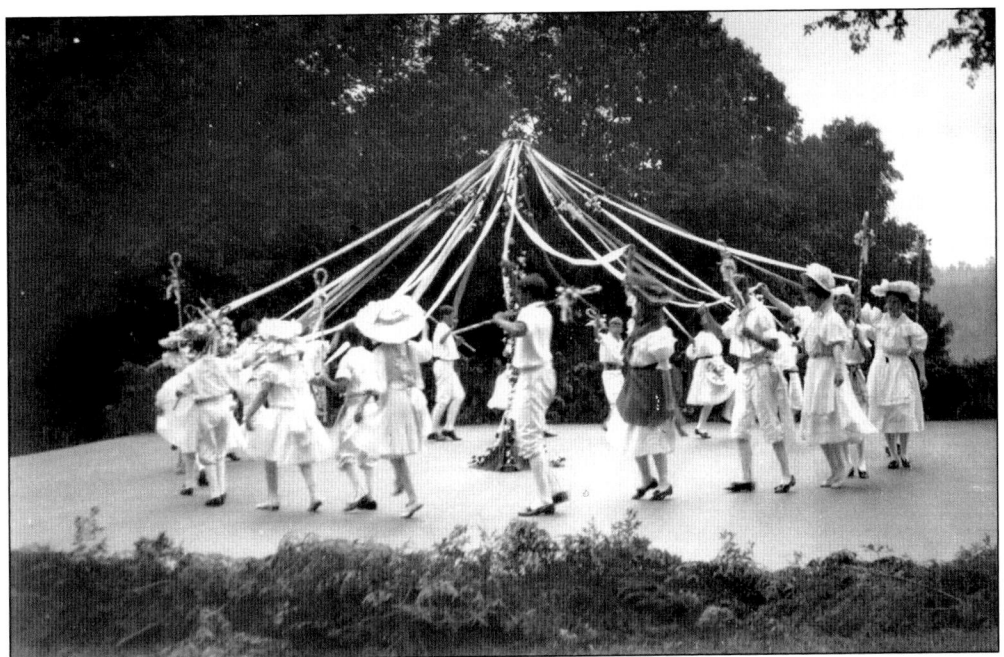

SUSANNE SAWYER'S OUTDOOR DANCE PAGEANT. Susanne Sawyer and her sister Jessie Sawyer started teaching dance c. 1897 at the Montclair Club. They taught ballet, tap, aesthetic, and social dancing. They also staged outdoor dance pageants. When Susanne died in 1946, she had classes in Montclair, Upper Montclair, Glen Ridge, and Essex Fells.

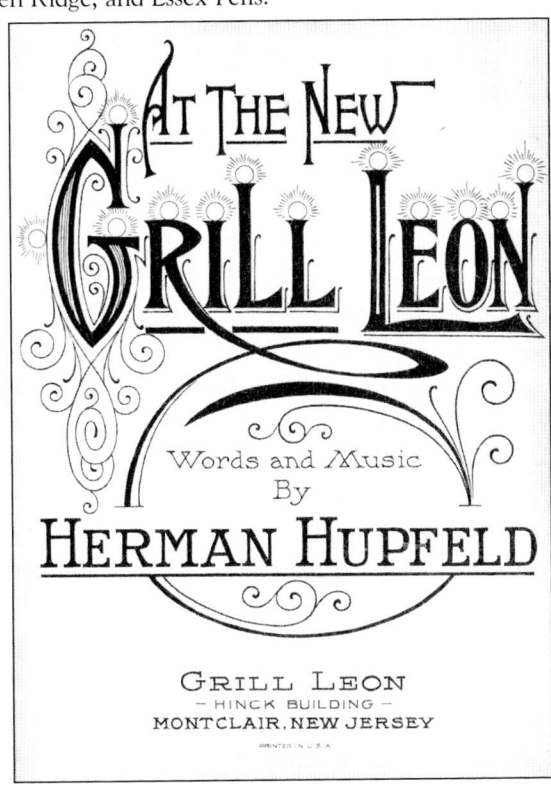

HERMAN HUPFELD. Composer Herman Hupfeld, best known for his song "As Times Goes By" in the movie *Casablanca*, wrote a song to promote the new Grill Leon in the Hinck building. The opening lines of "At the New Grill Leon" were "Are you wondering where to go for fun and recreation, without squandering too much dough?" When the Grill Leon was replaced by the Three Crowns, Hupfeld remained a regular patron. He lived at 259 Park Street. (Courtesy the Montclair Historical Society.)

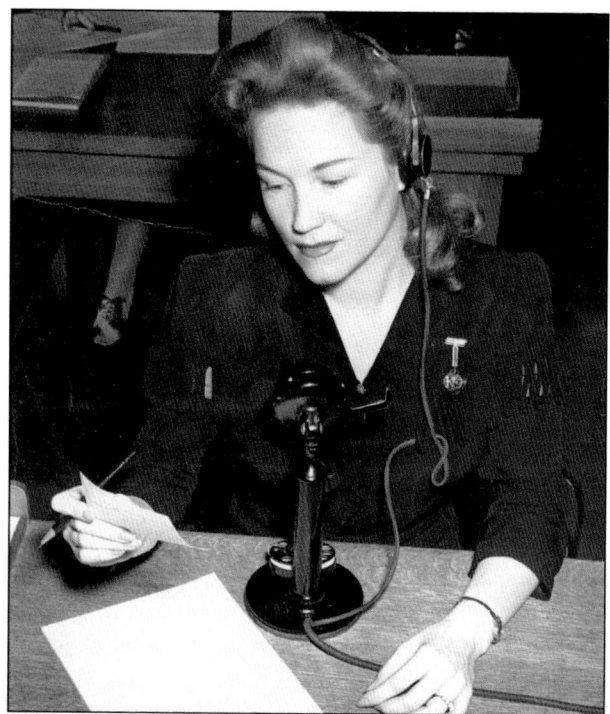

DOROTHY KIRSTEN. Lyric soprano Dorothy Kirsten worked as a telephone operator to pay for her singing lessons and sang popular music on the radio. Discovered by Grace Moore, her first opera contract was with the Chicago Civic Opera in November 1940. In 1945, she became principal soprano with both the San Francisco Opera (1945–1972) and the Metropolitan Opera (1945–1979). She also sang with Frank Sinatra, Bing Crosby, and Nelson Eddy. (Courtesy the *Montclair Times*.)

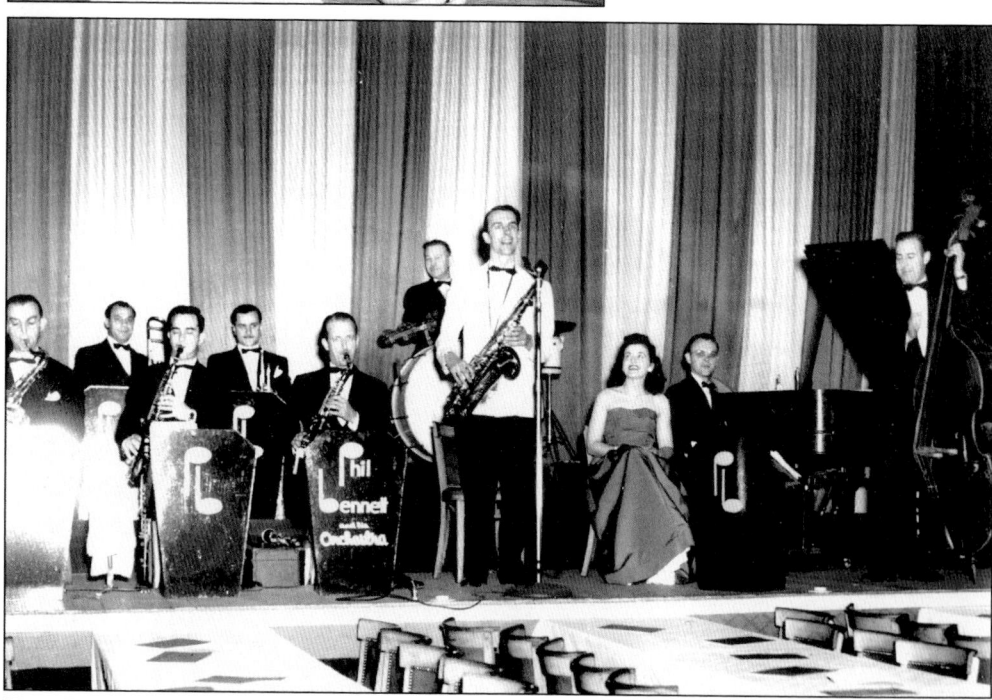

THE PHIL BENNETT ORCHESTRA. Musician-composer Phil Bennett came to Montclair c. 1926. Blind at birth, he learned new tunes by listening to the radio. Established in 1939, his Phil Bennett Orchestra played locally and in New York for various clubs and high school and college dances. Several musicians were on call to play in the band. Bennett composed music and played eight instruments, including the saxophone.

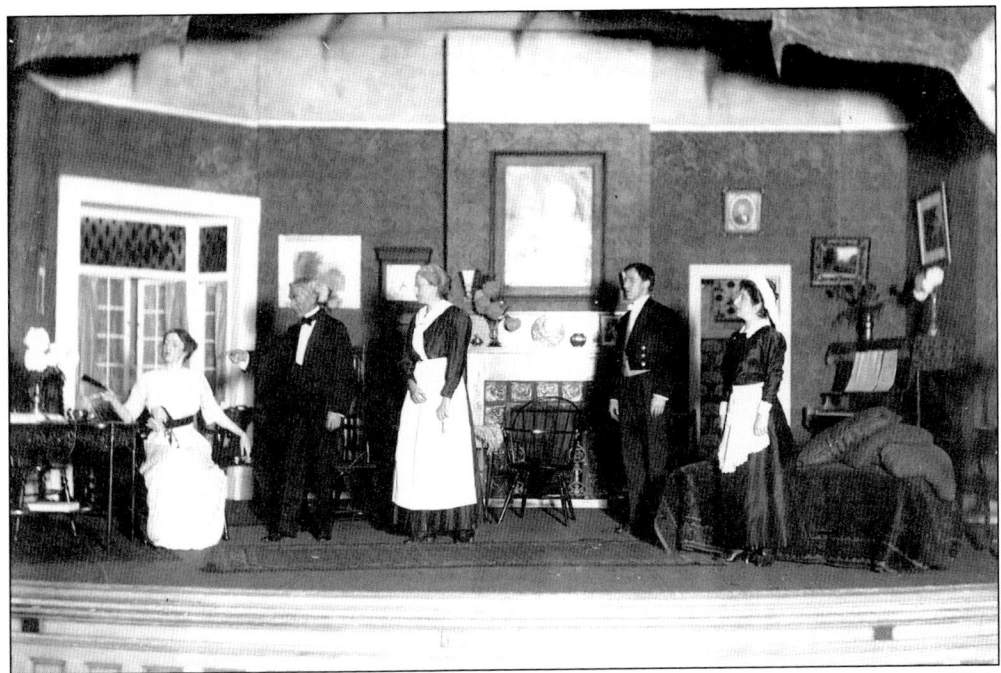

THE MONTCLAIR DRAMATIC CLUB. Founded on April 17, 1889, the Montclair Dramatic Club produced fall and spring amateur plays at the Montclair Club (1889–1924), Montclair Theater (1924–1928), George Inness School (1928–1930), and Mount Hebron School (1931–the early 1990s). During World War I, special plays for servicemen were performed. After 1893, the staff included a professional theater director and both member and non-member actors. It was the oldest amateur theater group in America when it dissolved in the early 1990s.

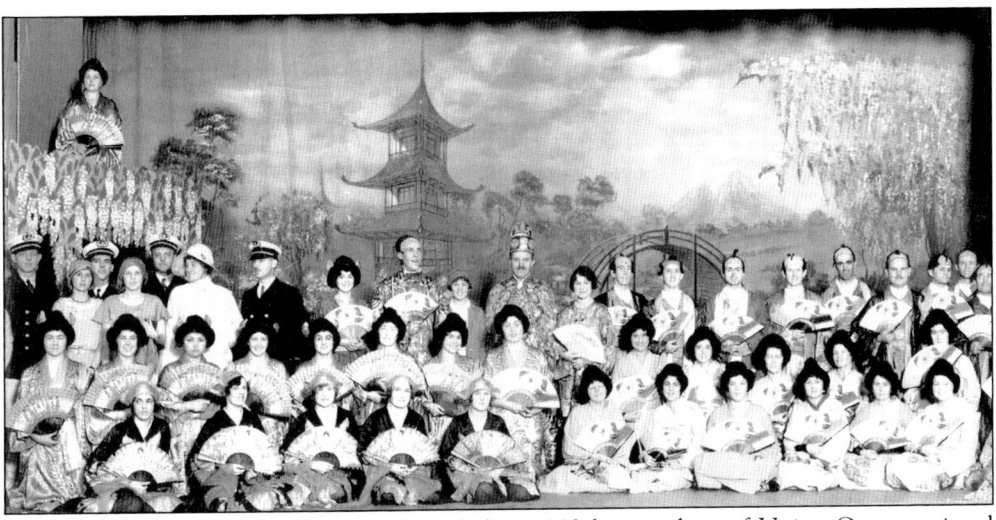

THE MONTCLAIR OPERETTA CLUB. Founded in 1923 by members of Union Congregational Church, the Montclair Operetta Club is the oldest theatrical organization of its kind in America. Chartered in 1925, the club at first performed only Gilbert and Sullivan operettas. In 1929, the repertoire expanded to other operetta composers. After the club incorporated as the Montclair Operetta Club in 1936, the leads, directors, and choreographers were professionals. In 1953, the club performed its first Broadway musical. (Photograph by Pictorial News Syndicate.)

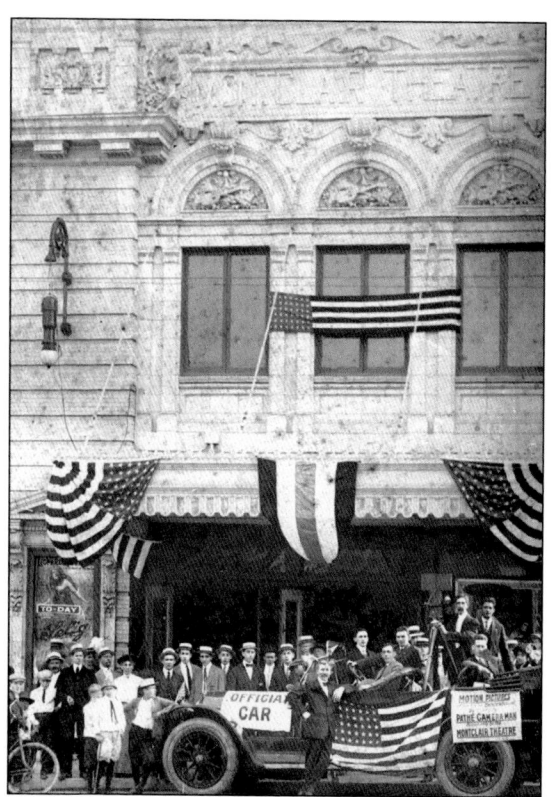

THE MONTCLAIR THEATER. The first movie theater in Montclair opened in 1913 at 634 Bloomfield Avenue. The Montclair Theater had a full stage for plays, vaudeville, and musical productions, as well as for movies. This photograph may show the grand opening for the theater. The Wellmont, Claridge, and Bellevue Theaters opened in 1922, featuring both live and movie entertainments.

OSCAR MICHEAUX. The Micheaux Film Corporation produced more than 30 melodramas, action movies, and musicals featuring black actors from 1919 to 1948. Although the films played at black movie theaters, Oscar Micheaux tirelessly promoted them at the other theaters, where they were shown at 2:00 a.m. or 3:00 a.m. to packed houses. Paul Robeson's first film, *Body and Soul*, was one of Micheaux's films. The first black talkie, *Exile* (1931), was another Micheaux production. Micheaux's wife was Montclair native Alice Russell.

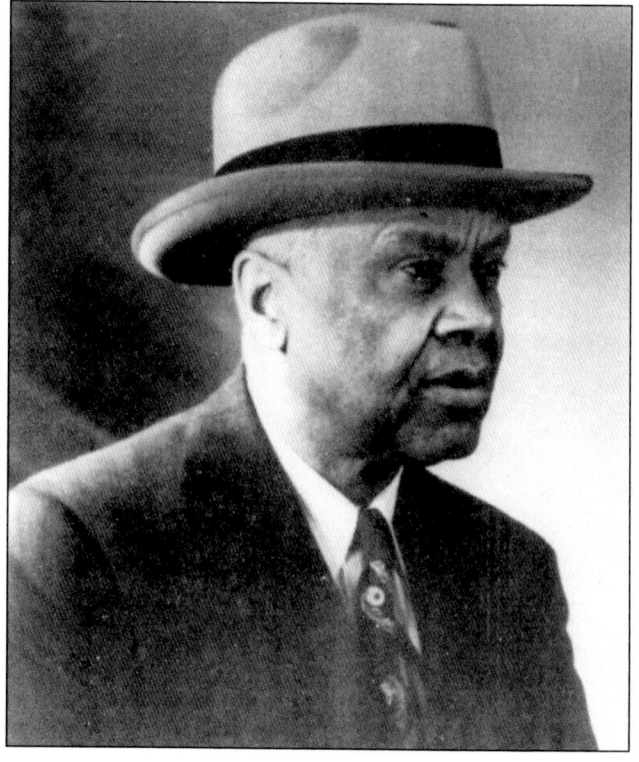

Five

EDUCATION

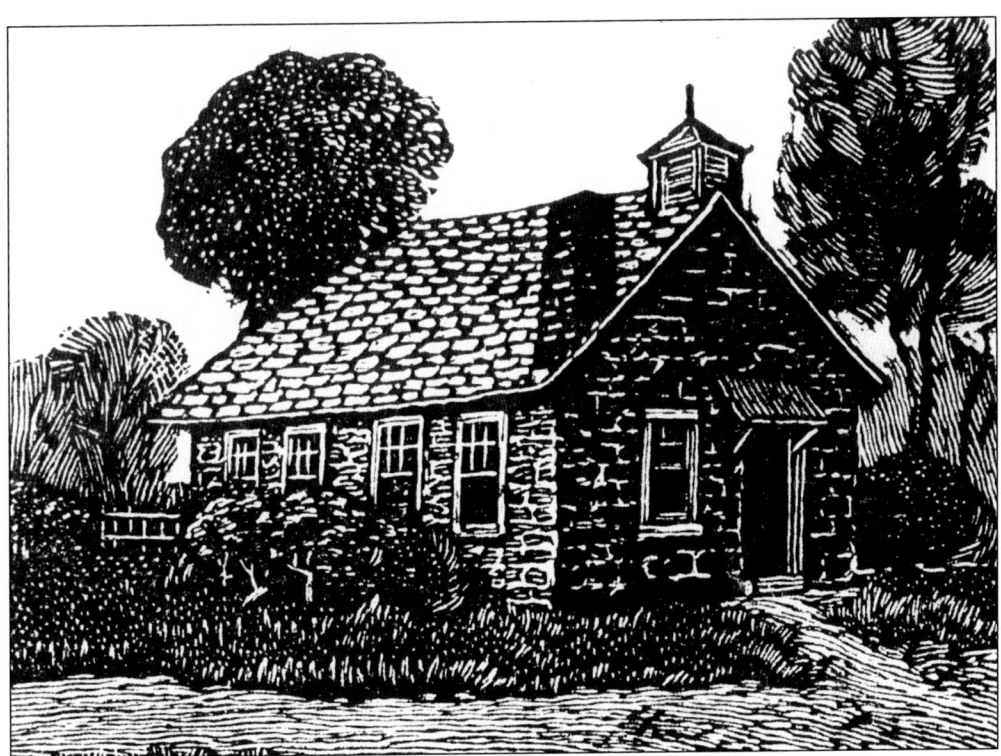

THE FIRST SCHOOLHOUSE. Built c. 1740, this school was situated near the northwest corner of Valley Road and Church Street. The seats were slabs with the bark side down. At one end of the room was the raised rostrum from which the teacher presided. Below him was a trap door through which miscreants might be dropped into the darkness. An early teacher was Isaac Watts Crane, named for the lyricist who set the Psalms to rime and meter for use as hymns.

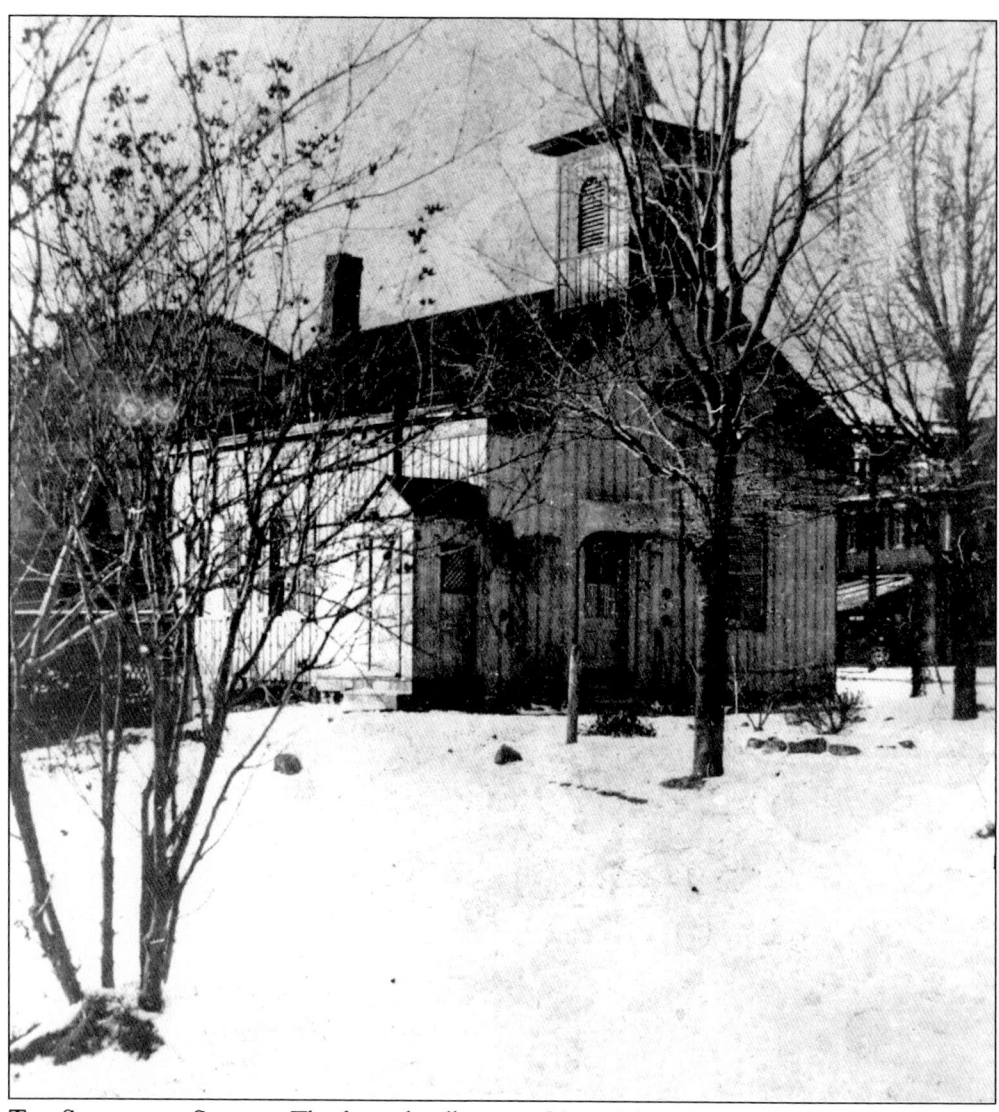

THE SPEERTOWN SCHOOL. The first schoolhouse in Upper Montclair was built c. 1827 near the southwest corner of Bellevue Avenue and Valley Road. The one shown here replaced the original c. 1849. What was known as the Trunk Building, containing offices and shops, appears in the background. The schoolhouse served briefly as the home of the Christian Union Church (later, the Union Congregational Church) and spent its last days housing offices of a lumberyard.

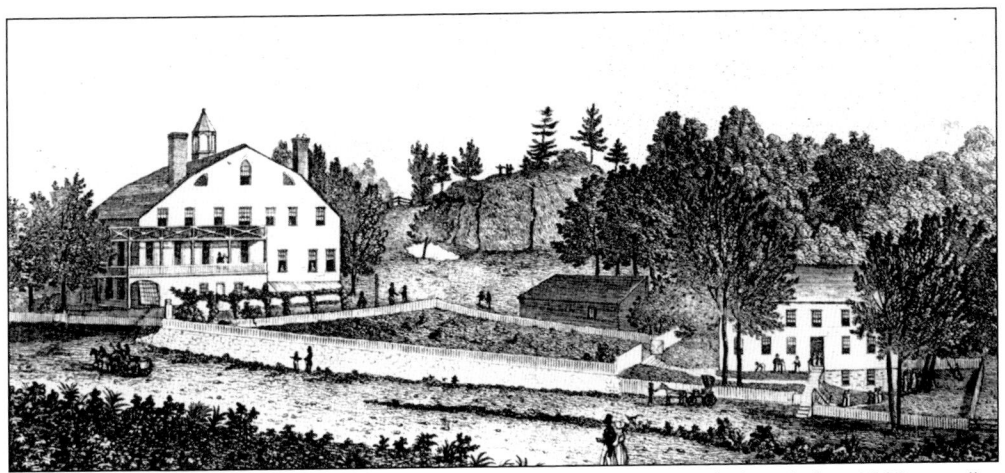

MOUNT PROSPECT INSTITUTE. The object of this boarding school, founded c. 1838, was "to prepare Young Gentlemen for entering college or business life." Boys wore single-breasted coats that buttoned at the throat with gilt buttons. Mount Prospect also had a department for young women. Four stages daily connected the school with the New York ferries. In 1850, five boarding schools were located in Montclair.

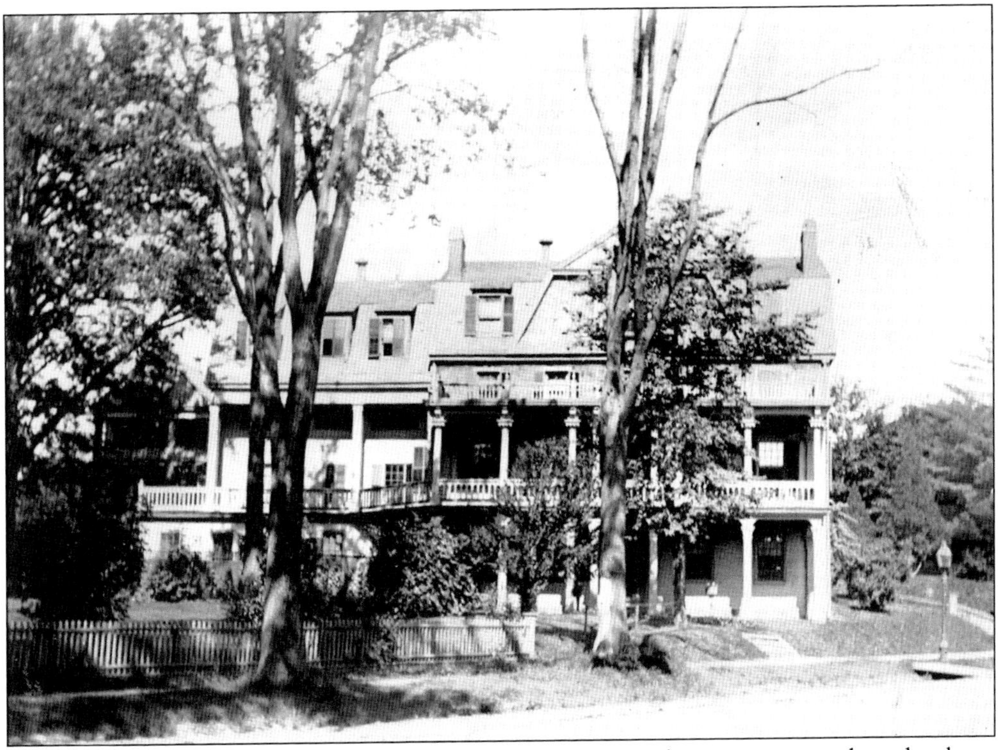

ASHLAND HALL. Located on Bloomfield Avenue across from the train station, this school was established in 1845 by Rev. David A. Frame, a native of Northern Ireland, as a small boarding school for boys. Ashland Hall helped make Montclair known to New York families who sent their sons here.

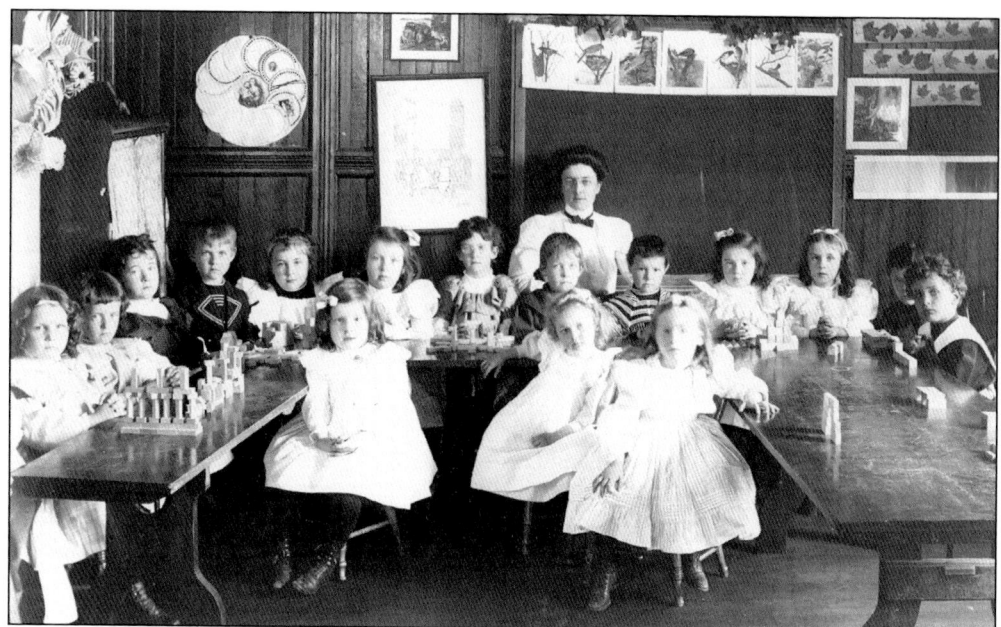

MRS. CARTER'S KINDERGARTEN. In the late 19th century, there were several small schools for young children conducted by women in Montclair. The kindergarten run by Mrs. J.L. Carter was held at 133 Chestnut Street in a home that still stands on the corner of Central Avenue. The photograph was taken in 1899.

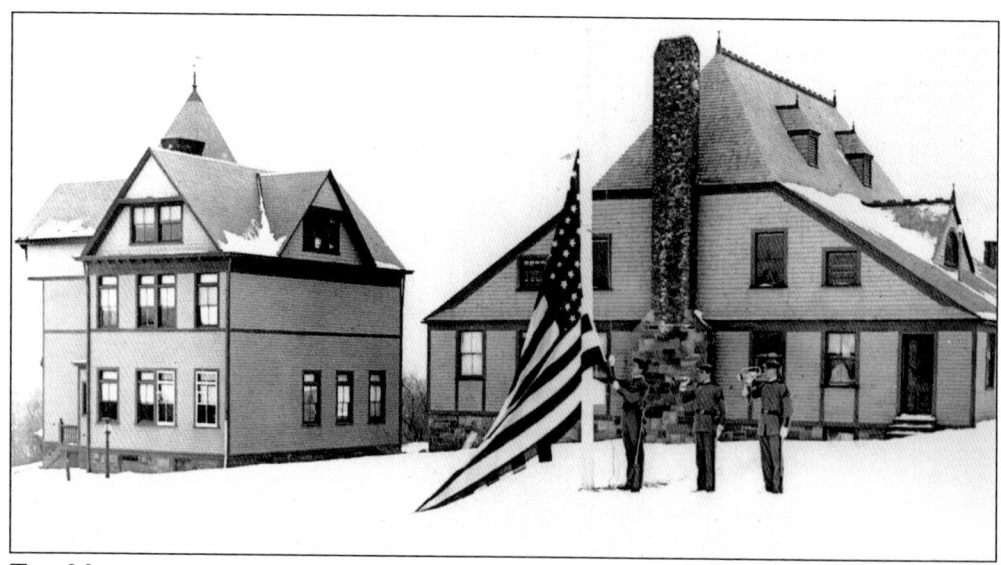

THE MONTCLAIR MILITARY ACADEMY. Seeking private instruction for their sons, several Montclair men recruited John G. MacVicar in 1887 to conduct a small school. After outgrowing premises on Clinton Avenue, the Montclair Military Academy moved to Walden Place. This 1890s photograph shows the recitation building on the left and the gymnasium to the right. Ceasing early on to be a military school, the academy joined with Kimberly School in 1974 to form Montclair Kimberly Academy.

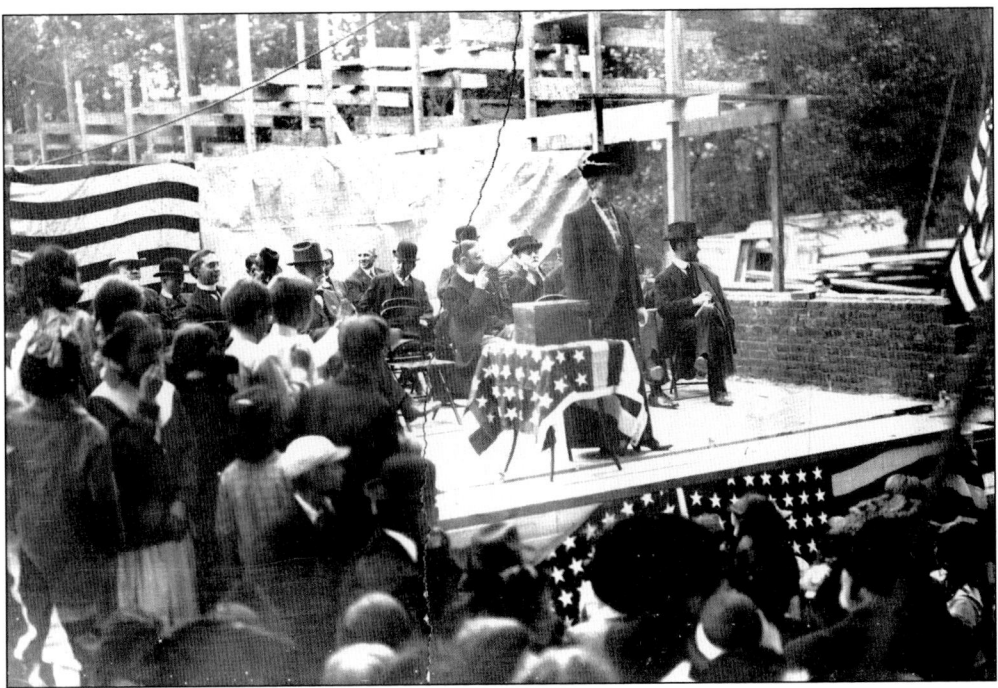

LOUISE C. HINCK. The first woman to serve on the Montclair Board of Education was Louise C. Hinck. She was also among the first women admitted to the New York State Bar. Here, she speaks at the cornerstone laying for the high school on Chestnut Street on October 6, 1914. William Balch, of the school's first graduating class, recalled that when Louise Hinck entered a room, "you felt that a queen had arrived."

PROGRAM	PROGRAM
Invocation REV. HENRY E. JACKSON	Gymnasium LOUISE C. HINCK
Introductory ELMER H. NEFF Chairman of Committee	Placing Box in Corner Stone WILLIAM WHITNEY AMES
History of the Enterprise ARTHUR C. HARRIS President	Laying Corner Stone RANDALL SPAULDING
Oration REV. HARRY EMERSON FOSDICK	Singing "Alma Mater" PUPILS OF HIGH SCHOOL
Architectural Features of the Building OTTO F. SEMSCH	Benediction REV. EDGAR SWAN WIERS

CORNERSTONE PROGRAM. Dedicated in 1914, the high school is still in use, although with important additions. Participating in the cornerstone laying are some of the people who also appear elsewhere in this book. It is a fair guess that the box placed inside the cornerstone is the one resting on the flag-draped table in the previous picture.

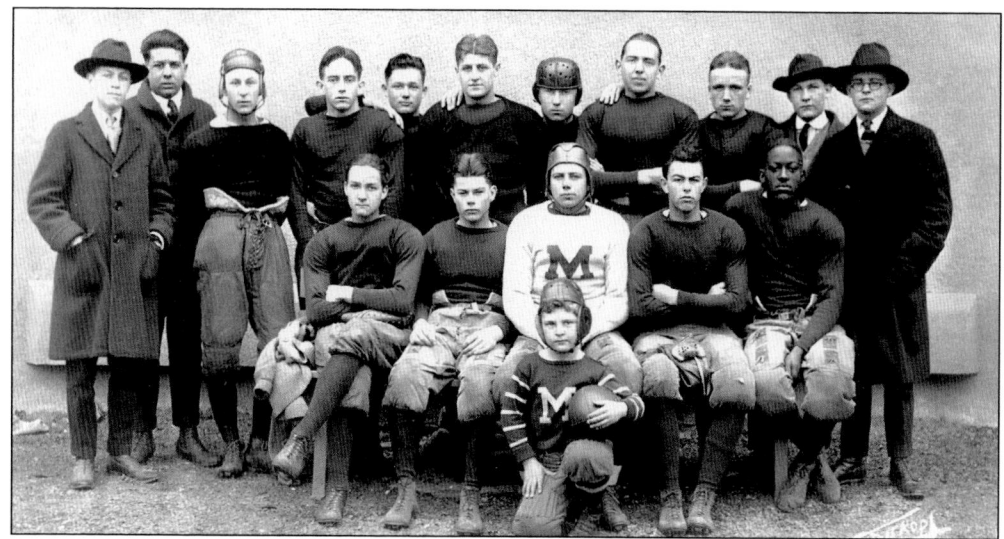

THE FOOTBALL TEAM, 1918. Football was already well established at the high school, although the great championship teams under Clary Anderson and Butch Fortunato were yet to come. The captain of the 1918 team was John Foster, who wears the white jersey. The lone African American on the team was John Fitzgerald, destined to become a well-known dentist in town.

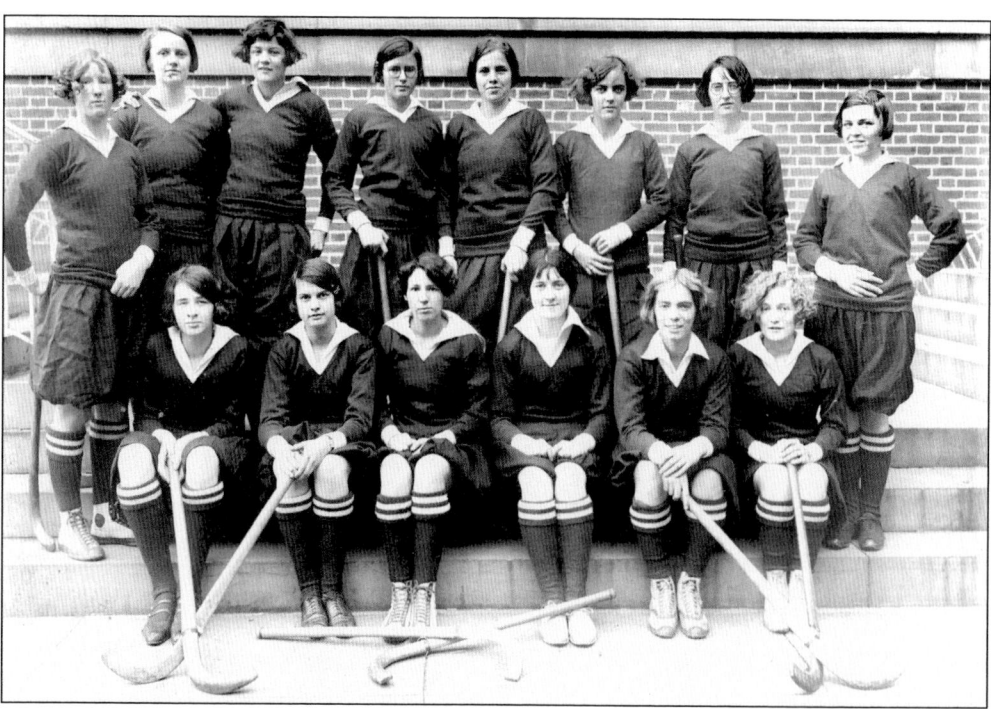

THE FIELD HOCKEY TEAM, 1925. Field hockey had become a popular sport for girls when this photograph was taken of the high school team. From left to right are the following: (seated) Ruth Lowelly, Lillian Kersey, Katherine Allen, Elizabeth Forde, Ethel Hesselbrock, and Janet Rockwell; (standing) Virginia Strothers, Jane Stearns, Pinky Brower, Constance MacDougall, Frances Wells, Natalie Sidman, Marion Ring, and Mary Dunning.

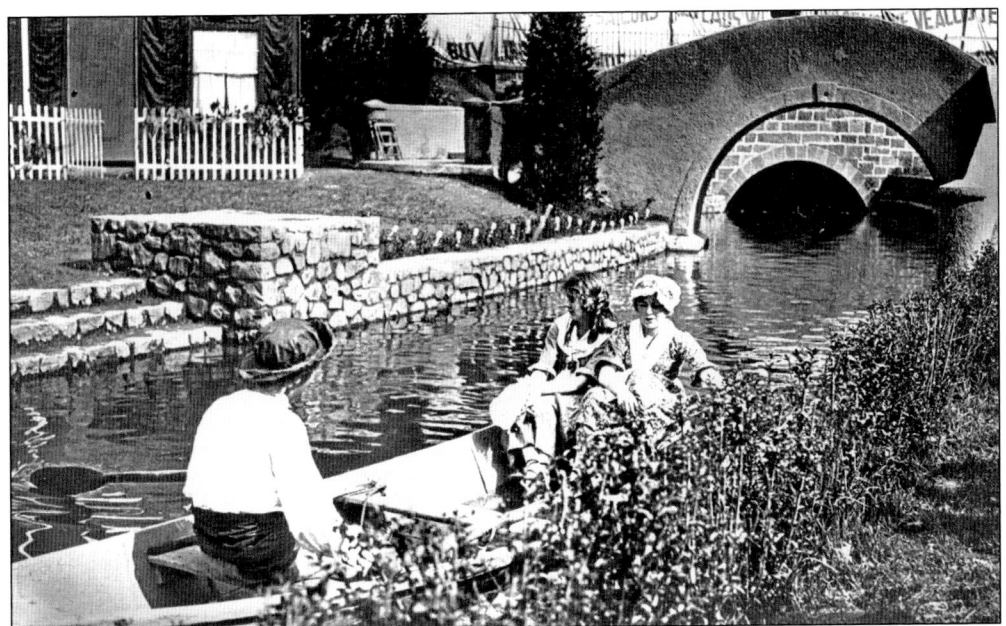

OUTDOOR DRAMA. *Pomander Walk* was the title of this play given at the high school amphitheater on May 31, 1918. It was a comedy in three acts by Louis N. Parker. The program states that Pomander Walk was "a crescent of five houses on a terrace by the river Thames" and that the action takes place in 1805. In this production, the part of the Thames is played by Toney's Brook.

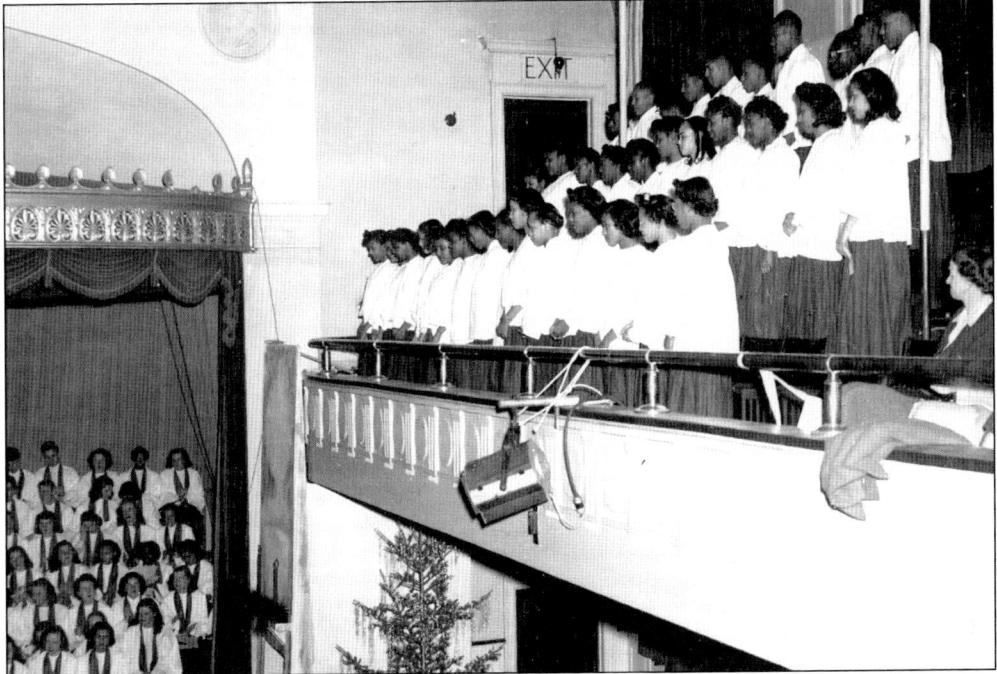

A SPIRITUAL CHOIR. This picture was taken in the old auditorium of the present high school, likely before 1960. The Christmas tree indicates a December date and suggests the theme for much of the music.

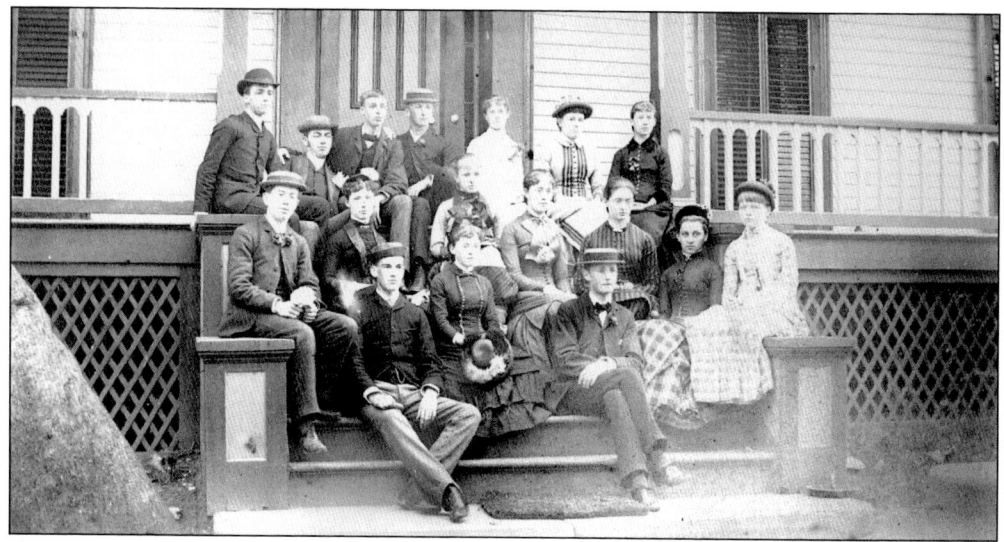

THE GRADUATING CLASS, 1883. At this early date, some of Montclair's wealthiest families thought well enough of the public high school to send their children there. The tall boy to the left on the lowest step is Washington Irving Lincoln Adams, whose father headed Scovil and Adams, manufacturers of photographic equipment. Also in the picture are Josephine Rand, daughter of Jasper, and Thomas W. Porter Jr., who later succeeded his father as president of Porter Brothers in New York.

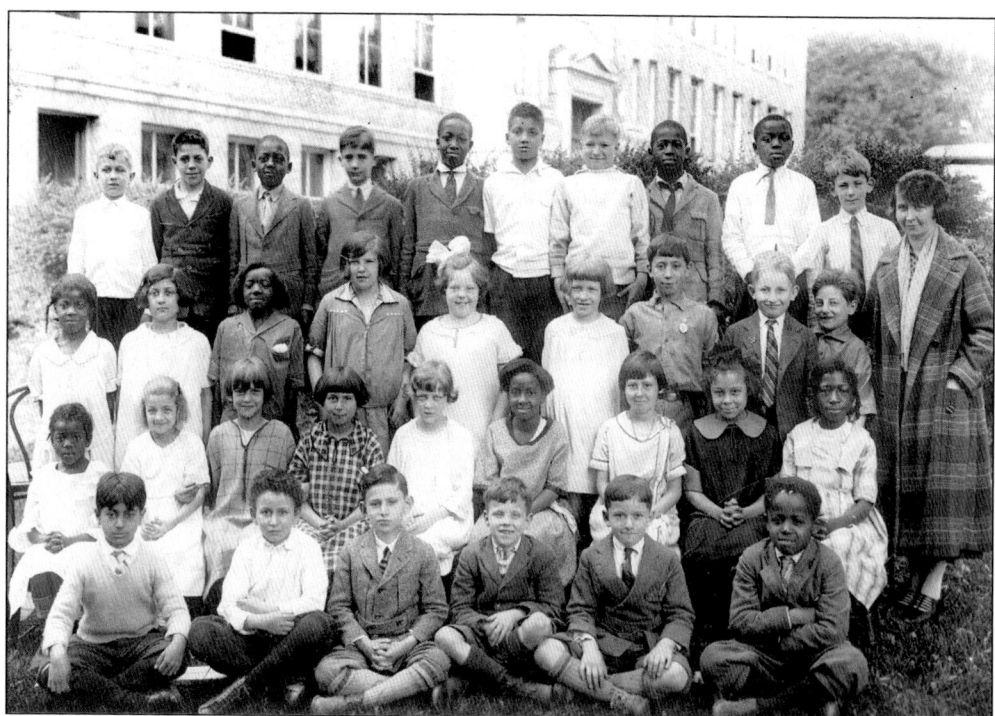

THE NISHUANE FIRST GRADE, 1922. The class reflects the racial diversity that already characterizes the town. However, a system of neighborhood elementary schools led to de facto segregation for some parts of the community. It was not until 1977 that a magnet school plan designed to remedy racial imbalance went into effect.

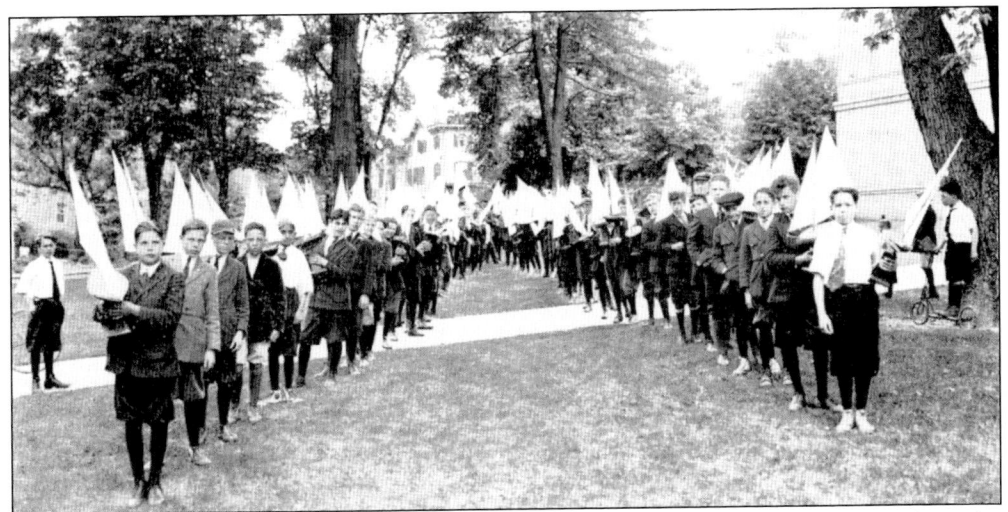

A SAILBOAT PARADE. These knickered boys at the Hillside School appear to be from the 1930s. Toy sailboat regattas were popular at that time, especially in the pond at Edgemont Memorial Park.

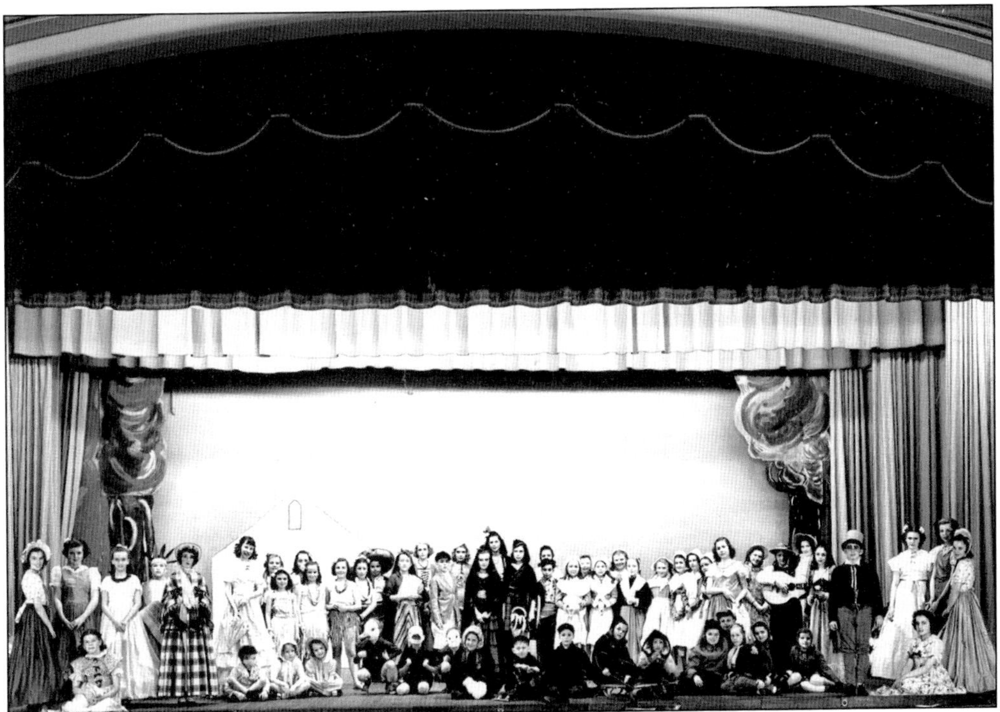

A SPRING CONCERT, MOUNT HEBRON SCHOOL. The title of the concert performed in April 1940 was "Music, Magic, Music." The large stage at Mount Hebron has witnessed not only that school's productions but also those of many other organizations, including the Montclair Operetta Club, the Montclair Dramatic Club, the New Jersey Symphony, and Unity Concerts of New Jersey.

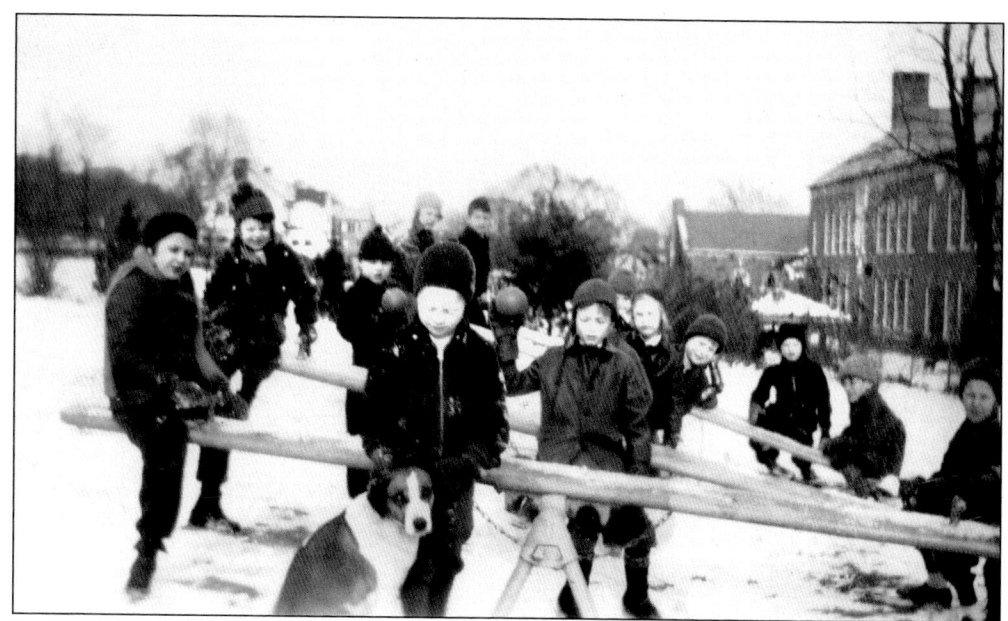

RECESS AT EDGEMONT SCHOOL. This 1930s photograph shows second-graders on the seesaws behind Edgemont School, which is located on Edgemont Road across from the park. The dog's name was Peter, and he attended class regularly with his companion Lynn C. "Lindy" Stoker.

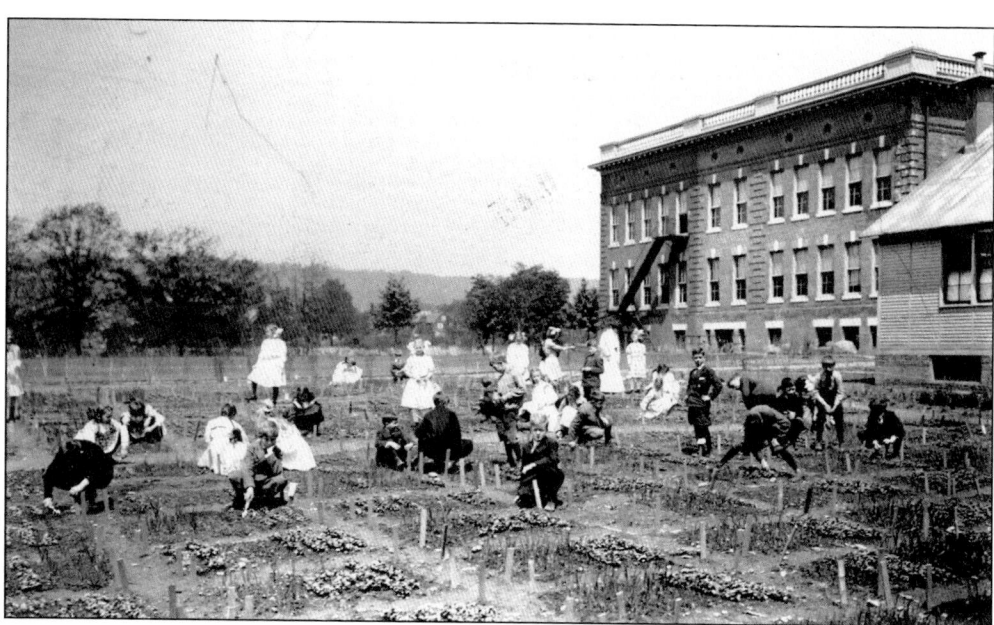

WATCHUNG HORTICULTURE. In the 1920s, Watchung School was still endowed with extensive grounds that lent themselves to training in raising crops. From the vantage point of a more casual age, the clothing worn for this activity seems strange. However, in those days, blue jeans would not have got you through the school door.

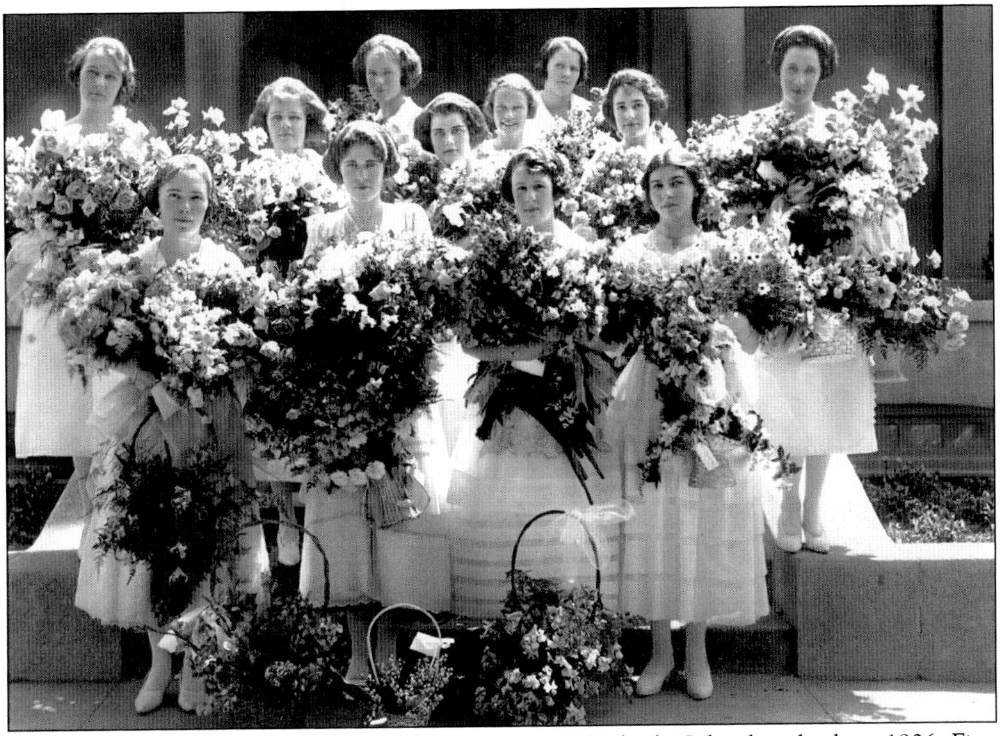

KIMBERLY SCHOOL, CLASS OF 1920. The origins of Kimberly School go back to 1906. First located at the site of the current Gibbs College, the school moved to the former property of the Montclair Athletic Club in 1950. Pictured here are Marian Williams, Ruth Broughton, Anna George, Margaret Moir, Eleanor Ellis, Margaret Elliot, Anna Lincoln, Juliet Dawes, Page Whelpley, Elizabeth Espaugh, Zillah Gray, and Barbara Harris.

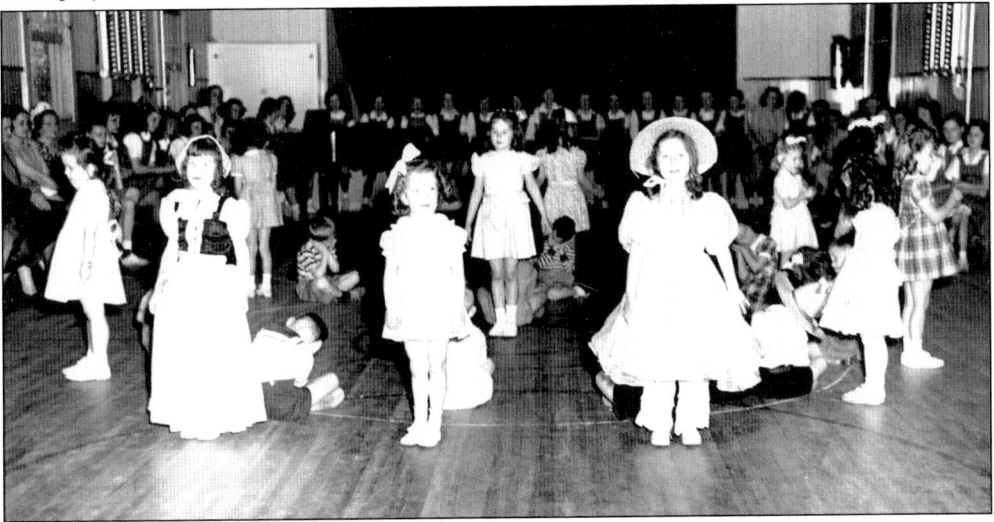

A LACORDAIRE EVENT. The kindergarten class performs in the gymnasium of Lacordaire Academy. The school was founded in 1920 by the Dominican Sisters of Caldwell, who purchased the former home and carriage house of prominent early physician Dr. Morgan W. Ayres, at the northwest corner of Lorraine Avenue and Park Street. A new building with more modern facilities was added in 1963.

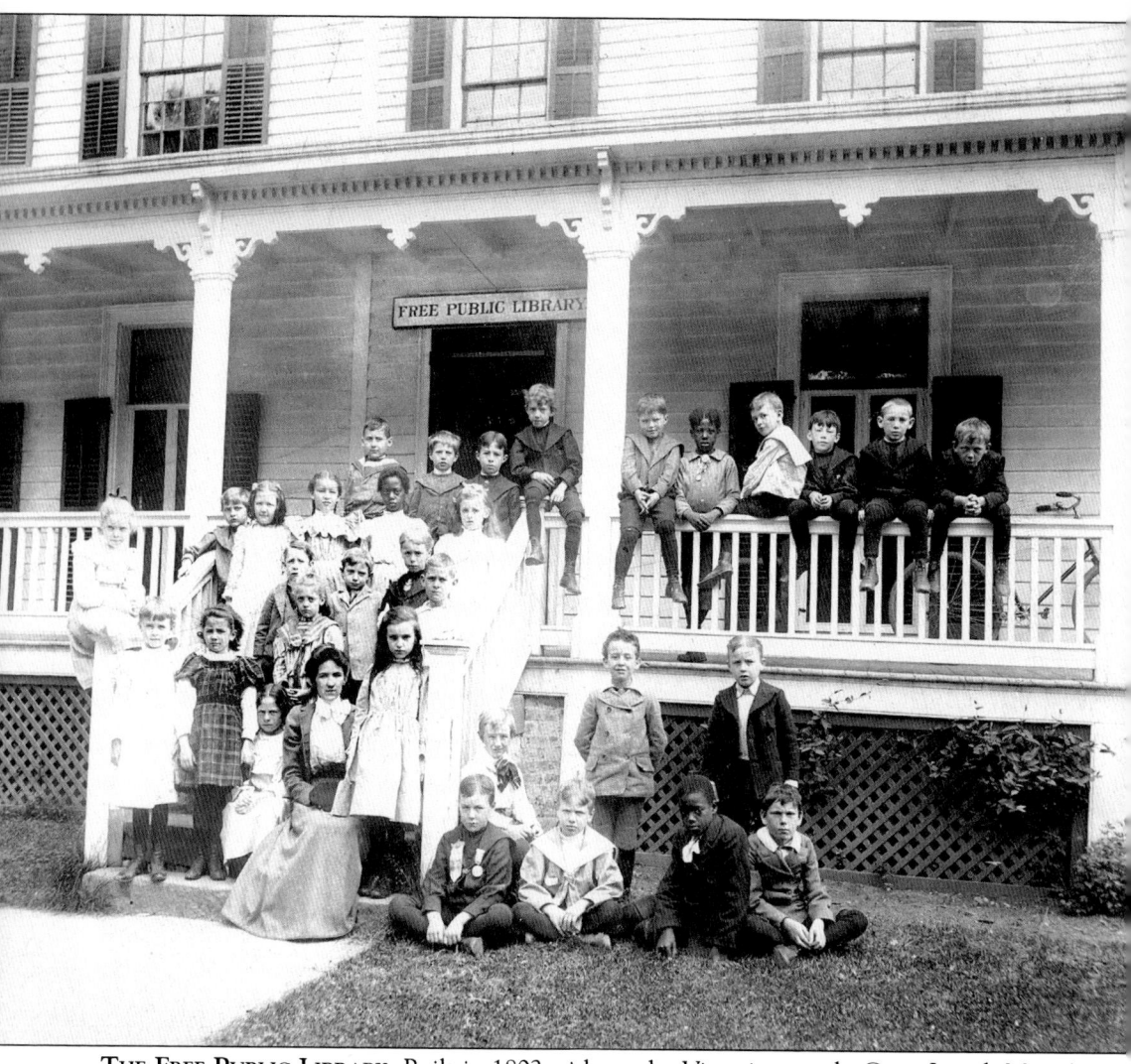

THE FREE PUBLIC LIBRARY. Built in 1802 without the Victorian porch, Capt. Joseph Munn's first tavern has seen many uses over two centuries. Here, it is home to the Montclair Free Public Library. Today, it provides space for the educational programs and other activities of the Evangelical Covenant Church.

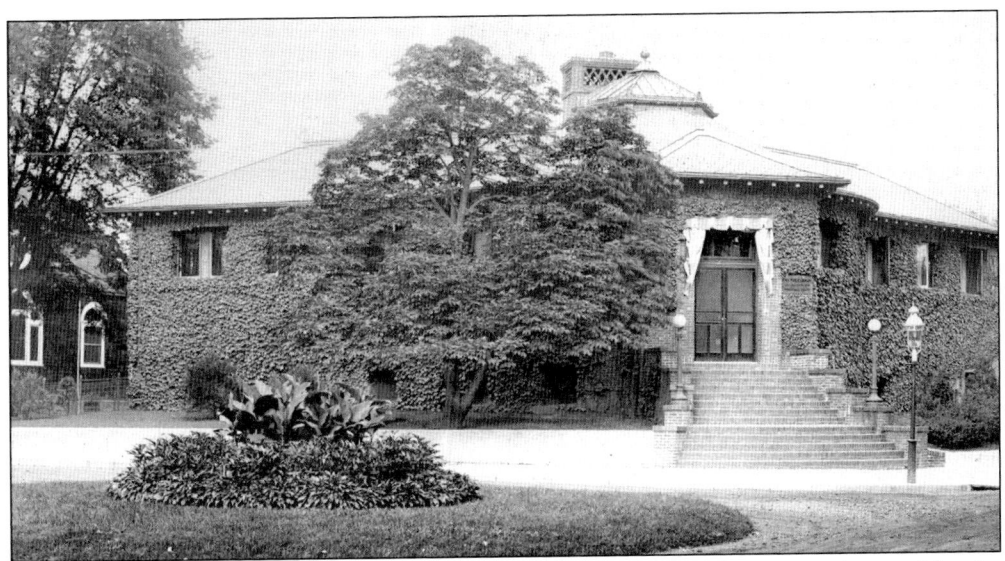

THE CARNAGIE LIBRARY. A gift of $40,000 from Andrew Carnegie made possible the construction of a library designed for the purpose. The former Munn Tavern was moved behind the Covenant Church, and the new library opened in 1904 at the northeast corner of Valley Road and Church Street. After much larger library facilities were built on South Fullerton Avenue in 1955, this building was acquired and remodeled by the Unitarian Church. Note the gas streetlight.

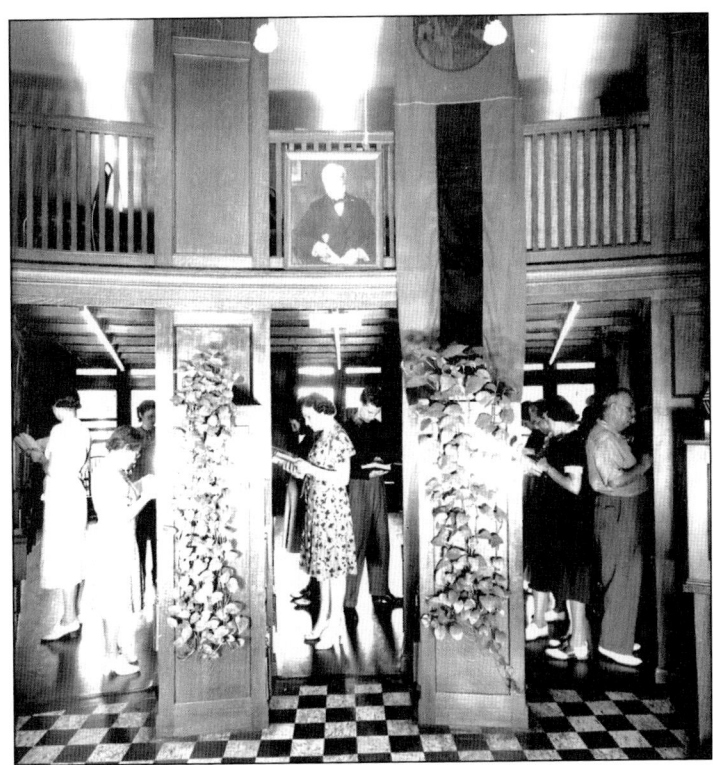

THE LIBRARY INTERIOR. Although cramped for space and forced to store many of its books elsewhere, the public library achieved a high reputation under the leadership of Marjorie Quigley, who introduced an IBM card system and conducted time-motion studies for checking out books with Dr. Lillian Gilbreth. Note the picture of benefactor Andrew Carnegie. (Photograph by L. Decker.)

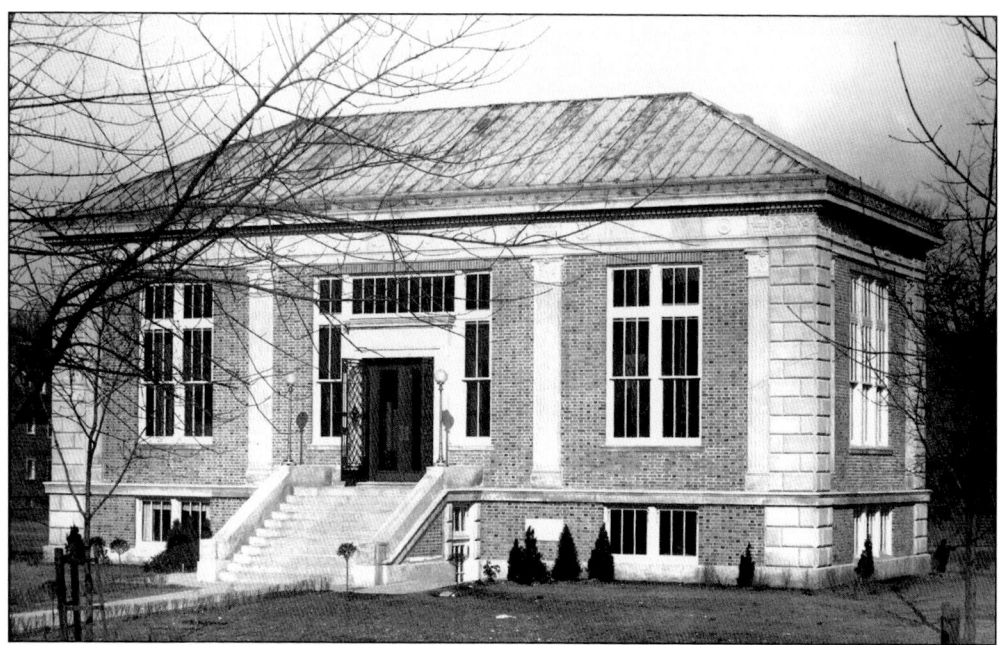

BRANCH LIBRARY. Opened on December 7, 1914, the library on Bellevue Avenue was designed by architect F.A. Nelson, whose work may be seen at several locations in the neighborhood. The exterior lamps were stolen in the early 1990s but replaced according to the original plans. Also made possible by Andrew Carnegie, whose picture hangs within, the building is on the National Register of Historic Places. (Photograph by Tebbs Architectural Photo Company.)

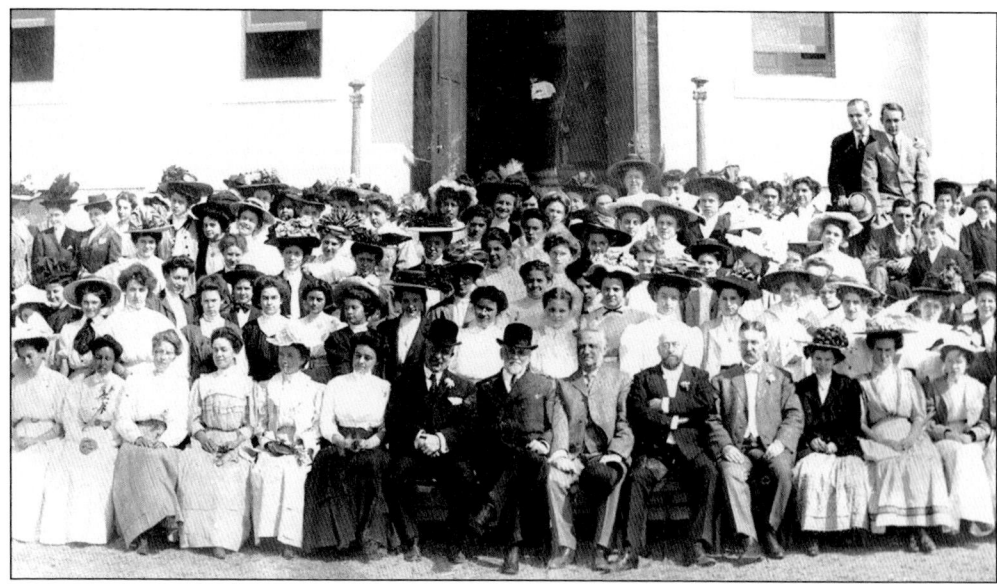

THE NEW NORMAL SCHOOL. These people are gathered for the dedication of the Montclair State Normal School on October 3, 1908. Students that year included 178 women and 5 men preparing to be elementary school teachers. The opening of the school led to extending the Valley Road trolley line to Normal Avenue. The school eventually evolved into Montclair State University.

Six
RELIGIOUS LIFE

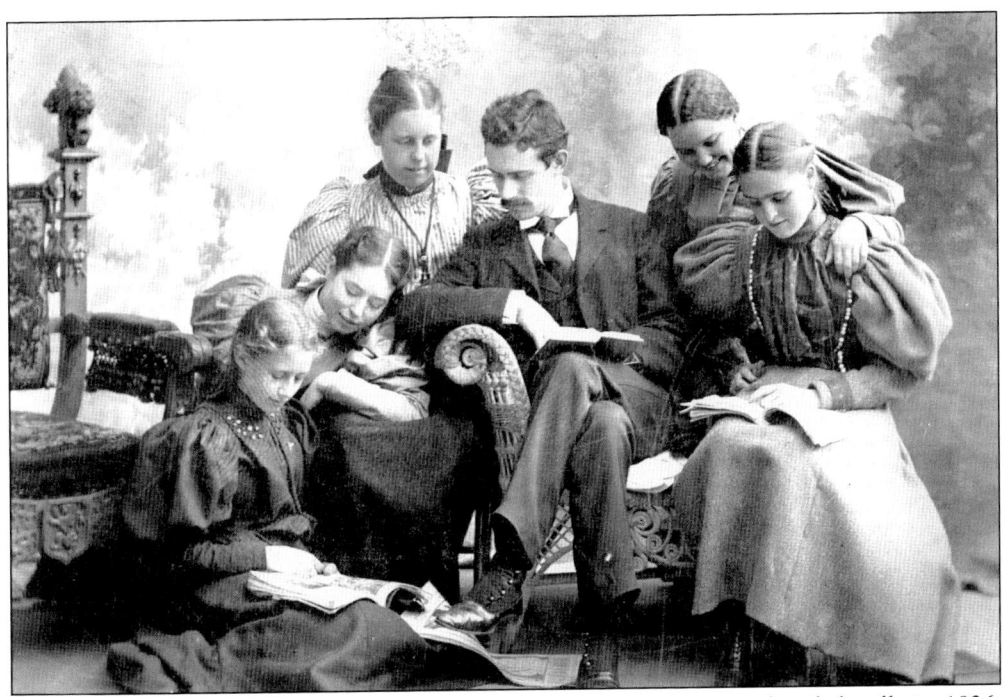

THE METHODIST SUNDAY SCHOOL CLASS, 1894. First to organize a church locally in 1836, the First Methodist Episcopal Church moved from its original home on Bloomfield Avenue to North Fullerton Avenue in 1879. Pictured with their teacher, Fred Hall, from left to right, are Lillian Goman, Sadie Brundage, Ida Madison, Maie Wright, and Harriet Lockwood.

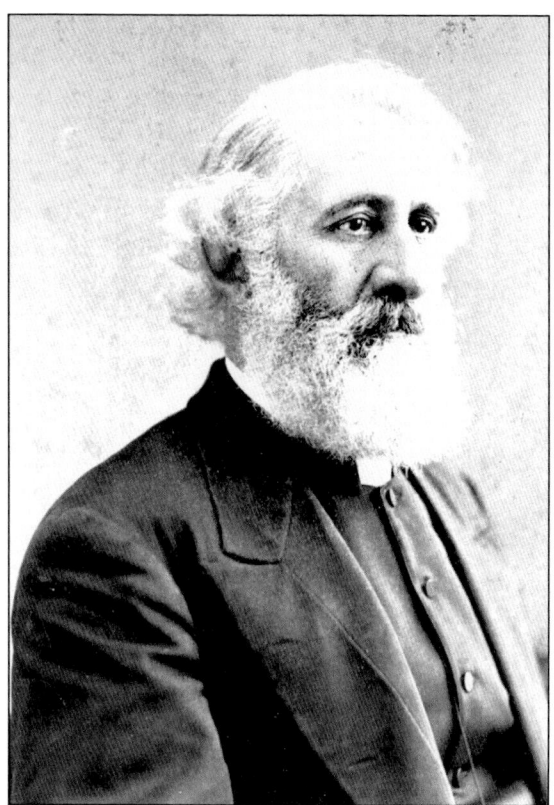

DR. J. ROMEYN BERRY. "A very patriarchal looking man," wrote Dr. Samuel Watkins, "who looked as if he might have been one of the genuine old Bible characters." Dr. J. Romeyn Berry came in 1870 to serve as pastor of the Presbyterian church and remained until 1887.

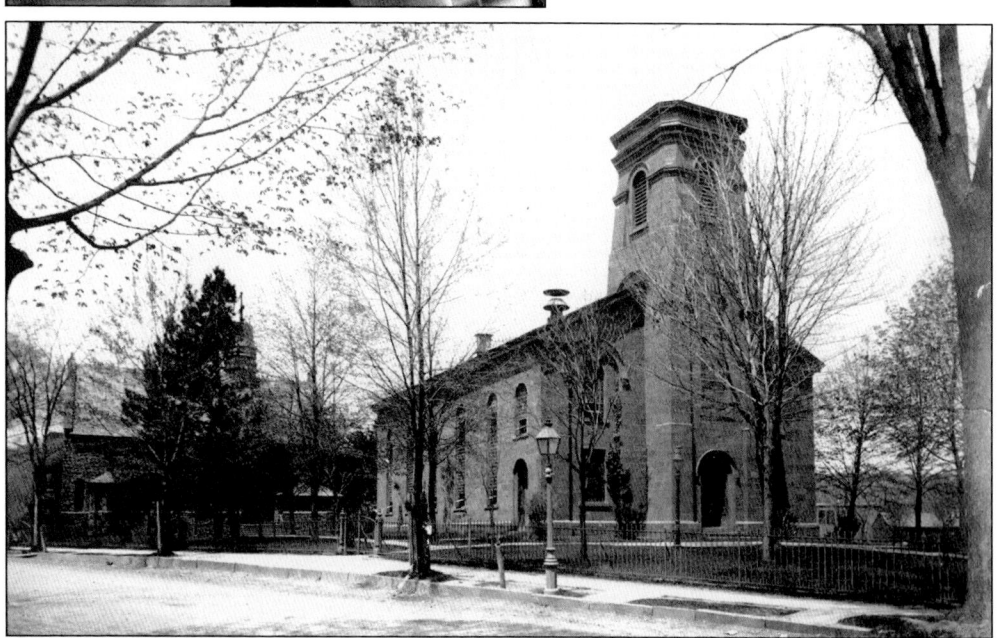

THE "OLD FIRST" PRESBYTERIAN. Dr. J. Romeyn Berry preached in this sturdy house of worship at the corner of Church Street and Bloomfield Avenue. It stood here from 1856 to 1921 and hosted the first town meetings, and in 1876, a celebration of the national centennial. The bell in the tower was contributed by Mary Crane, daughter of Israel Crane.

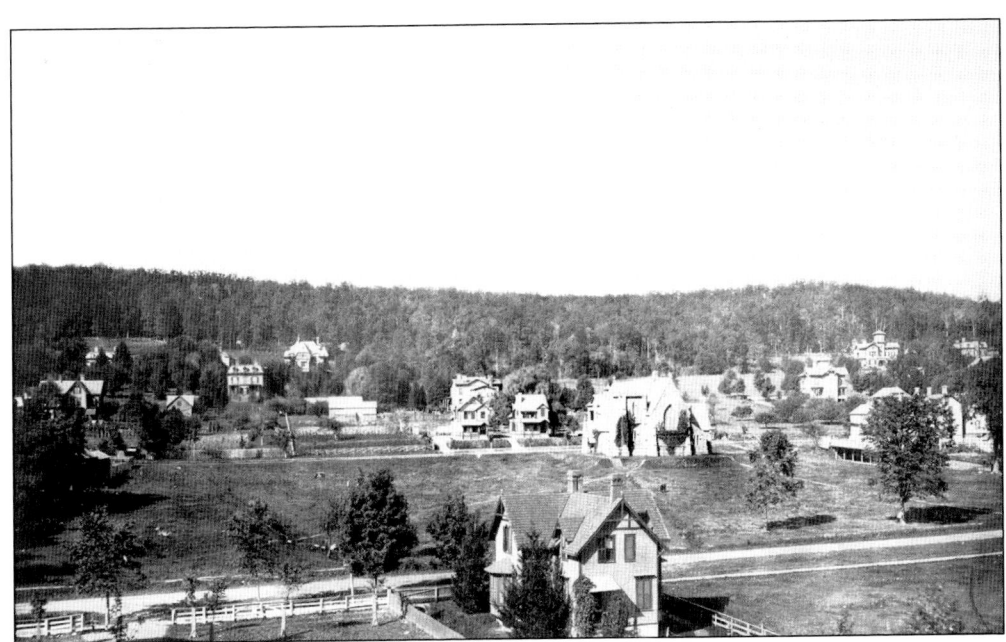

ST. LUKE'S EPISCOPAL CHURCH. In this view looking west from Orange Road, St. Luke's Episcopal Church rises a little to the right of center on St. Luke's Place. Much open space remained along the hillside when the cornerstone was laid in 1865. This building was soon outgrown, and by 1889, a new St. Luke's was going up on South Fullerton Avenue.

THE WILLIAM BRADBURY MONUMENT. Organist, piano manufacturer, and Sunday school singing teacher William Bradbury (1816–1868) composed and published religious songs for children, including, "Jesus Loves Me," and the tunes for gospel hymns still sung across the land, such as "Sweet Hour of Prayer," "Savior Like a Shepherd Lead Us," and "Just as I Am." His last years were spent in West Bloomfield, now Montclair. The monument is in Bloomfield Cemetery. (Photograph by Amy Dahn.)

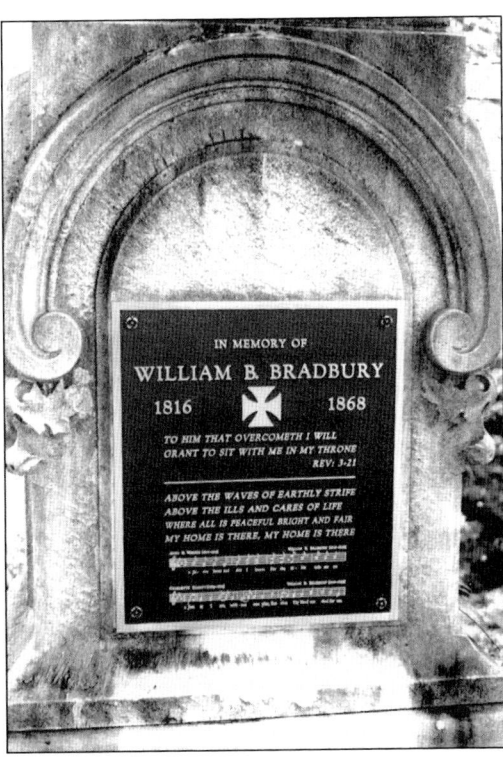

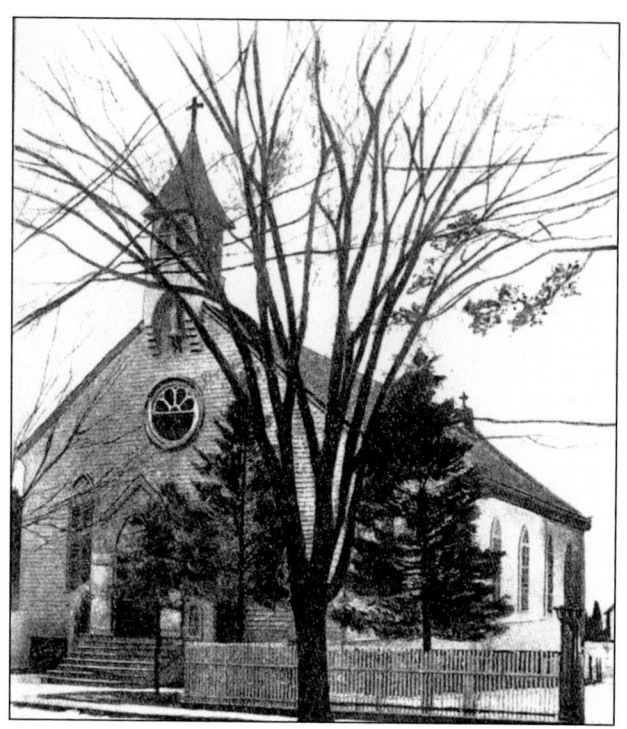

IMMACULATE CONCEPTION CHURCH. Described by the New York *Tablet* as "a new and beautiful frame Gothic church with green venetian blinds," this humble house of worship was built in 1856 from timber cut locally. It stood on Washington Street, a site central to a parish that included Bloomfield. The present church on North Fullerton Avenue was restored recently with the help of a grant by the New Jersey Historic Trust. (Courtesy Msgr. Timothy J. Shugrue.)

REV. JOSEPH MENDL. Born in Austria, Rev. Joseph Mendl came to Immaculate Conception Church in 1879. He envisioned a larger church more central to Montclair, and in 1892, work began on North Fullerton Avenue. When Mendl died in 1907, the *Montclair Times* reported that "clergymen of all the Protestant churches attended the service in a body to show their respect for their dead co-laborer." (Courtesy Msgr. Timothy J. Shugrue.)

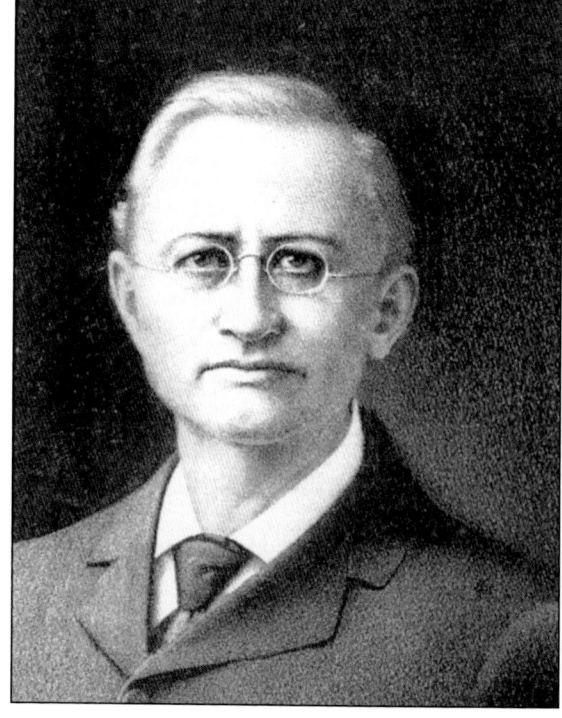

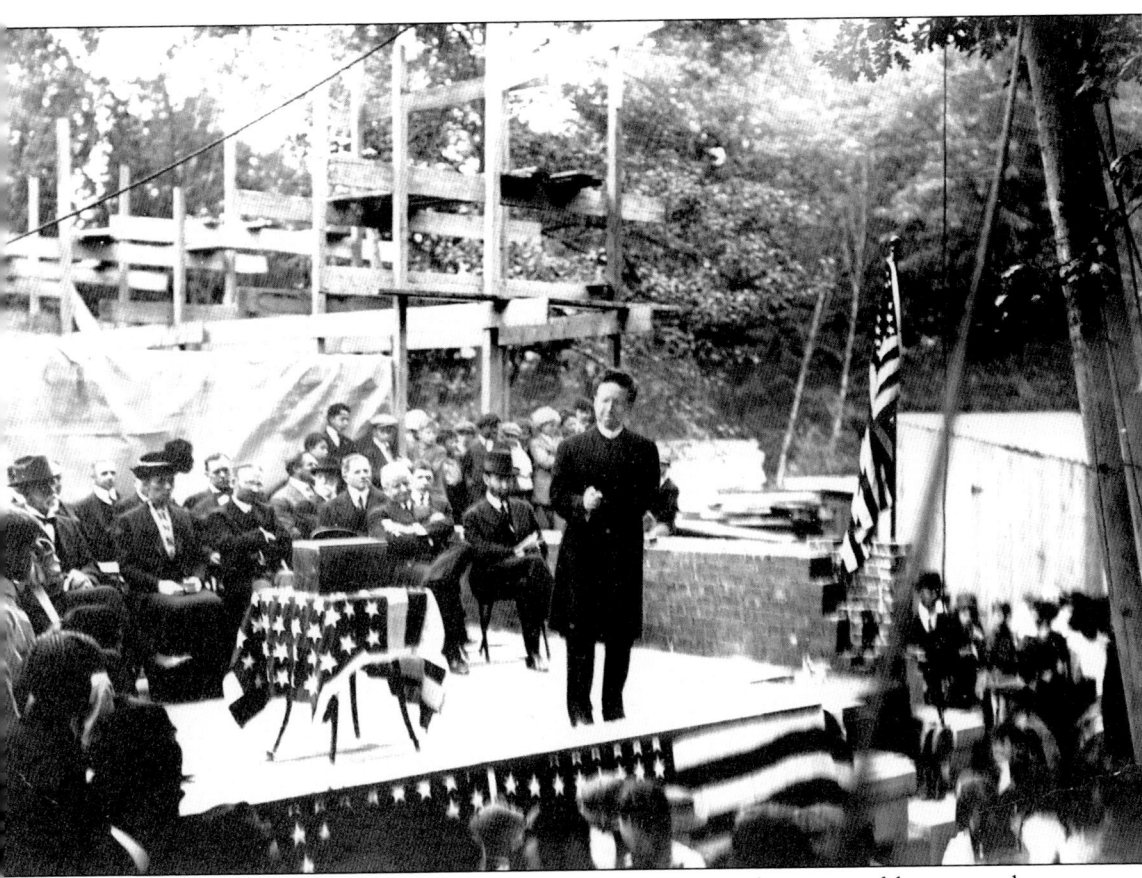

HARRY EMERSON FOSDICK. One of the most widely known clergymen of his time, the Reverend Harry Emerson Fosdick came to Montclair as a young man in 1904 to serve the First Baptist Church. When the church's home, later the Masonic Hall, proved too small, Fosdick undertook to build a new one at the corner of Church Street and Trinity Place. Later the founding minister of Riverside Church in New York, Fosdick described his Montclair experiences in his autobiography, The Living of These Days. Here, he speaks at the laying of the cornerstone of the Montclair High School on October 6, 1914. (Courtesy of Montclair Historical Society.)

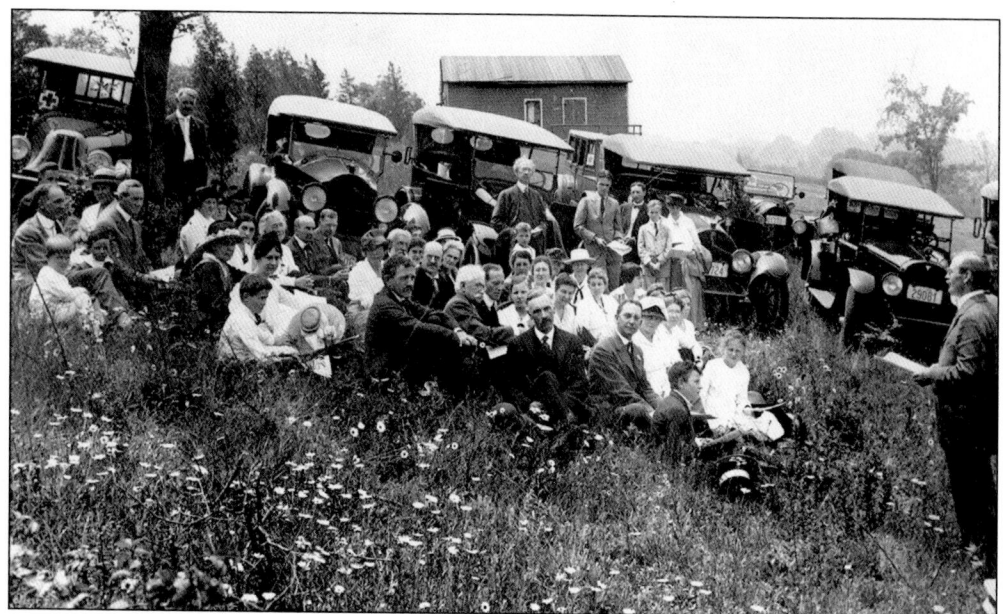

A UNITARIAN OUTING. Members of the Unity (Unitarian) Church gather on a hillside on June 29, 1918, to be addressed by their congregation's president, Arthur Hunter. Seated near the front and facing the camera is the minister, Edgar Swan Wiers. Under his leadership, the church established the Unity Institute with its concerts and lectures. In July 1914, the Ladies Home Journal featured Wiers and his church in an article entitled "An Effective Suburban Church."

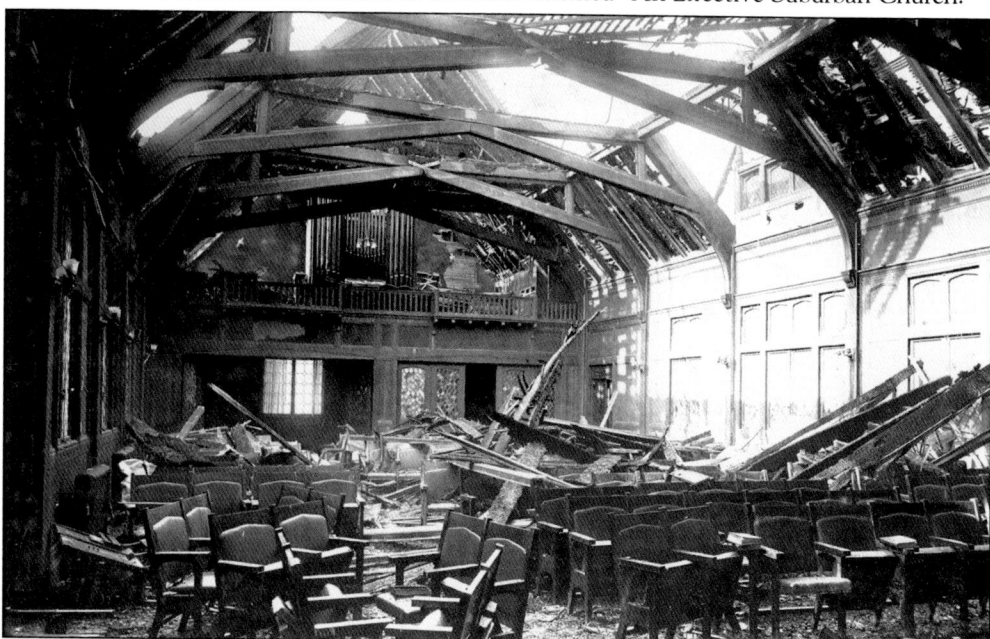

A DISASTROUS FIRE. On March 2, 1919, some rubbish behind the Carnegie Library caught fire and sparks ignited the roof of the Unity (Unitarian) Church. The members rallied to restore the building. Meanwhile, they met in the Wilde Chapel of the First Congregational Church. Fund-raising events included poetry readings by Amy Lowell, Robert Frost, and Vachel Lindsay and a concert by Australian pianist and composer Percy Granger.

THE FIRE AT THE FIRST CONGREGATIONAL CHURCH. The Congregationalists had reason to sympathize with the Unitarians, for on March 3, 1914, their magnificent building, constructed in 1873, was largely destroyed. By 1916, an even larger edifice had risen on the site of the old one. It was designed by architect Bertram Goodhue, still celebrated for his design of St. Bartholomew's Church in New York.

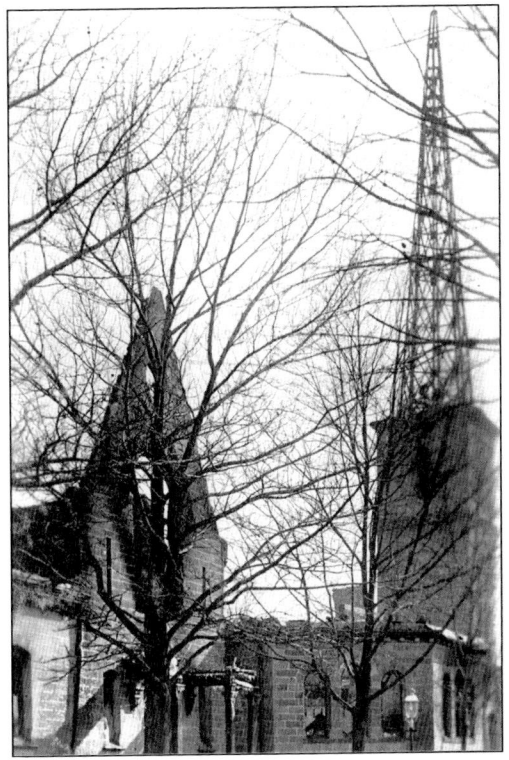

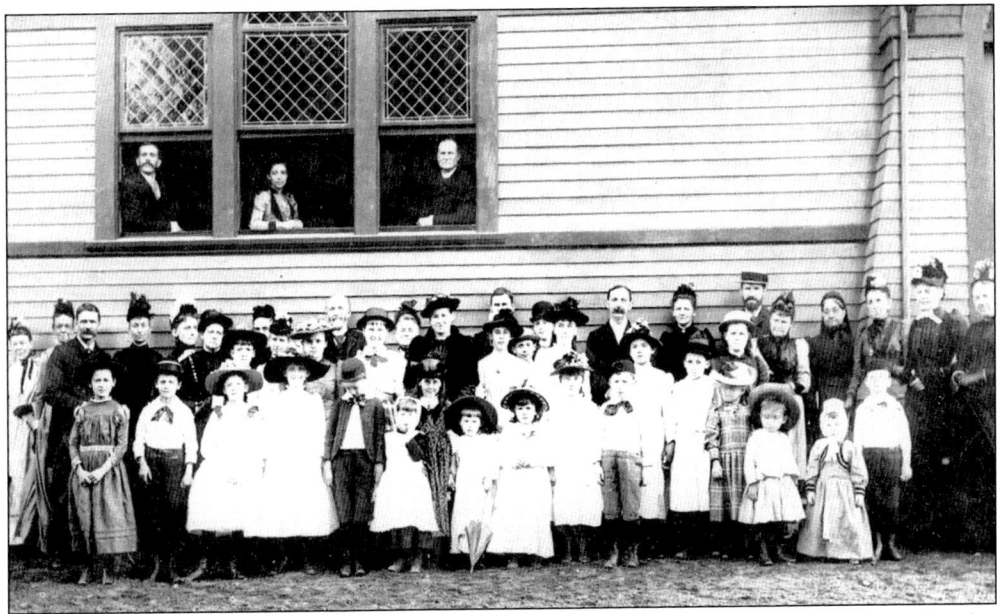

THE GRACE PRESBYTERIAN SUNDAY SCHOOL. First meetings of the Grace Presbyterian Sunday school were held at the Walnut Street depot, pictured on page 24. When this photograph was taken in 1891, the school was meeting at the Chestnut Street chapel at the corner of Forest Street. Shown in the window to the right is Rev. William Finney Junkin. In the center window is Helen Taylor, the first director of the Montclair Art Museum. The church came into being officially in 1892.

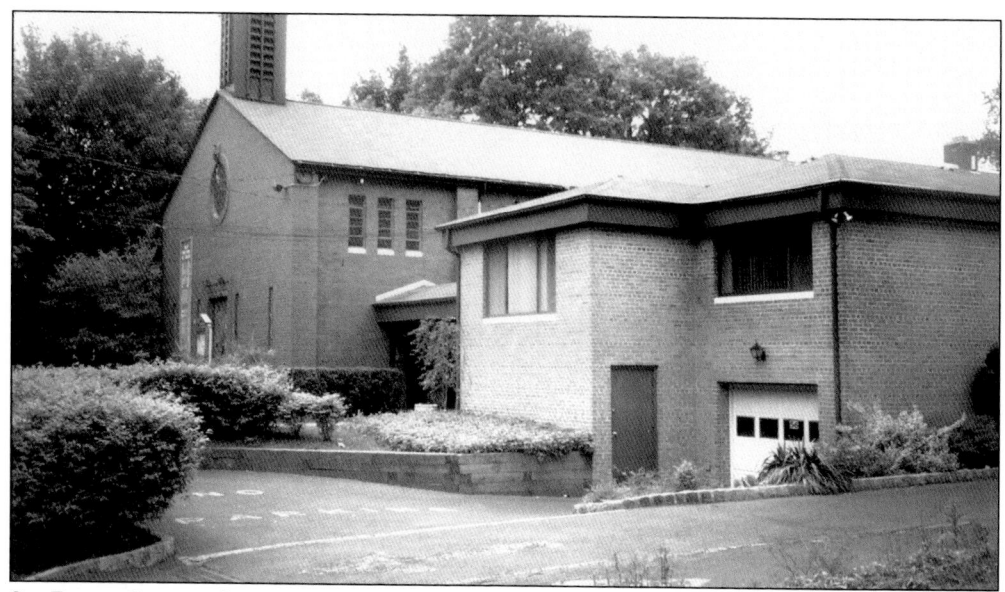

ST. PETER CLAVER CATHOLIC CHURCH. The cornerstone for this church on Elmwood Avenue was laid on November 5, 1939. Earlier, the congregation met in the basement of Immaculate Conception Church and on Elm Street. Although continuing to celebrate its African American heritage, the parish has grown increasingly cosmopolitan.

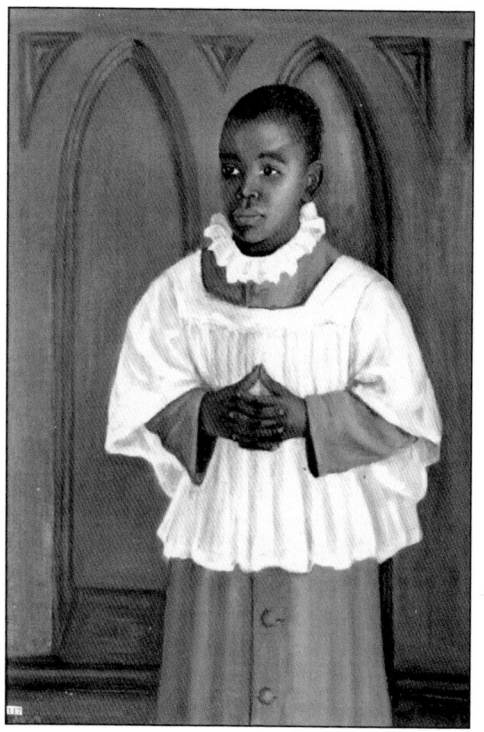

AN ACOLYTE. Edmond Deshong Jr. is the subject of this painting by Colin Osborne. Edmond lived at 16 Talbot Street and served at Trinity Episcopal Church on North Willow Street. His red-and-white vestments were imported from England. The painting was exhibited at a New Jersey state exhibition held at the Montclair Art Museum in November 1938 and at the Newark Art Museum the following year. Trinity Church was founded in 1916 by African Americans, mostly of Caribbean ancestry.

REV. MORGAN P. NOYES.
A renowned pastor and preacher, Dr. Morgan P. Noyes served Central Presbyterian Church from 1932 to 1957. Yale University recognized his gifts by inviting him to deliver the prestigious Lyman Beecher Lectures in 1942. In illustrating a saying of St. Paul's, Noyes observed that none may "have" the view from Eagle Rock, the books in the public library, or the pictures in the Montclair Art Museum, but all may learn to possess them. (Photograph copyright © Bachrach; courtesy Sarah N. Emmel.)

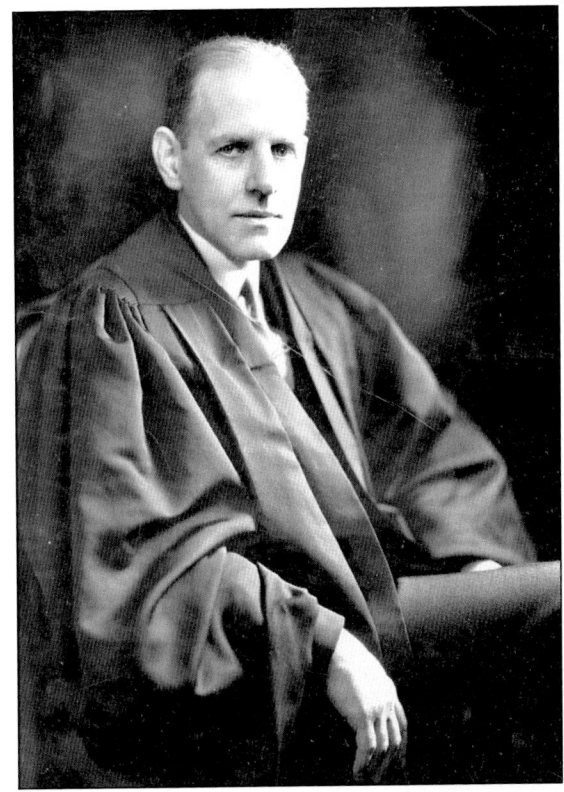

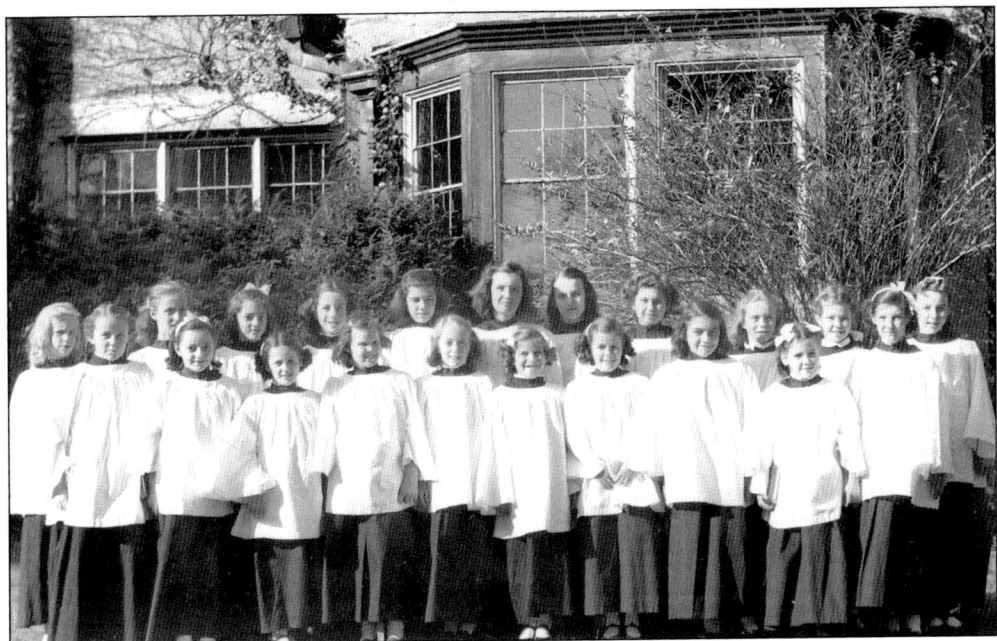

THE GIRLS CHOIR. The choir stands outside the Presbyterian Church of Upper Montclair in 1944. The church owes much to Timothy Sellew, a dedicated layman who built a chapel on Norwood Avenue in 1907. Later, he contributed to the building of the church's current sanctuary. The church received its charter from the Presbytery of Newark in 1908.

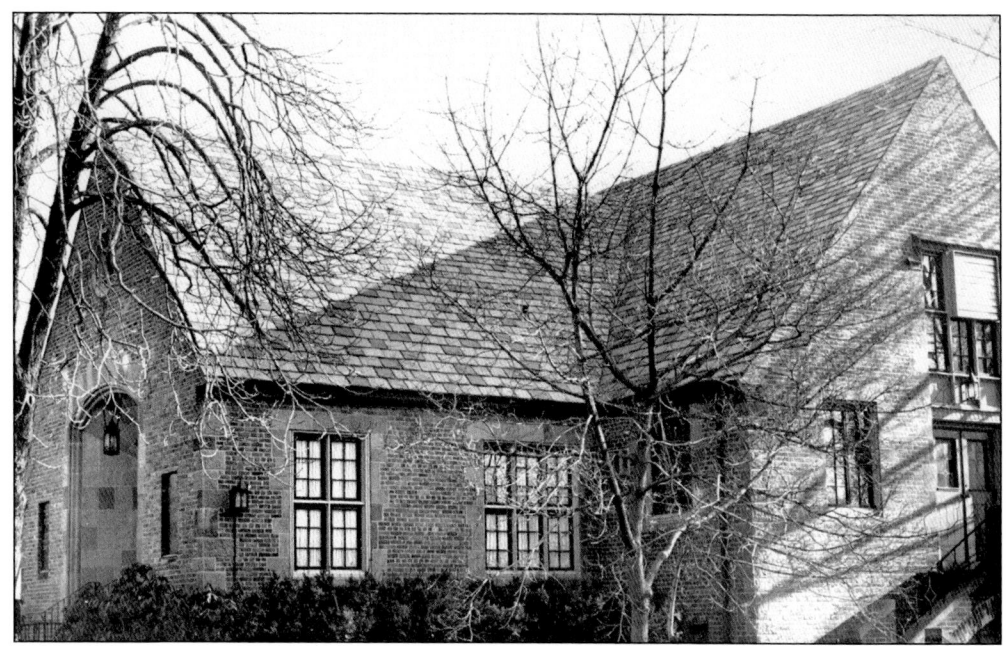

TEMPLE SHOMREI EMUNAH. Formed in Bloomfield in 1905 as Congregation Shomar Ammuno of Bloomfield and Montclair, this Jewish congregation met for many years on Bloomfield Avenue in Glen Ridge. Land was purchased at 67 Park Street in Montclair by the early 1940s, and on February 22, 1953, the temple shown above was dedicated.

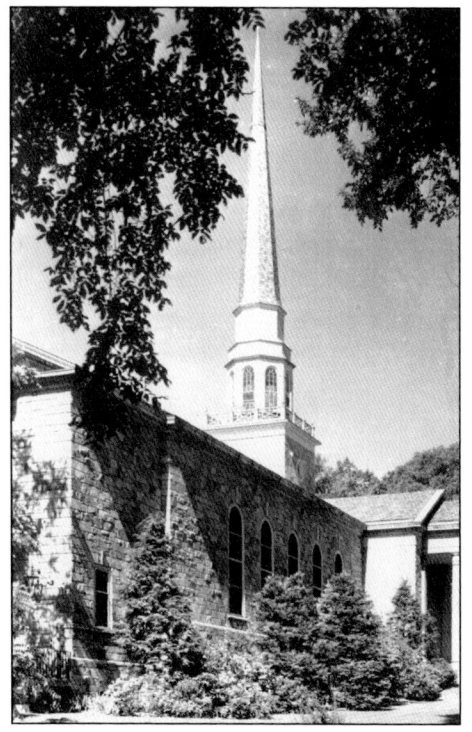

THE FIRST CHURCH OF CHRIST, SCIENTIST. In 1898, a group of Christian Scientists met in a private home. By 1901, they had organized a church in Arcanum Hall in the Doremus Building. Another early meeting place was the former Montclair Theater. On March 26, 1926, ground was broken on Hillside Avenue for the beautiful edifice made of Vermont granite. Services began here in October 1927.

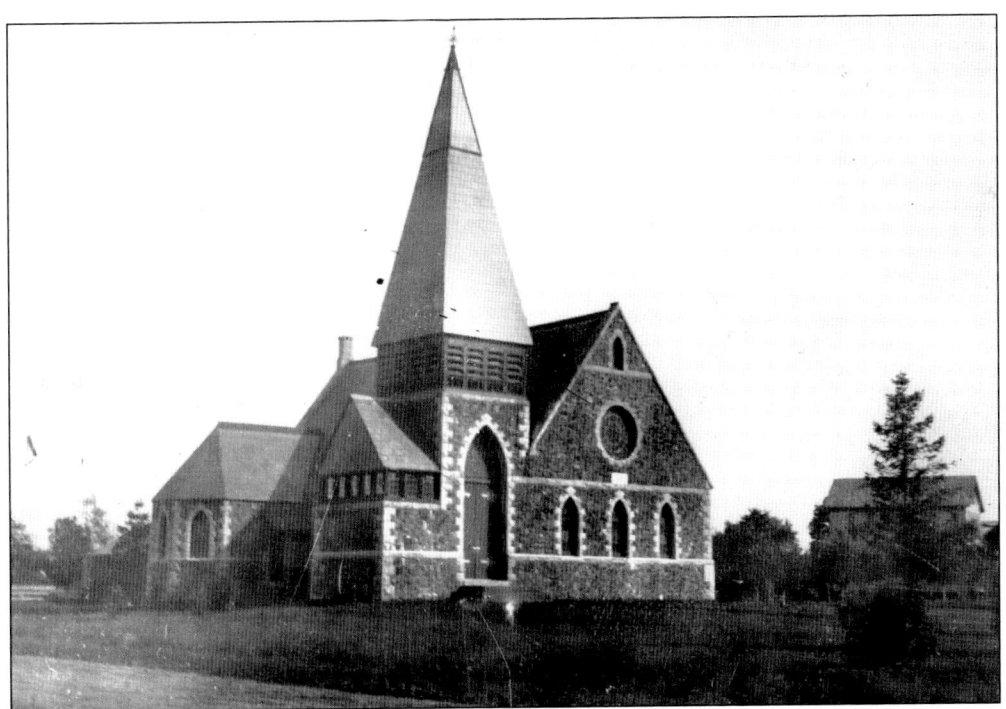

THE CLIFFSIDE CHAPEL. In 1878, people of several Christian denominations came together to build a chapel on Valley Road at Bellevue Avenue, a neighborhood then known as Cliffside. The chapel helped spawn Union Congregational Church, and in 1888, the property was acquired by the new Episcopal parish of St. James. Although changes have been made, including replacement of the steeple by a bell tower, the basic building stands as the oldest house of worship in Montclair.

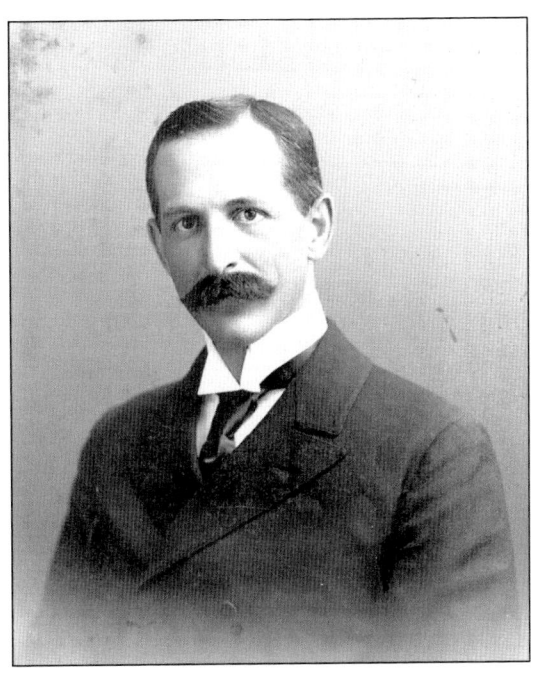

REV. HOWARD S. BLISS. From 1894 to 1902, Rev. Howard S. Bliss served as pastor of Union Congregational Church. This was a period of growth and vitality when the church members moved into their building on a large tract given them by sisters Harriet and Mary Cooper, who were opening Cooper Avenue. Bliss left Montclair to become president of the American University in Beirut.

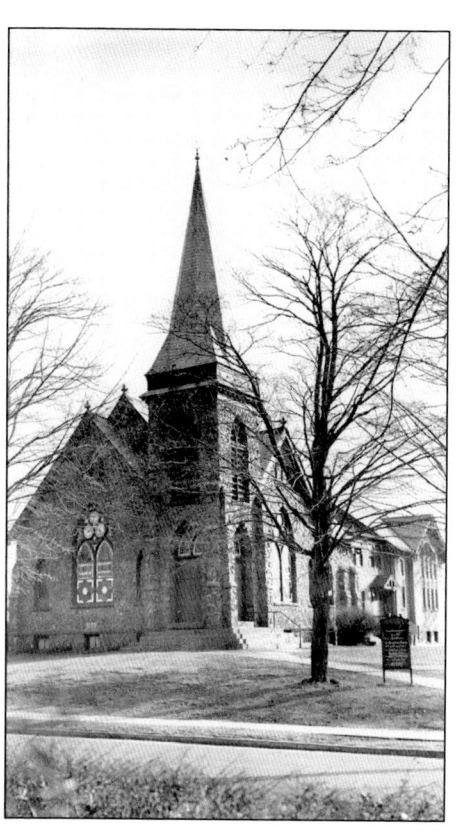

MONTCLAIR HEIGHTS REFORMED CHURCH. Like the people of Cranetown, the early Dutch settlers of Speertown had to travel long distances to attend church. In 1897, some of their descendants organized a congregation of the Reformed Church of America on land set aside by Thomas and Caroline Van Reyper.

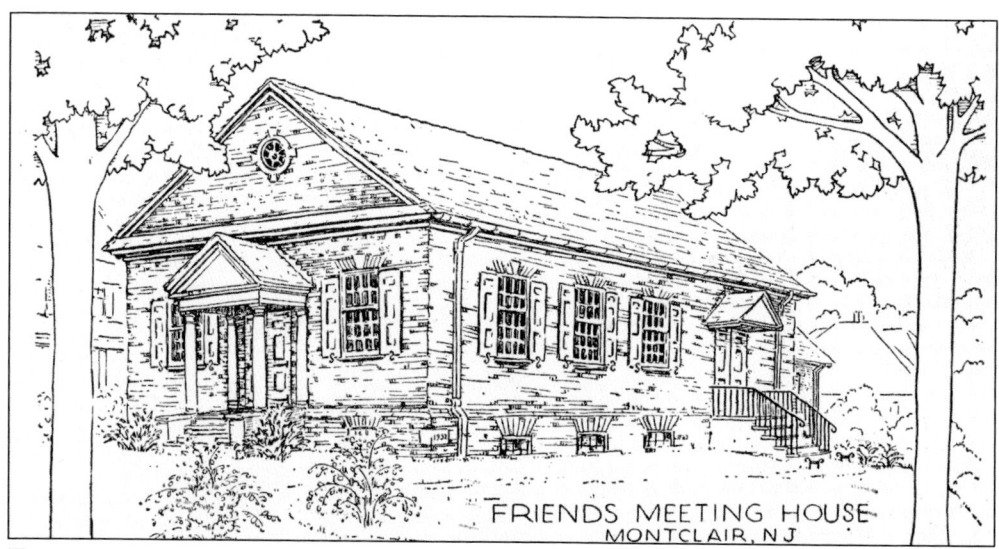

THE FRIENDS MEETINGHOUSE. The Montclair Meeting of the Religious Society of Friends (Quakers) was formed in 1926 and met for a time on the Crescent. In 1932, the meeting built this place of worship, with its wood-paneled interior, on Park Street at the corner of Gordonhurst Avenue. The clerk of the meeting at the time was the well-known neurologist Dr. Harvey Haines.

Seven
GOVERNMENT

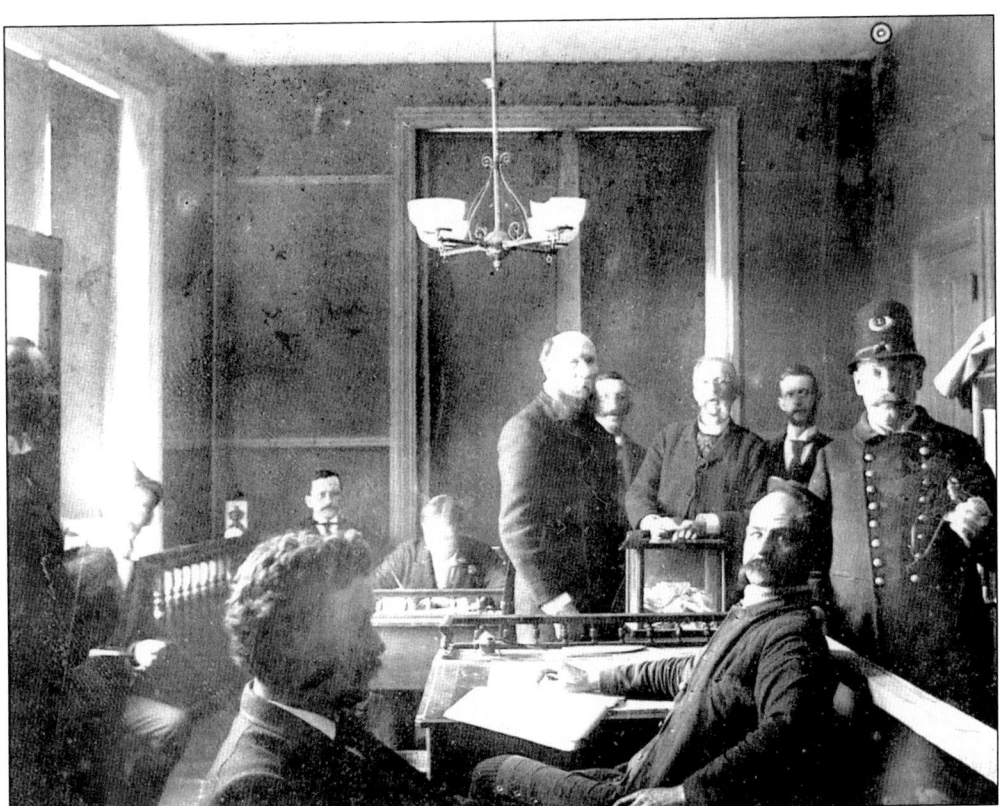

COUNTING THE VOTES. A clerk of election and two inspectors from each major party are shown in the Speertown Schoolhouse on April 11, 1893. They include Philip Young (seated to the right front, facing the viewer), who ran a bicycle shop; Edwin B. Littell (behind the police officer), Democratic clerk; and Theodore Bagley (leaning over the records in the background), Republican clerk.

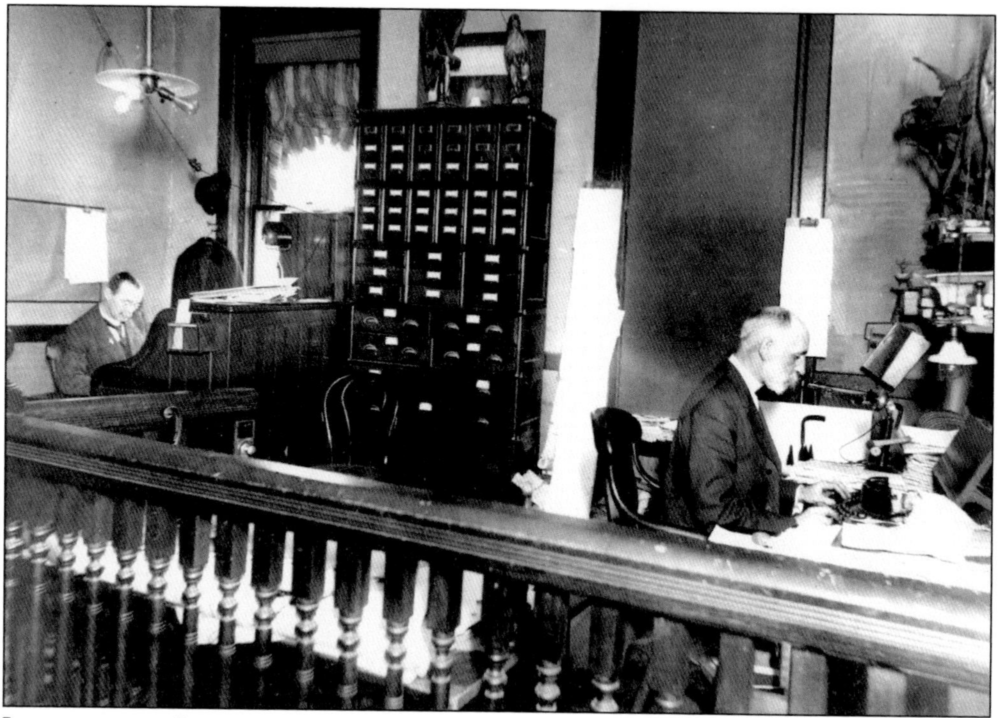

LONGEVITY IN OFFICE. Harry Trippett (seated to the right) served Montclair as clerk from May 1894 to October 1944. It is a record not likely to be equaled very soon. At the time he was elected, Montclair changed from a township to a town under the Short Law. Among other things, the change gave Montclair a unified school district and control over liquor licenses.

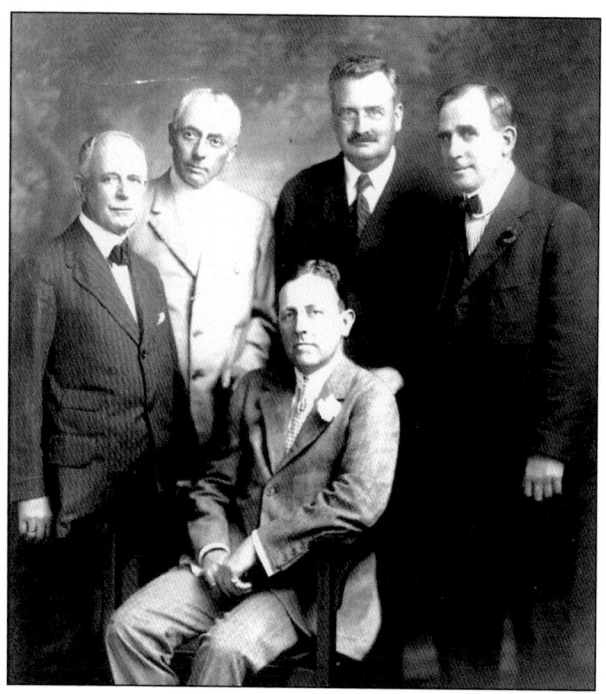

THE FIRST BOARD OF COMMISSIONERS. In a referendum held on July 11, 1916, Montclair decided to adopt the commission form of government, a system that prevailed until 1980. The first mayor under the new system was Louis F. Dodd (seated), who also bore the title of commissioner of Public Affairs. Standing, from left to right, are Charles G. Phillips, Revenue and Finance; John C. Barclay, Water Supply; John Picken, Public Safety; and E. Mortimer Harrison, Streets and Public Improvements.

THE CHANGE OF GUARD. In 1932, Frederick E. Kip organized the Town Affairs Committee to oust Commissioners Charles G. Phillips and Arthur P. Heyer. The committee supported incumbents John Picken and Howard F. McConnell, and put forward three new candidates, W.I. Lincoln Adams, Oscar Carlson, and James McMahon. In a record-breaking turnout at the polls, the entire Town Affairs slate was elected.

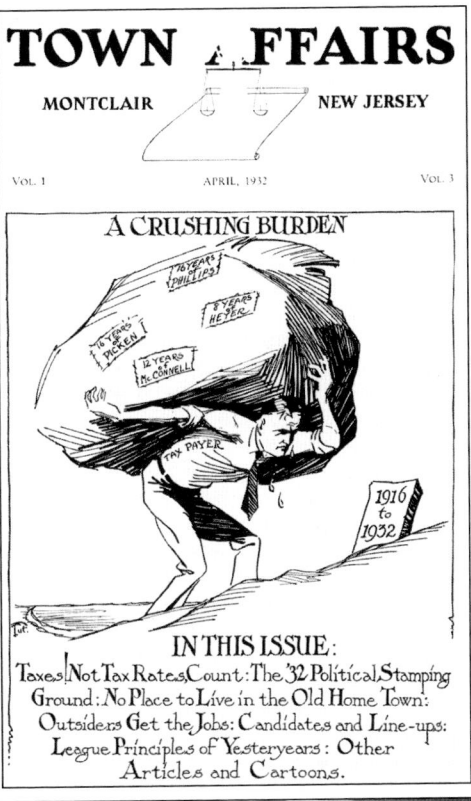

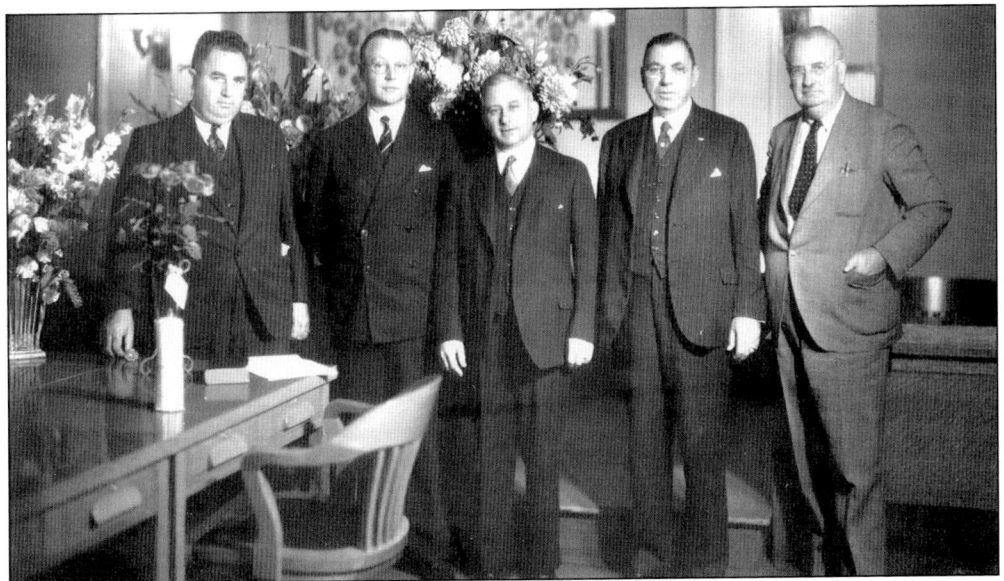

LOCAL OFFICIALS, 1933. Pictured, from left to right, are James J. McMahon, commissioner of Public Safety; Oscar L. Carlson, mayor; James McKee, town clerk; John Scott; county clerk; and John Picken, commissioner of Public Works. McMahon led the Democrats in a largely Republican town. Carlson, a building contractor, represented Montclair's Swedish community. Not shown are Commissioners Howard F. McConnell and W.I. Lincoln Adams. (Photograph by Enoch Gabrielle.)

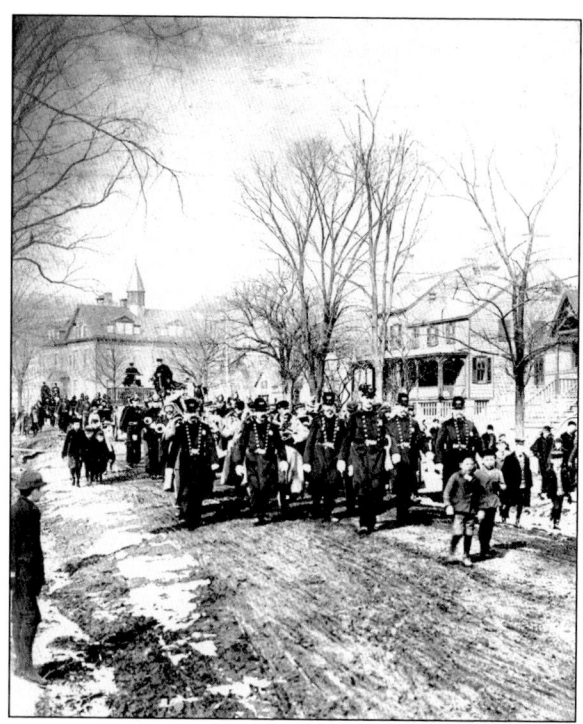

A Parade. Led by six-year-old Rufus Trimble, mascot of Hose Company No. 2, and his companion, the police and fire department march past Munn's Tavern and along Church Street on Washington's Birthday 1894. Young American elms stand at attention.

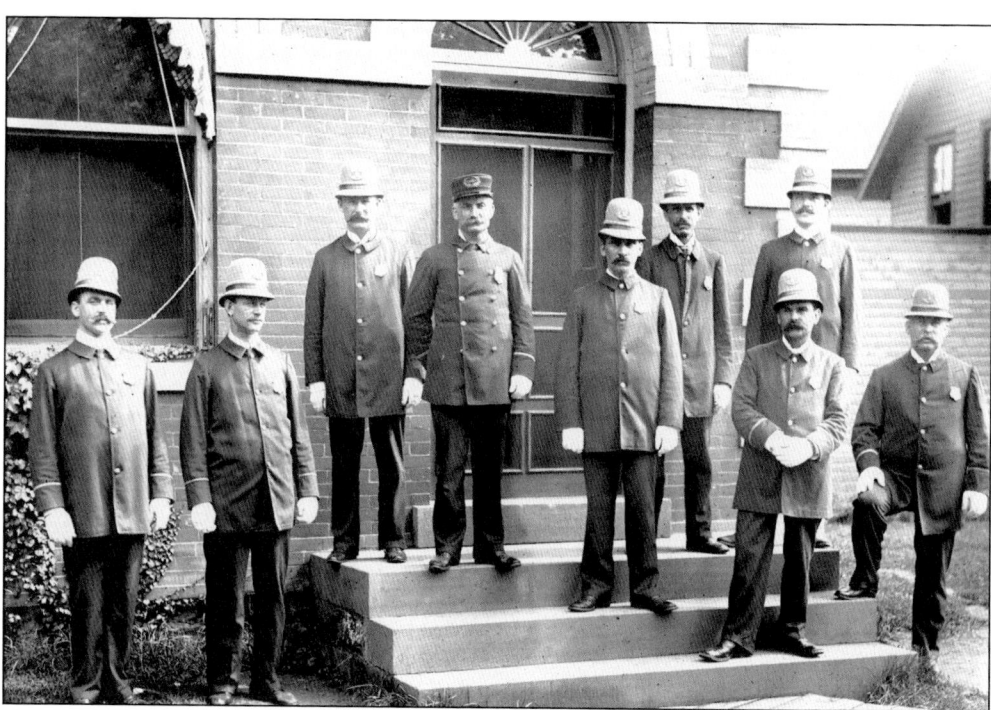

The Law. It seems a small force to keep the peace in a town of 15,000. However, it is possible that people were more law-abiding in 1901 than they are today. From left to right are John Gannon, Edward Ackerman, Thomas Dockery, Chief Henry Gallagher, Edward F. Reilly, William Lawler, Thomas Claver, John Perrin, and James McGarry.

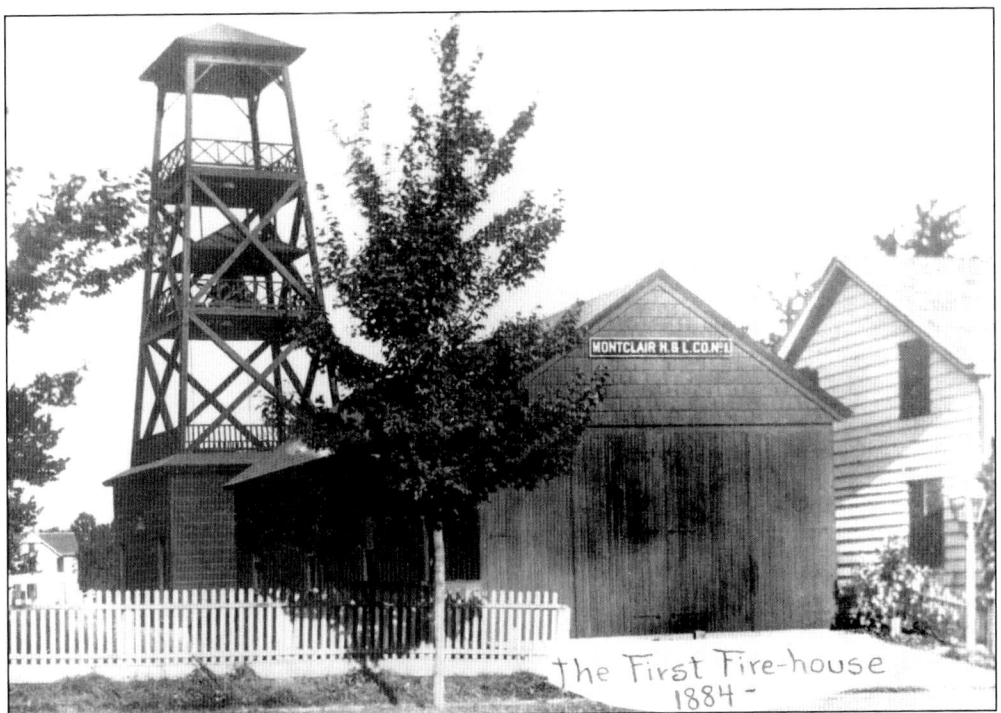

HOOK AND LADDER COMPANY NO. 1. Following several disastrous fires and years of unproductive discussion, Montclair citizens finally built this firehouse in 1882. Located on Bloomfield Avenue near Valley Road, it housed a fire truck and a chemical engine known as a Babcock Extinguisher. The bell tower was 54 feet high.

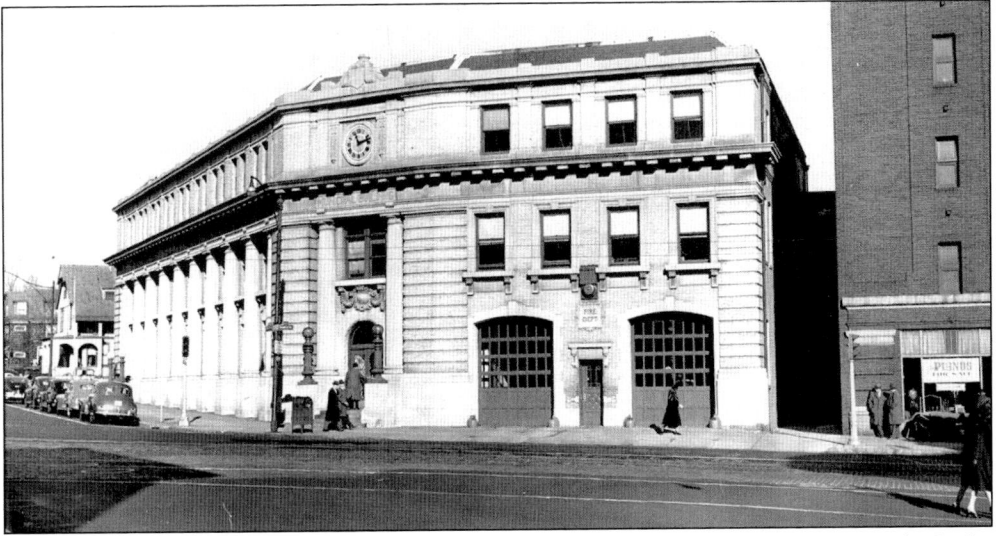

THE MUNICIPAL BUILDING. The Nolen Plan of 1909 called for a civic center in which the principal public buildings would be gathered attractively in one place. Talk of a civic center has never died, but in 1913, during Mayor Ernest Hinck's administration, this building was constructed to house town offices. It incorporated the earlier fire station. In 1929, Public Safety Commissioner George F. Lewis complained of the need for fire trucks "to swing out into heavy traffic." He called for a new headquarters.

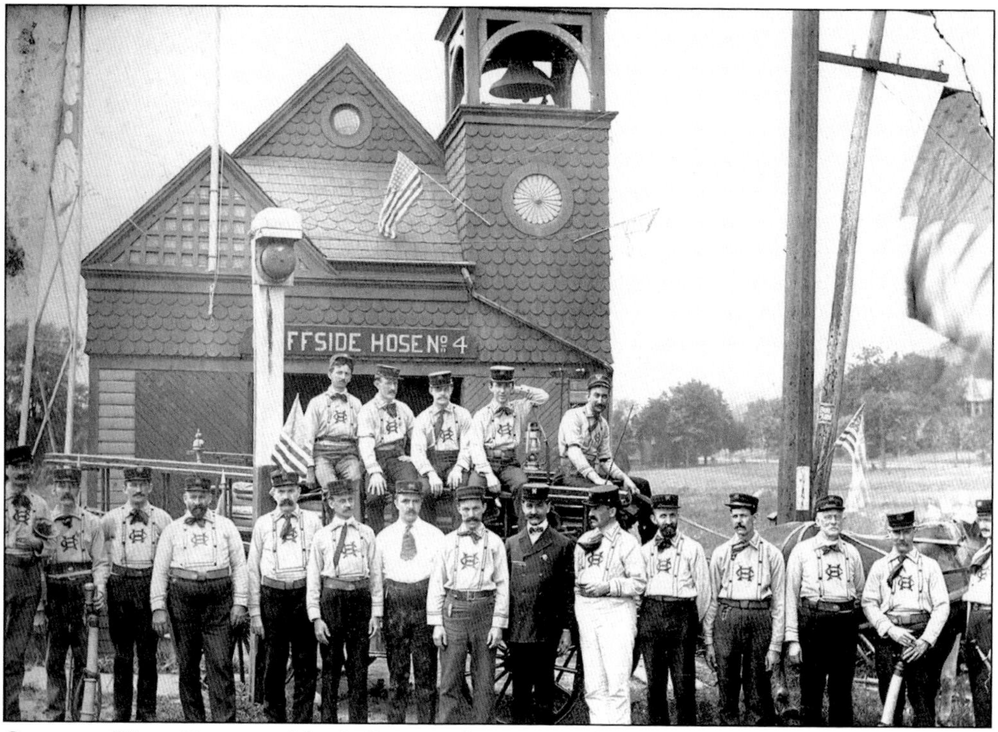

CLIFFSIDE HOSE COMPANY NO 4. Organized in 1888 with the aim of enlisting "all able-bodied citizens north of Watchung Avenue," the Cliffside Hose Company was known as "the Van Gieson Brigade" after its first foreman, A. Eben Van Gieson. The firehouse was located on Bellevue Avenue at the edge of the future Anderson Park.

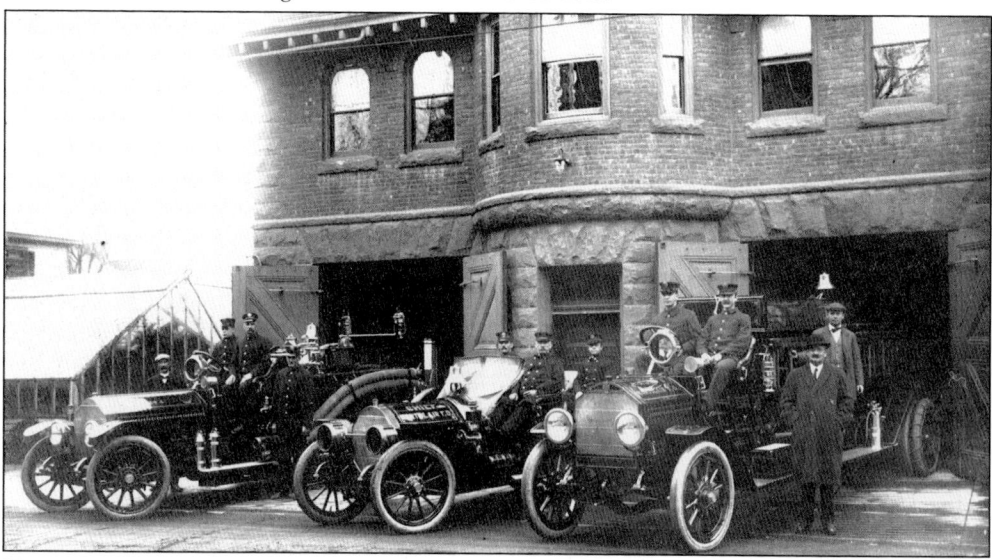

THE NEW FACILITY. In 1902, the Cliffside Hose Company moved into a stone structure designed in the Queen Anne style by local architect Ephraim North. The building remains, although one doorway has been widened. This 1920s photograph shows, from left to right, the first fire department motor truck, the fire chief's car with Chief Fred Williams, the first motor truck serving Upper Montclair, and Public Safety Commissioner John Picken.

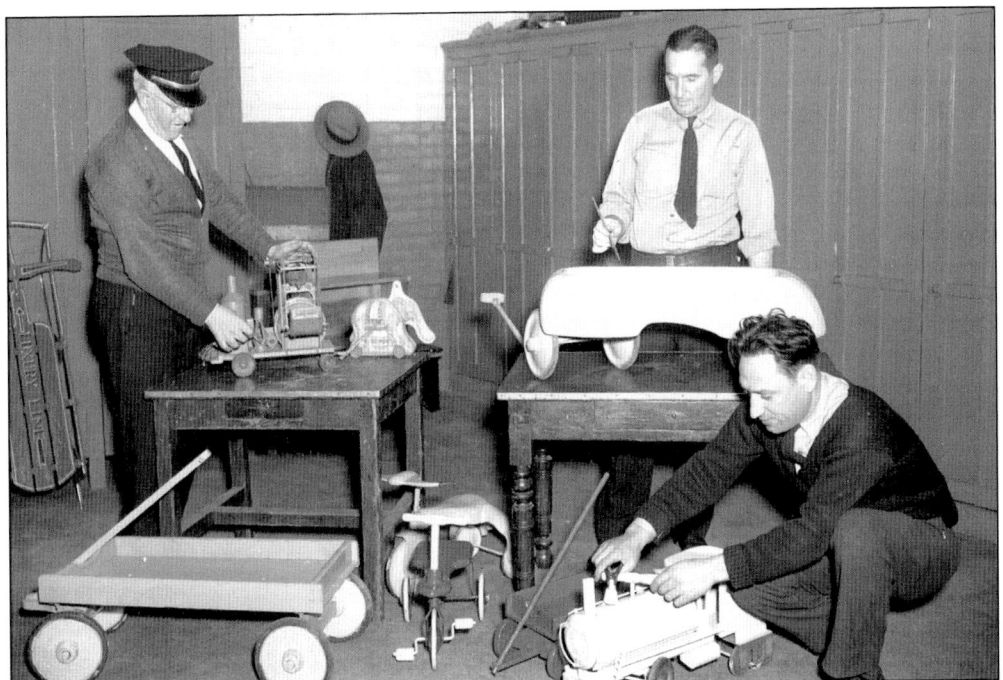

TOY REPAIR. A Montclair tradition for many years was taking toys to the fire department to be repaired for distribution to poor children at Christmas. The toys were donated by more privileged children.

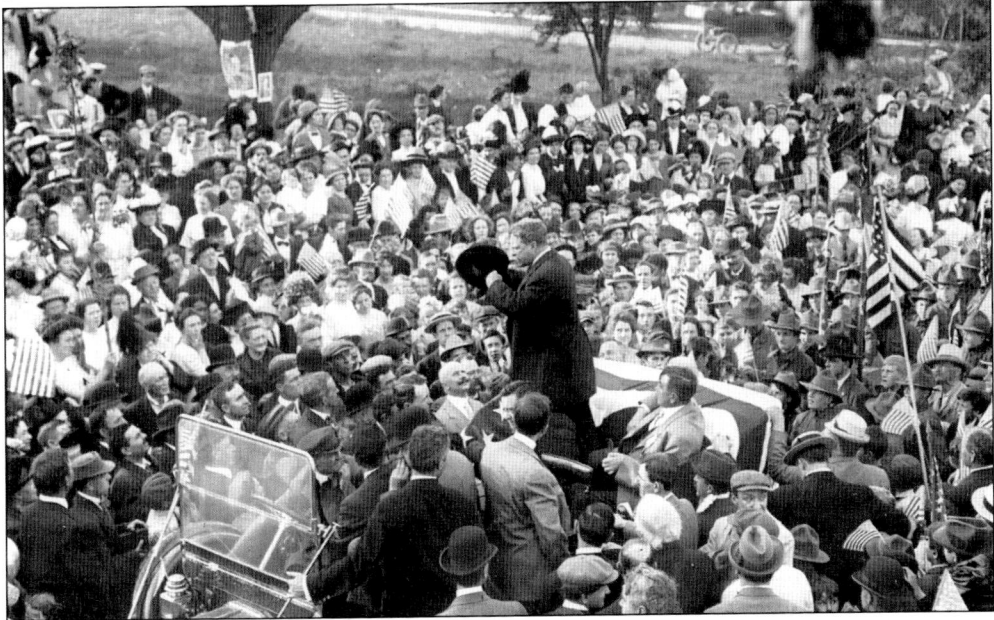

THE 1912 CAMPAIGN. This photograph came near to rejection on the grounds that it was taken between Hackensack and Rutherford. But Theodore Roosevelt stands in a car belonging to Montclair Mayor Ernest Hinck and carrying as well Montclair citizens F.M. and P.S. Crawley and Ellworth Young. Roosevelt's party-splitting comeback failed nationally, but he carried Montclair, defeating both Woodrow Wilson and William Howard Taft by substantial margins.

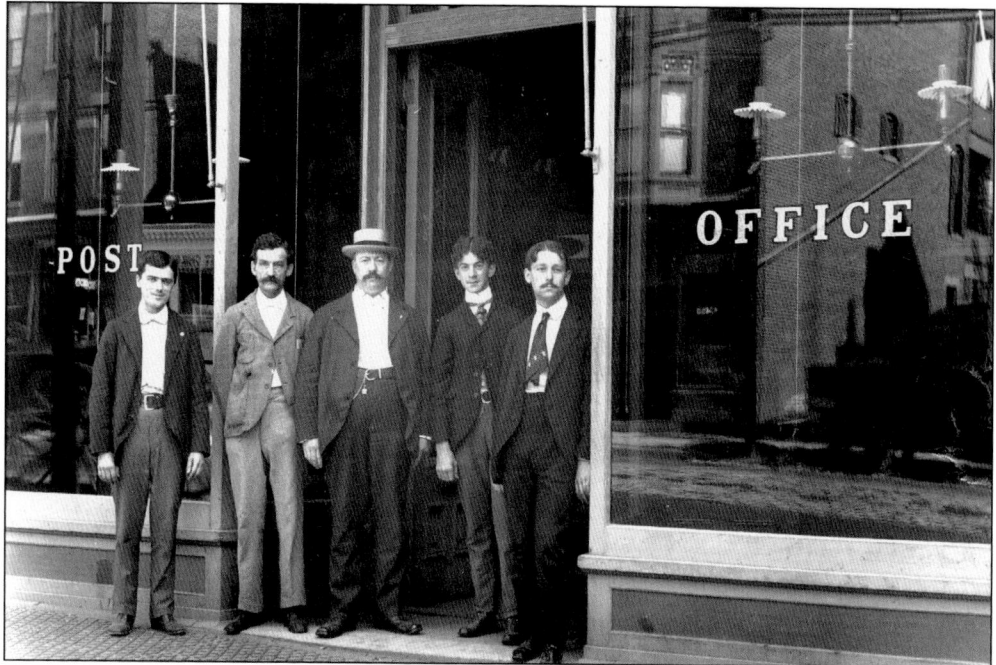

THE POSTAL STAFF. The first postmaster to serve locally was Nathaniel H. Baldwin, appointed in 1830. His office was in Capt. Joseph Munn's new tavern on the turnpike (Bloomfield Avenue). In this 1900 photograph, postmaster George A. Van Gieson (center), appointed in 1890, is flanked by, from left to right, Michael Kaveny, Amedee Tunison, Louis Bowlby, and John Holmes.

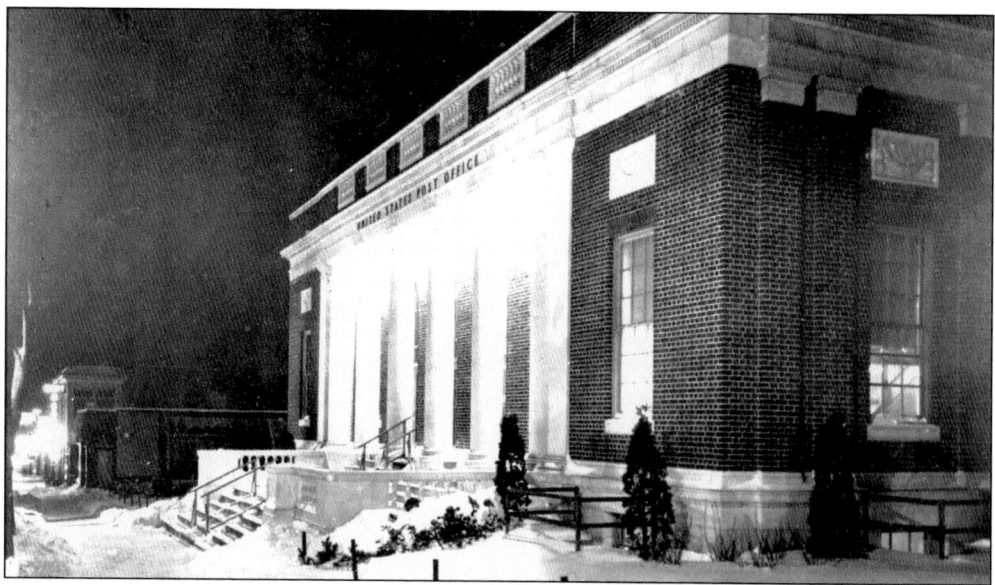

A CLASSIC POST OFFICE. Many alive still recall this building that looked the way a post office is supposed to look. On September 24, 1927, the cornerstone of the federal building was laid by Most Worshipful Howard R. Cruse, grand master of Masons for the state of New Jersey. Howard F. McConnell, former mayor, presided at the "Civic Celebration." The Social Security Building now stands at the site. (Courtesy the *Montclair Times*.)

Eight
COMMERCE

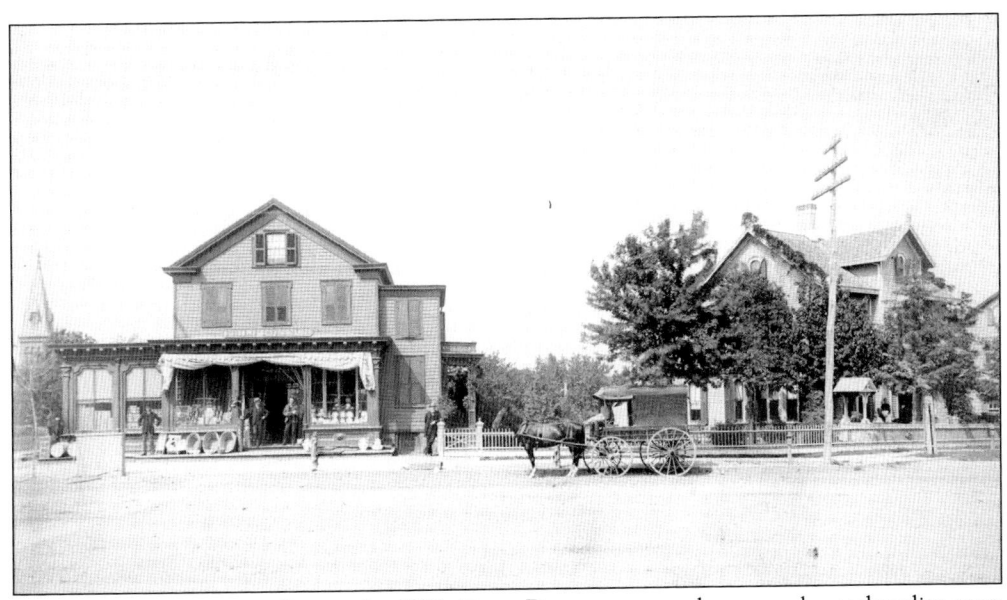

THE SECOND DOREMUS STORE. In 1811, Peter Doremus opened a general merchandise store on the new turnpike (Bloomfield Avenue). His knowledge of Dutch led to a large business with Dutch-speaking farmers. In 1848, son Philip Doremus took over the business and, in 1853, built the store shown here. White-bearded, he leans against the fence to the store's right. The steeple of First Methodist Church rises to the left on North Fullerton Avenue.

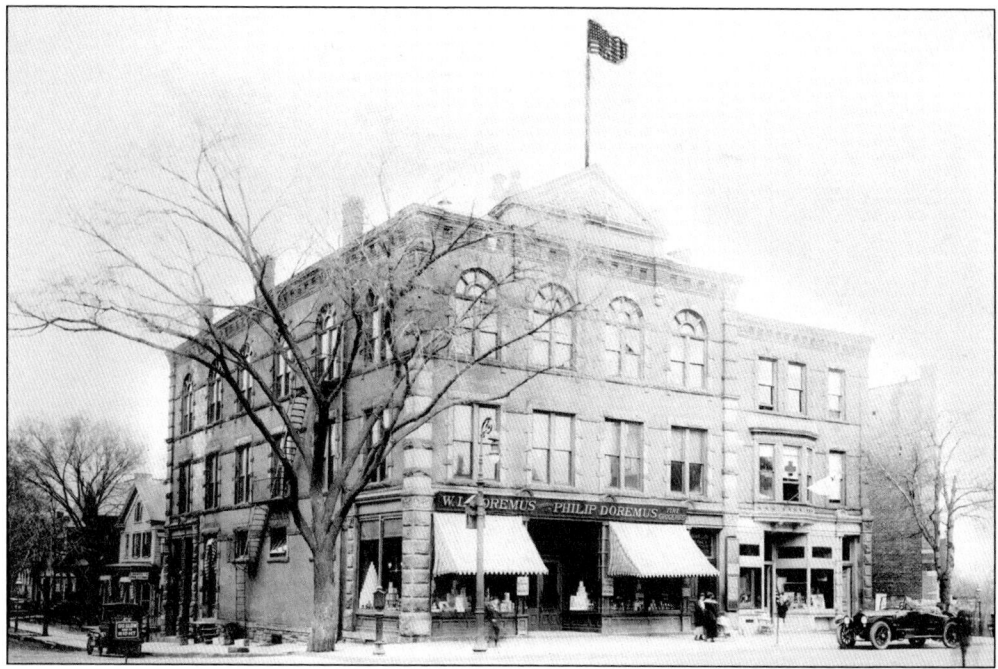

THE THIRD DOREMUS STORE. When this building was completed in 1890, the store's business focused on groceries for the upscale commuter trade. The top floor contained a meeting room called Arcanum Hall. The sign shows that Philip Doremus's nephew W.L. (Lou) Doremus had joined the business. Lou Doremus took over after his uncle's death in 1910. In 1947, after the building had received an Art Moderne facade, Carl Fisch opened here the Hampton House furniture store.

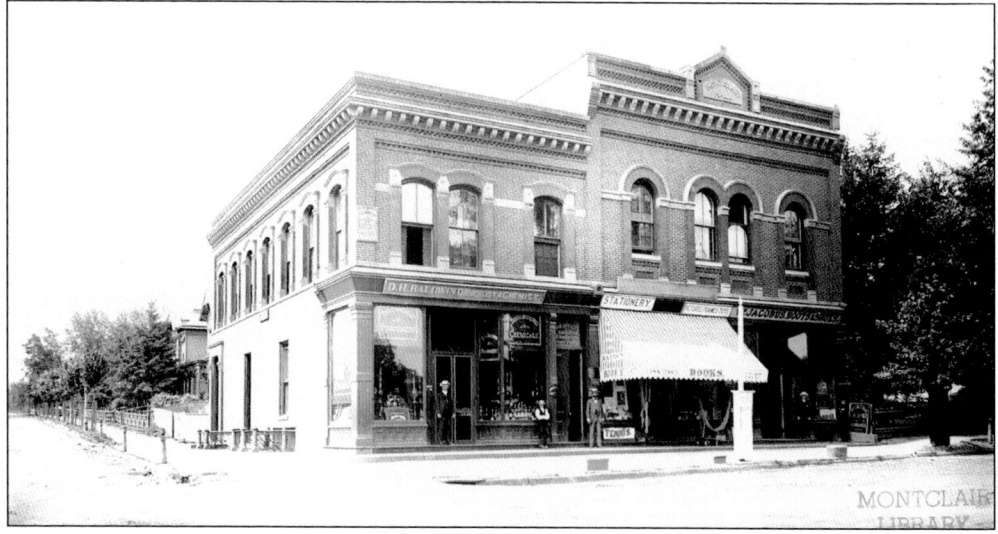

THE JACOBUS BLOCK. Situated on Church Street at South Fullerton Avenue, this important building housed Baldwin's Drug Store, Madison Books and Stationery, Jacobus Boots and Shoes, the town of Montclair offices, the *Montclair Times*, law offices, and an upstairs meeting hall. On January 27, 1878, fire destroyed the building. The *Times* publisher wrote later of his own enterprise, "Not a type or sheet of paper was saved."

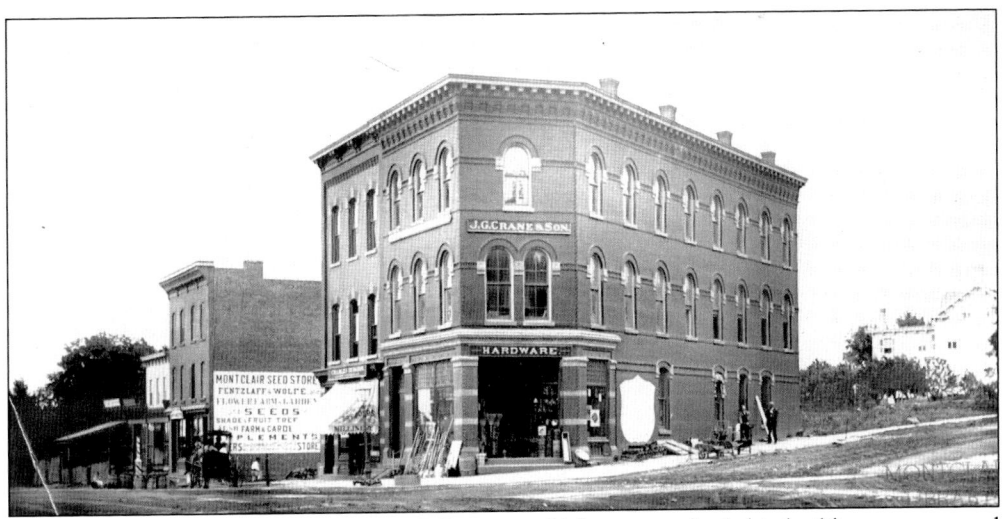

THE CRANE BUILDING, C. 1885. Jacob Ditmars of Morristown had this building constructed in 1879–1880. He opened a hardware store and then sold the business to Jarvis Crane, whose son, Ira Seymour Crane, took over in 1888. In 1902, the building received an addition on the Bloomfield Avenue side. For many years, a clock on the roof marked the hours using the 12 letters of the name Seymour Crane. The building has been restored.

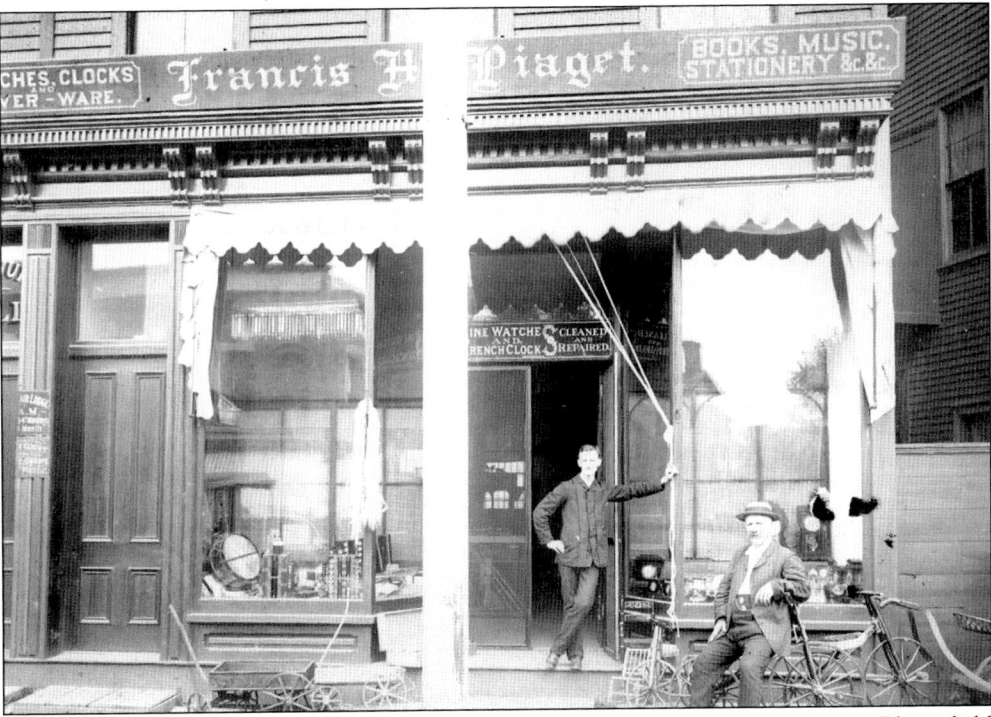

BLOOMFIELD AVENUE BUSINESSES. By 1889, Francis Piaget was in business at 458 Bloomfield Avenue. In 1898, Augustus Henke ran a shop at 462 Bloomfield Avenue. A year later the two businesses had merged at 460 Bloomfield Avenue. After a fire in 1901, the enterprise moved to Glenridge Avenue. Soon after that, Piaget's name disappeared from the directories, but in 1919, Henke jewelers was to be found at 32 Church Street. The Henke name remained on Church Street for many years.

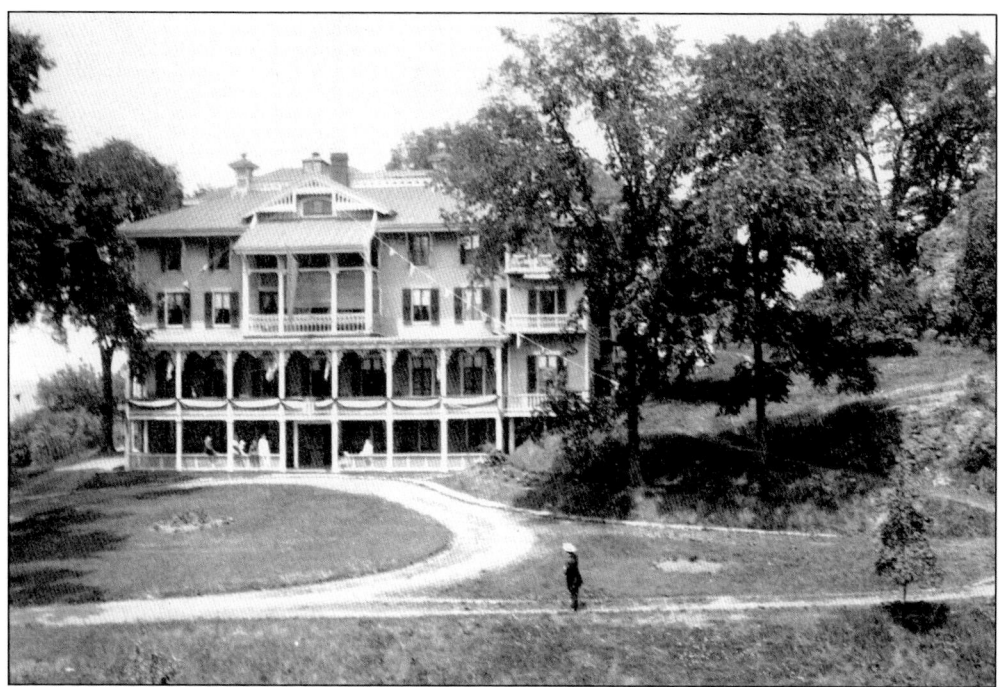

THE MOUNTAIN HOUSE. In the 19th century, New York City families looked for a pleasant place with healthy air to spend their vacations. In response, a number of boarding establishments arose in Montclair, including this one at the highest point on Claremont Avenue. The owners of the small hotel enlarged the former premises of the Mount Prospect Institute.

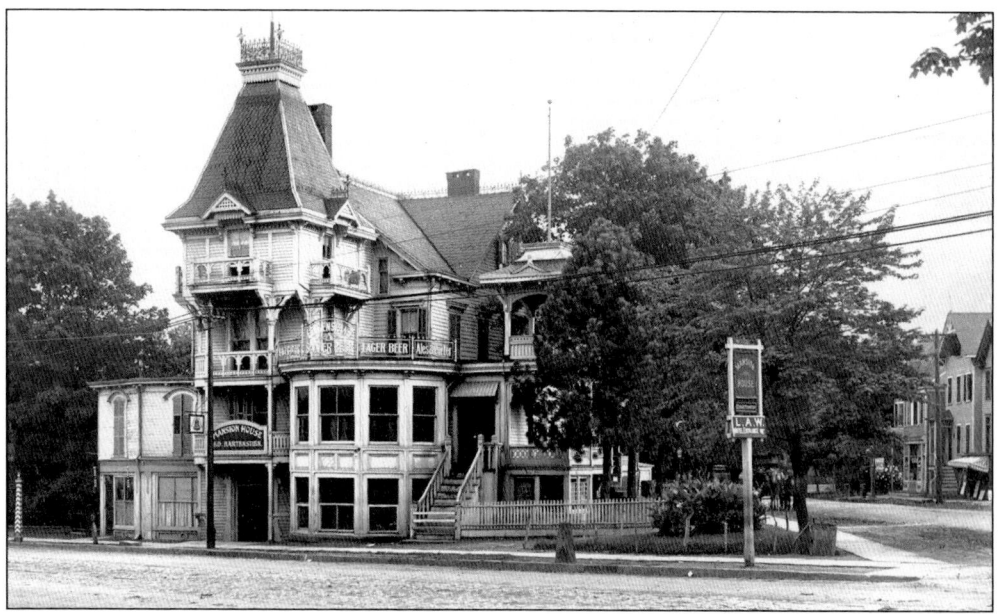

THE MANSION HOUSE. Beginning with Joseph Munn, a series of proprietors operated taverns and small hotels on the southeast corner of Bloomfield Avenue and Valley Road. The hotels had various names before Edward Wright gave his establishment the fantastic shape shown here. The building was replaced by the Montclair Theater.

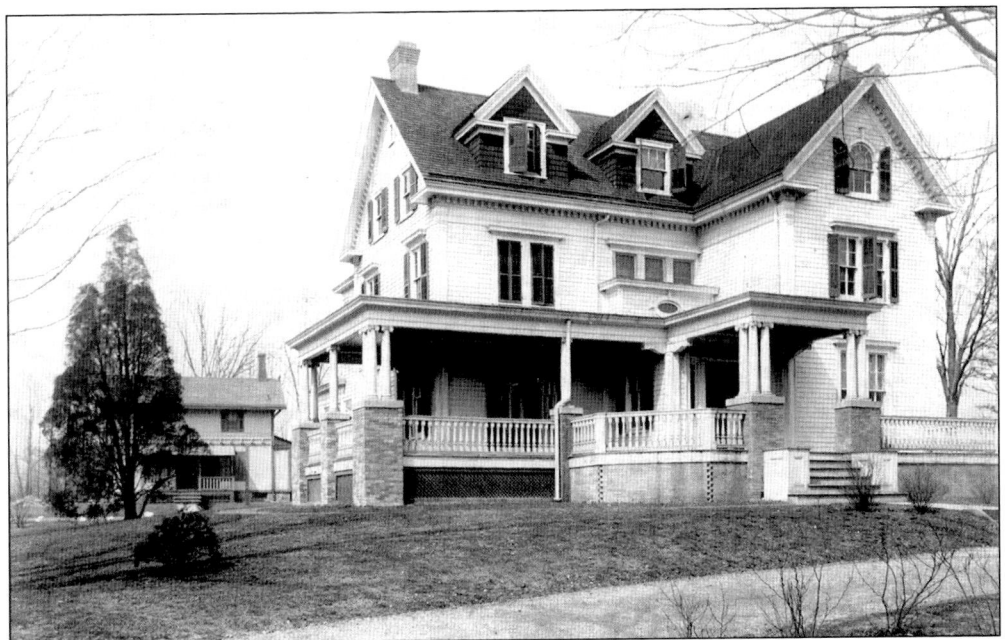

THE MARLBORO INN, C. 1905. A native of Waterbury, Connecticut, Samuel Holmes acquired 100 acres in Montclair in 1867, including this house, which he named Holmeswood. After his death in 1897, the Montclair Reality Company continued to develop his land and converted his home to an inn. In 1928, the much enlarged Marlboro Inn received a Tudor exterior but incorporated the original house. Marlboro, Massachusetts, was the birthplace of Mrs. Holmes.

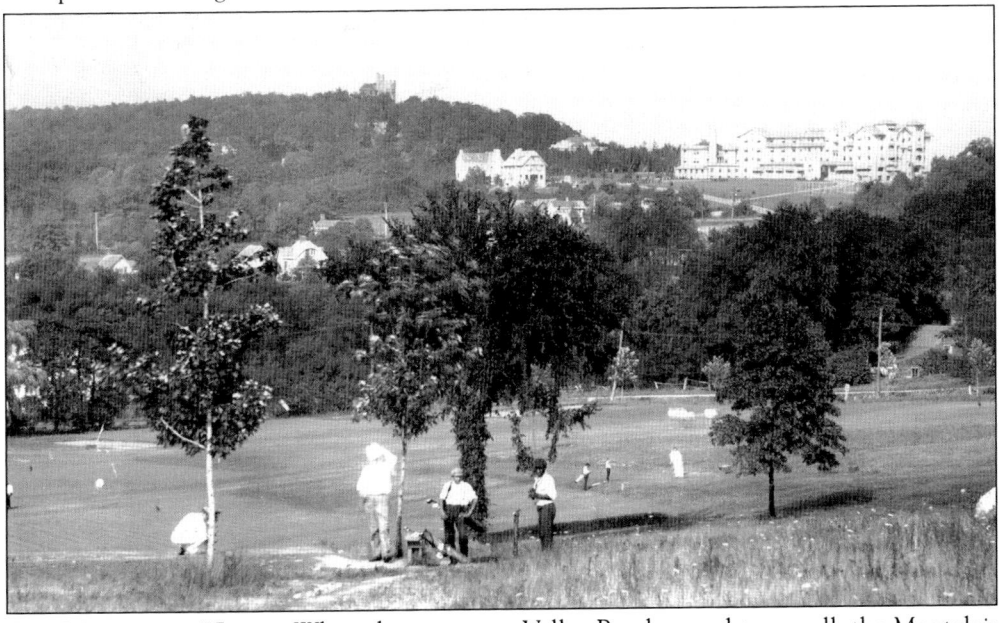

THE MONTCLAIR HOTEL. When the course on Valley Road proved too small, the Montclair Golf Club moved over the mountain to Verona. The links afforded an excellent view of the Montclair Hotel, which remained Montclair's largest hostelry until 1938. Higher up on the ridge is Kuypsberg, commonly known as Kip's Castle. It was completed in 1905 as the home of Frederick and Charlotte Kip.

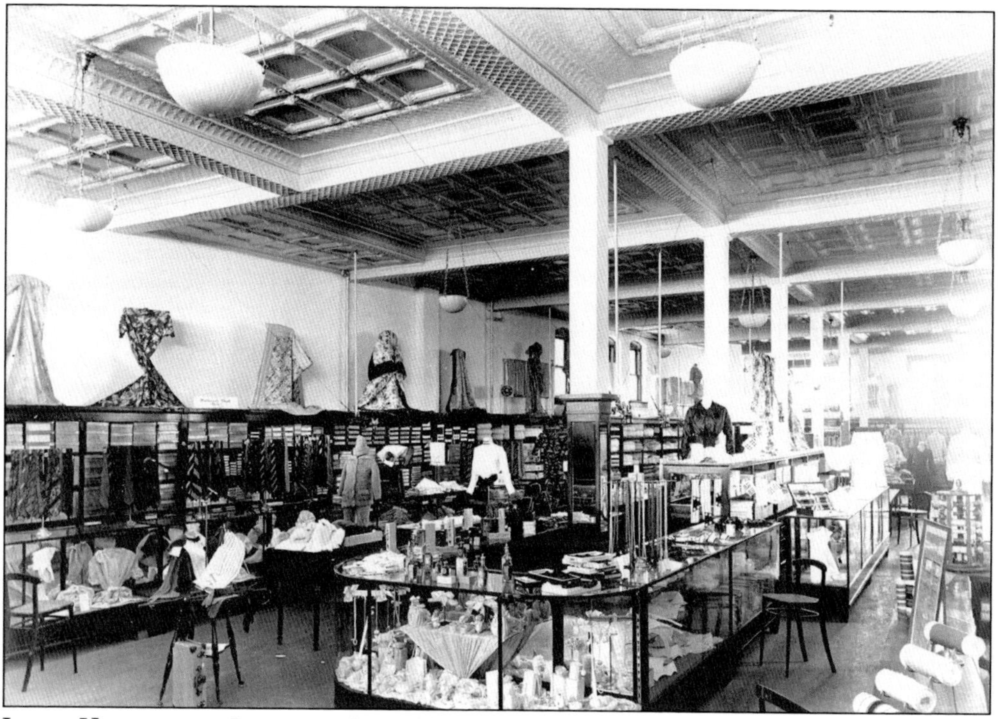

LOUIS HARRIS, THE INTERIOR. Louis Harris came to America from Germany at the age of 12 and, in 1875, opened Louis Harris Dry and Fancy Goods on Bloomfield Avenue. Later, the business became known as the Louis Harris Department Store.

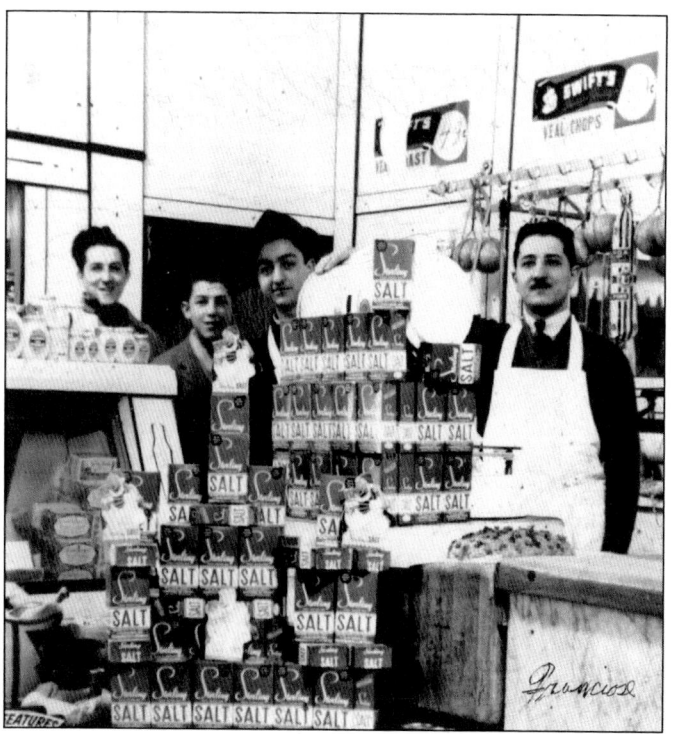

THE FRANCIOSE BUTCHER SHOP. Carlo Franciose, one of two brothers who came to America from Italy, opened a butcher shop on Glenridge Avenue in the 1920s. The shop, which was licensed to sell beer, was taken over in time by Franciose's sons Michael and John. As a sideline, the father brought in grapes by rail to Walnut Street Station. These he sold to the Italian-American community for making homemade wine. (Courtesy Fred Ruccio.)

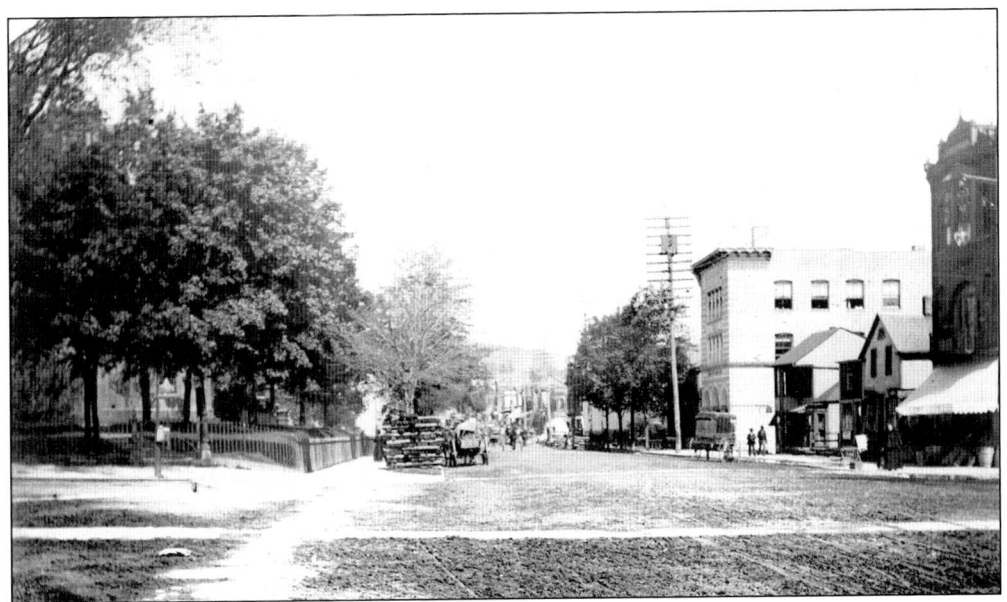

BANK OF MONTCLAIR. Montclair's first commercial bank opened for business in June 1889 in rented space at 418 Bloomfield Avenue. The first officers were Jasper R. Rand, president; William D. Van Vleck, vice president; and Thomas W. Stephens, cashier. The bank prospered and, in 1992, erected the light-colored building (made of yellow brick) to the right above. The trees to the left are in front of the First Presbyterian Church.

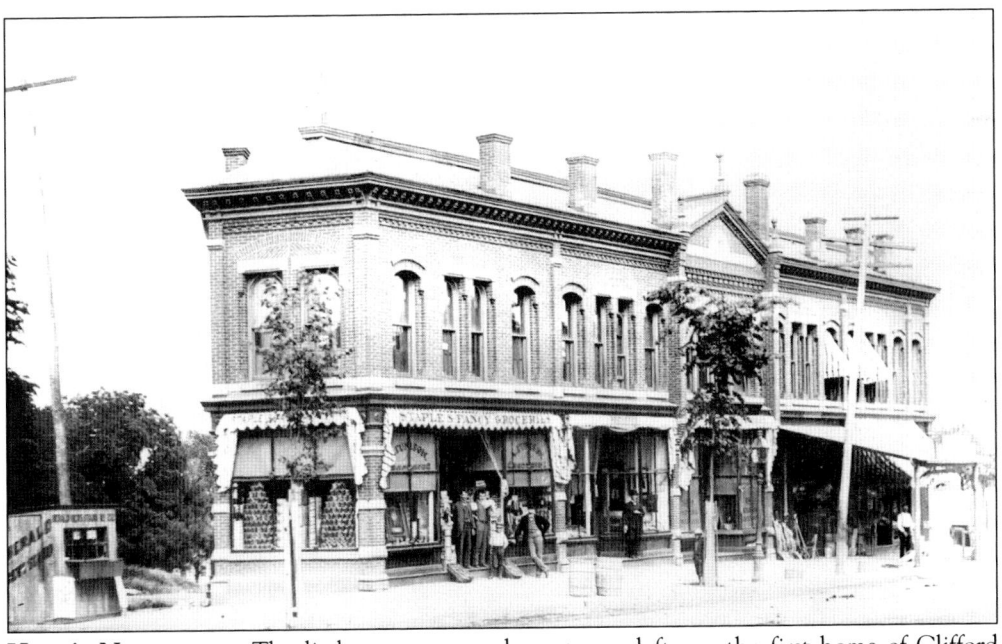

HOOE'S NEWSSTAND. The little structure at the extreme left was the first home of Clifford Hooe's newspaper business. Located at the point where Glenridge and Bloomfield Avenues meet, it was the first business known to have been owned and operated by an African American in Montclair. The large building was known as the Morris Building.

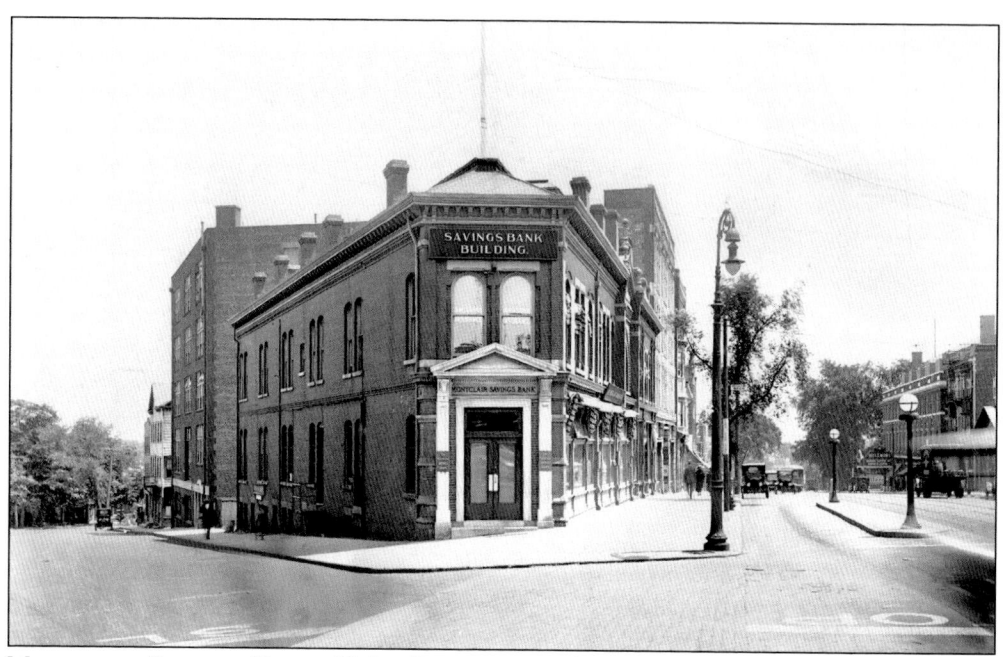

MONTCLAIR SAVINGS BANK. Philip Doremus was the first president of the savings bank, organized in 1893. In 1905, the bank acquired the Morris Building. In this c. 1924 photograph, the Edward Madison building appears behind the savings bank. It was the first building in Montclair with an elevator. On the other side of Bloomfield Avenue is the Wellmont Theater, which opened with much fanfare in 1922. Note the island for trolley riders.

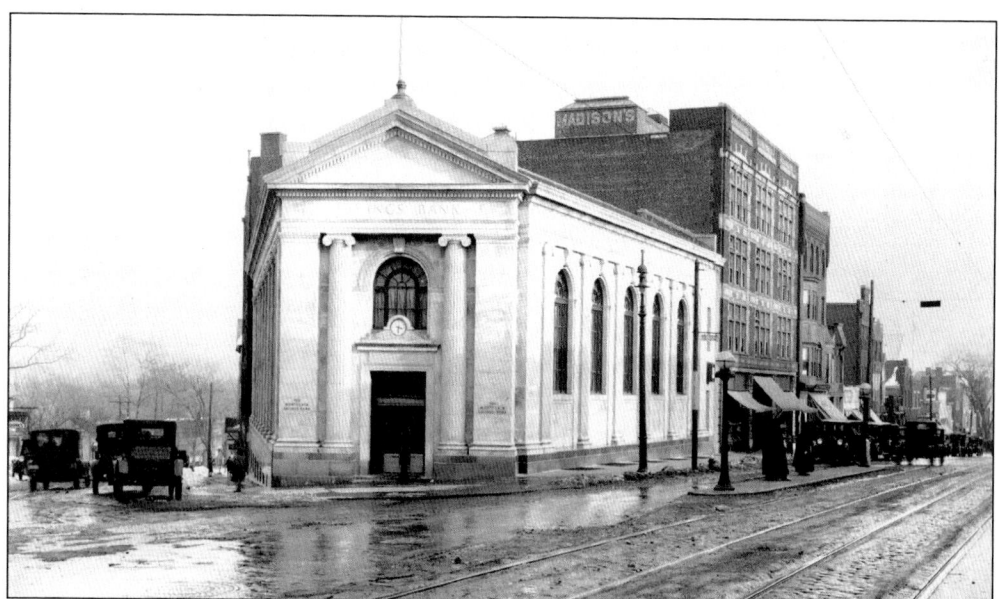

A GREEK TEMPLE. In 1925, the Montclair Savings Bank replaced its old building with this one in a style that conveyed to potential savers a feeling of strength and endurance. Also in clear view is the Madison Building. After fire destroyed the Jacobus block, the Edward Madison Company moved to several locations before erecting this building in 1911. It has an atrium with a skylight and space for artists' studios.

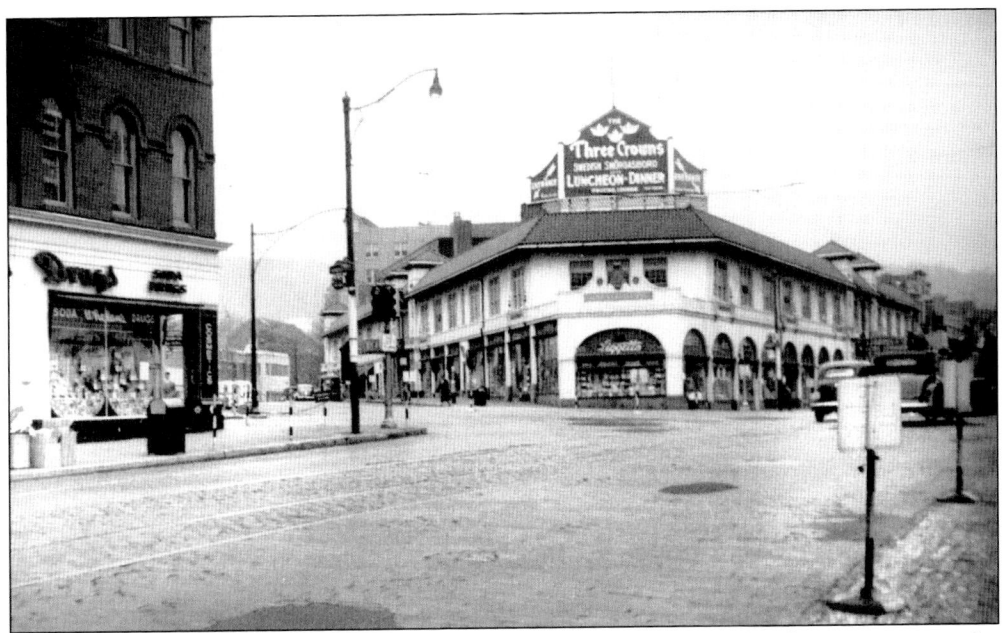

THE THREE CROWNS. This popular Swedish restaurant with a smorgasbord came to occupy the space in the Hinck Building that formerly housed the Grill Leon. A Liggett's drugstore is at the end of the building, and on the corner opposite is a Whelan's. Both were pharmacy chains with numerous stores in the New York metropolitan area.

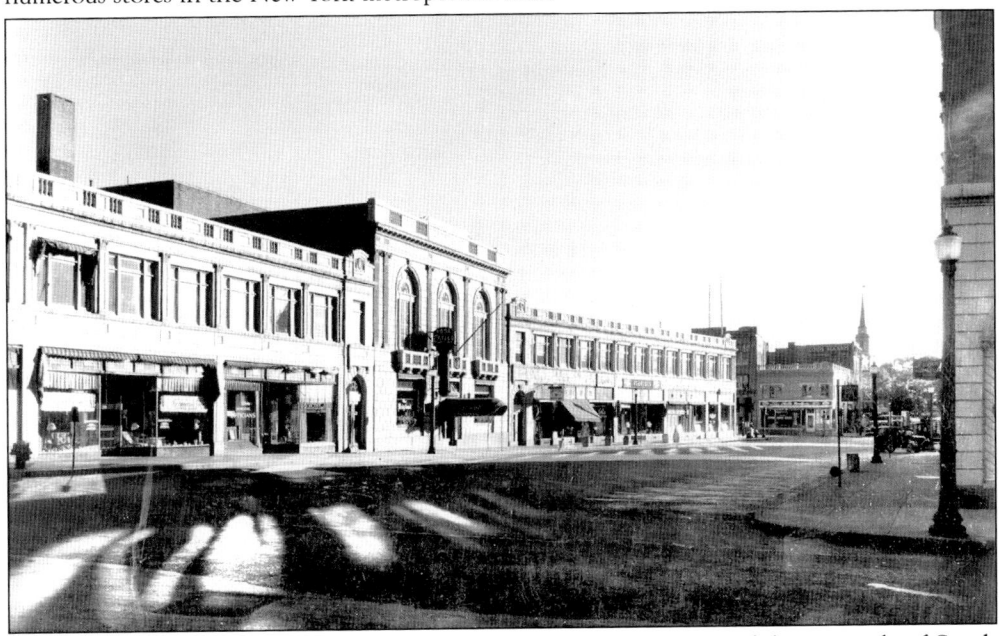

SOUTH PARK STREET, WEST SIDE. This long building covers most of the west side of South Park Street between Church Street and Bloomfield Avenue. The central portion housed briefly the post office. From 1929 to 1986, it was home to the famous Wedgewood Cafeteria. This part of South Park Street was opened later than that between Church Street and the Crescent. The latter was originally named Bradford Place after Rev. Amory H. Bradford. The steeple belongs to Central Presbyterian Church.

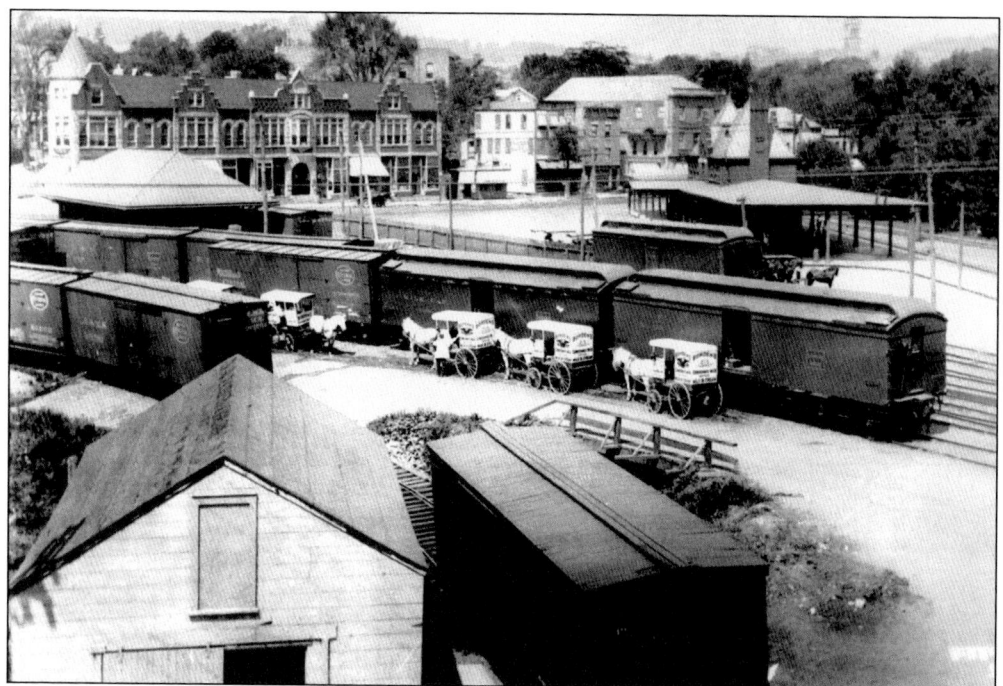

MILK DELIVERY. Borden milk wagons unload at Lackawanna Station c. 1910. In the distance is the tower of the recently completed Immaculate Conception Catholic Church. The long building behind the freight station at the left is the Crawford Block, built in 1895. It was cited in John Nolen's plan for Montclair as a good example of the right kind of commercial building for "a country town."

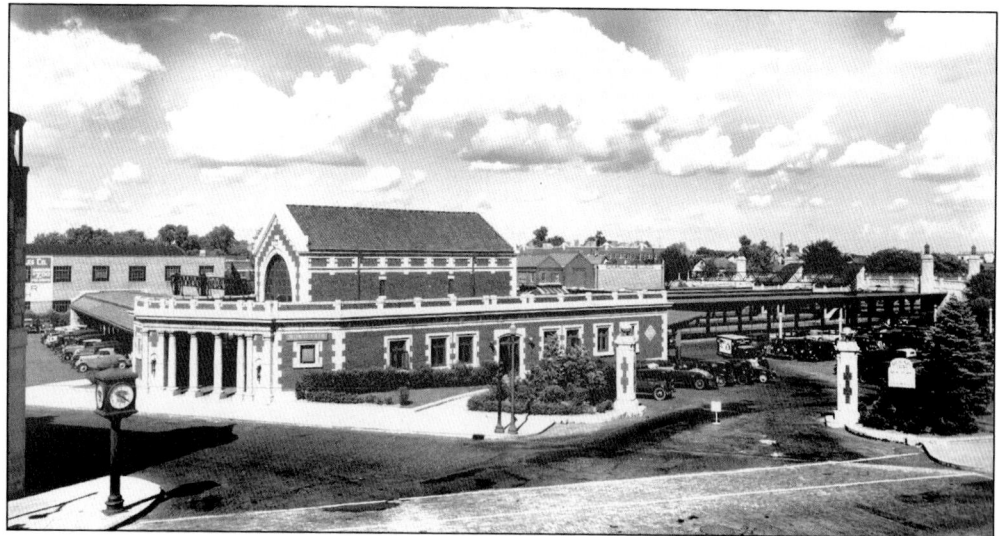

THE LACKAWANNA TERMINAL. Architect William Hull Botsford went down with the *Titanic* in 1912 and thus never saw his design for the Lackawanna terminal embodied. Dedicated on June 1913, the station was described as the "handsomest and best-arranged suburban railroad terminal in the United States." Many who were hurrying to catch the train found their pace accelerated by the clock on the corner. (Photograph by George French; courtesy the *Montclair Times*.)

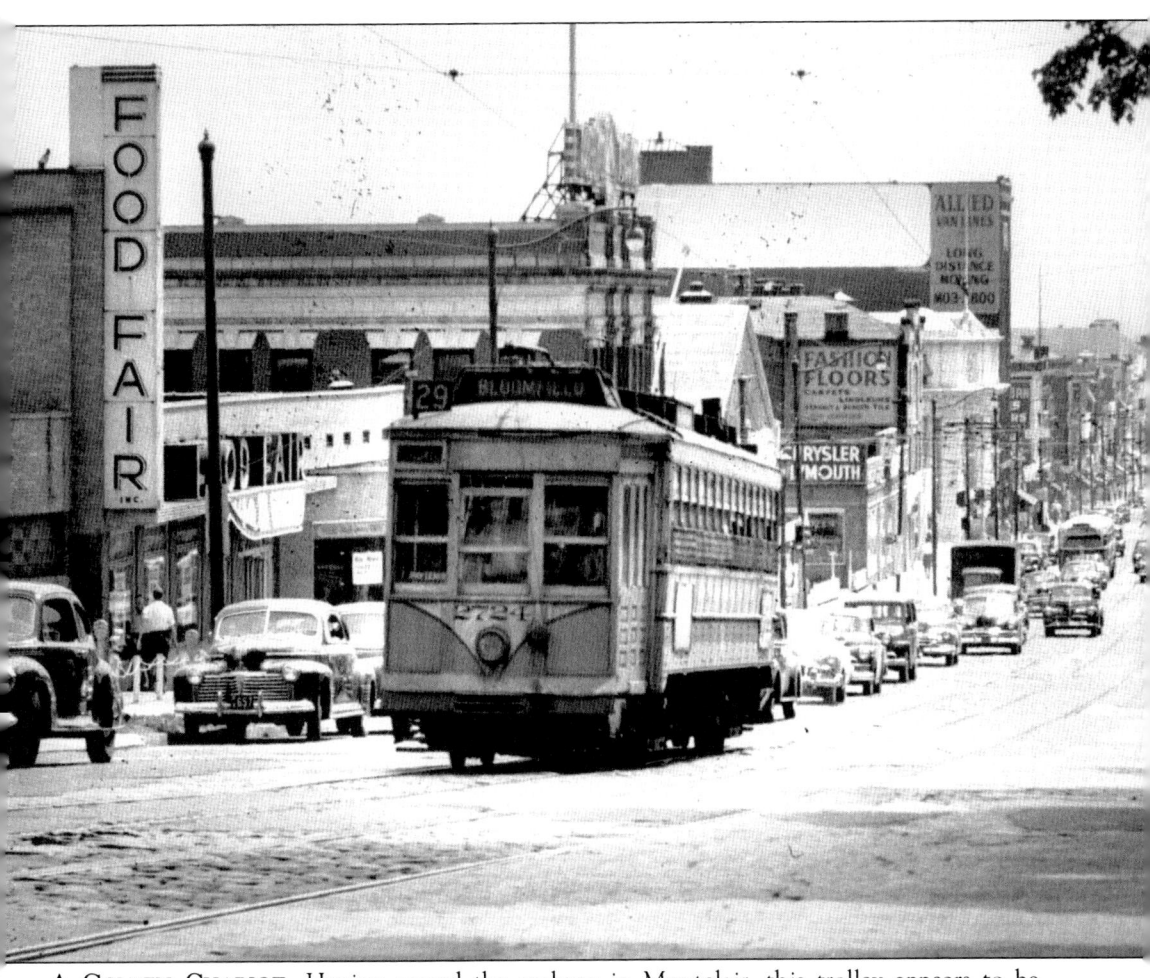

A GOLDEN CHARIOT. Having passed the carbarn in Montclair, this trolley appears to be heading for Caldwell. It would have begun at Penn Station in Newark. The Food Fair was one of Montclair's early supermarkets. The last trolley came through Montclair on March 30, 1952. (Photograph by Robert B. Chamberlin.)

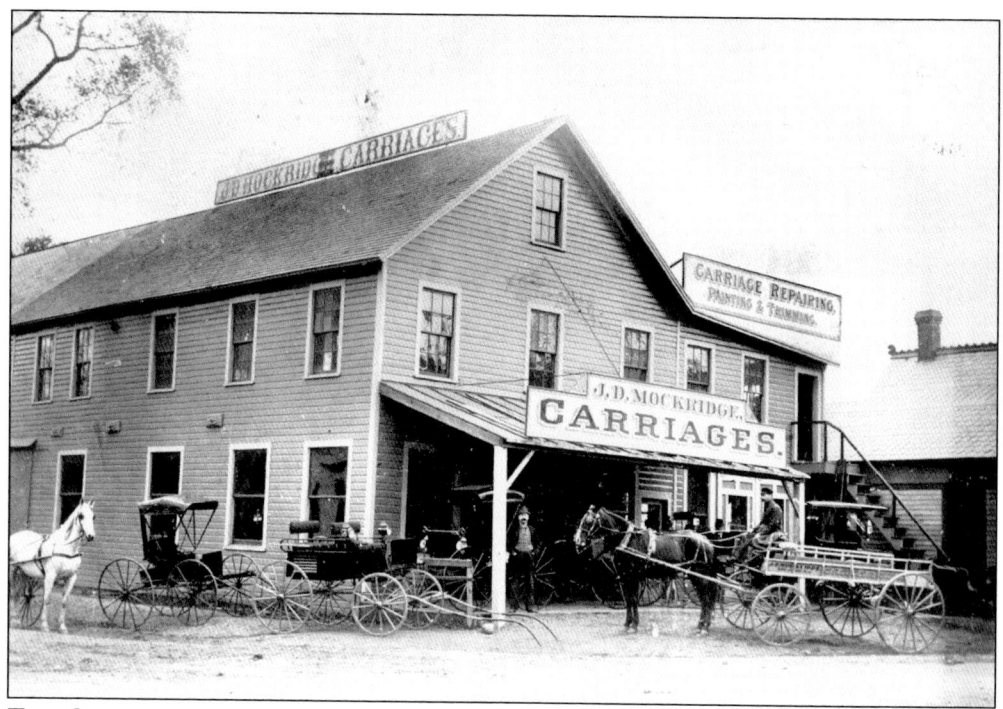

THE CARRIAGE SHOP. This photograph cleverly displays some of the variety of vehicles that were sold and repaired by the J.D. Mockridge establishment at 21 Greenwood Avenue. In August 1892, Mountainside Hospital's first ambulance, "almost complete," was on display here.

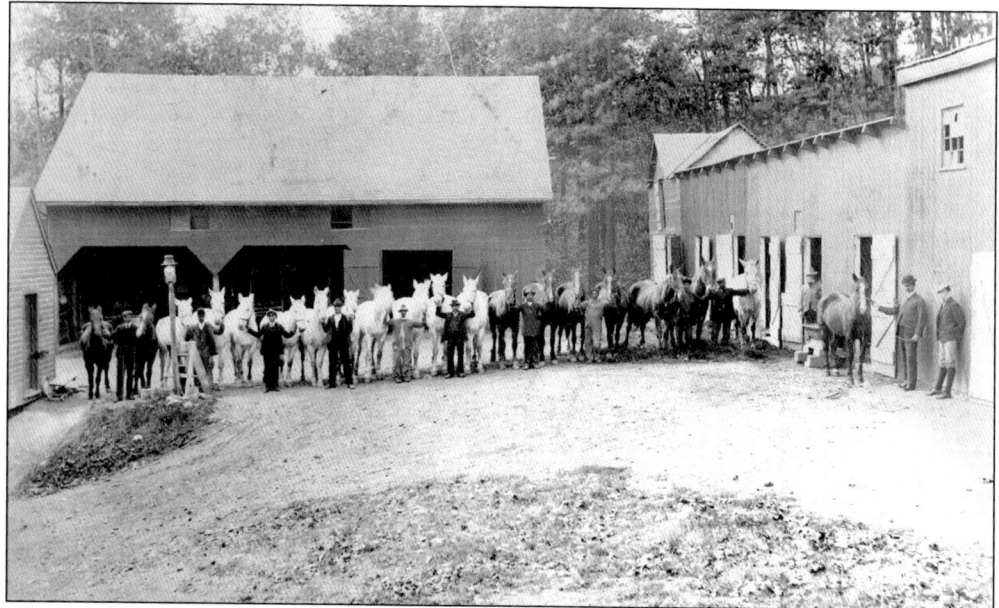

READY FOR ACTION. It is not the start of a race but the men and horses of the Osborne & Marsellis Company lined up for work at their Bradford Quarry atop the mountain c. 1903. The company also owned a lumberyard that was located in the area now occupied by Upper Montclair Plaza.

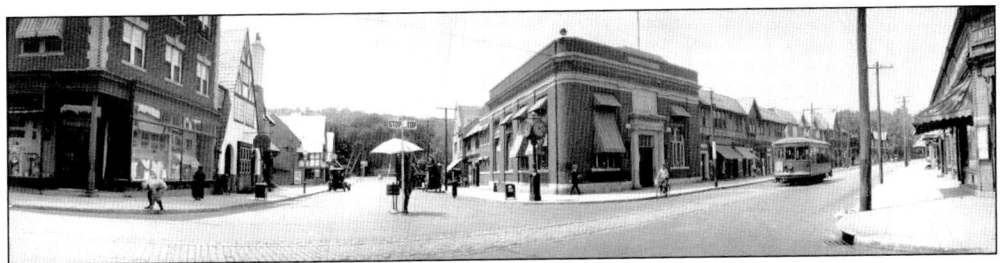

UPPER MONTCLAIR CENTER. The trolley, which ran for the last time in January 1928, approaches the building of the Montclair National Bank and Trust Company, erected in 1914. The clock by the bank is the first of three to appear on that corner. On Bellevue Avenue is the steep gable of the Tudor post office and, farther down, the Bellevue Theater, which opened in 1922.

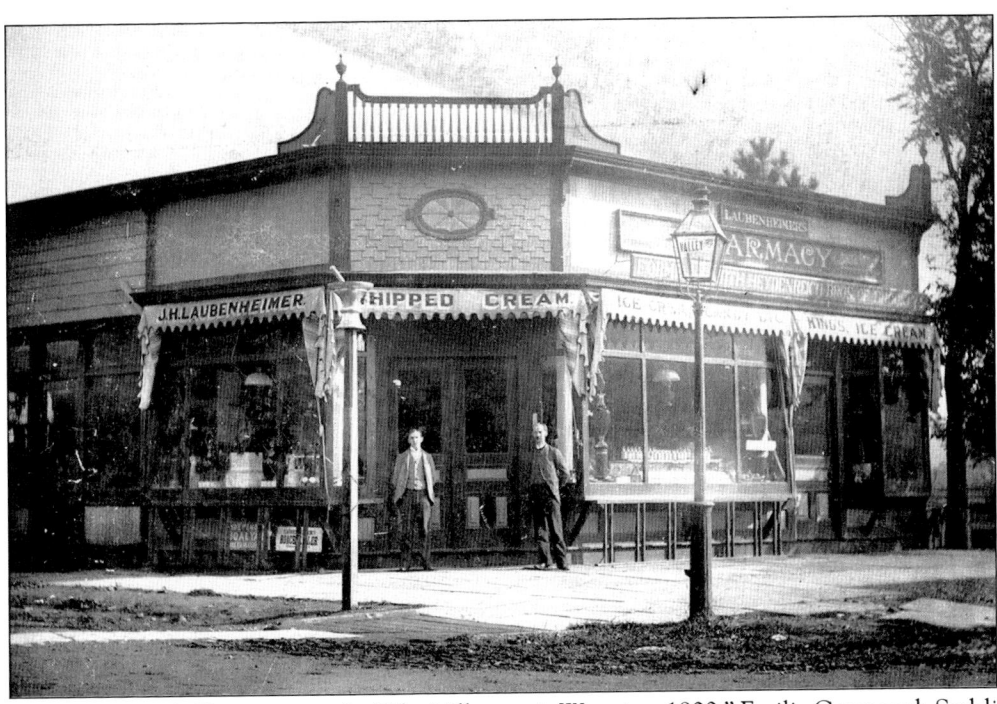

LAUBENHEIMER'S DRUGSTORE. In "The Village as it Was circa 1900," Emilie Greenough Stehli reports, "On down a little way where Valley Road crosses Bellevue, is Mr. Laubenheimer's drugstore" (the *Villager*, 1976). Located on the northeast corner of the intersection, the store was a fixture in Upper Montclair village for many years.

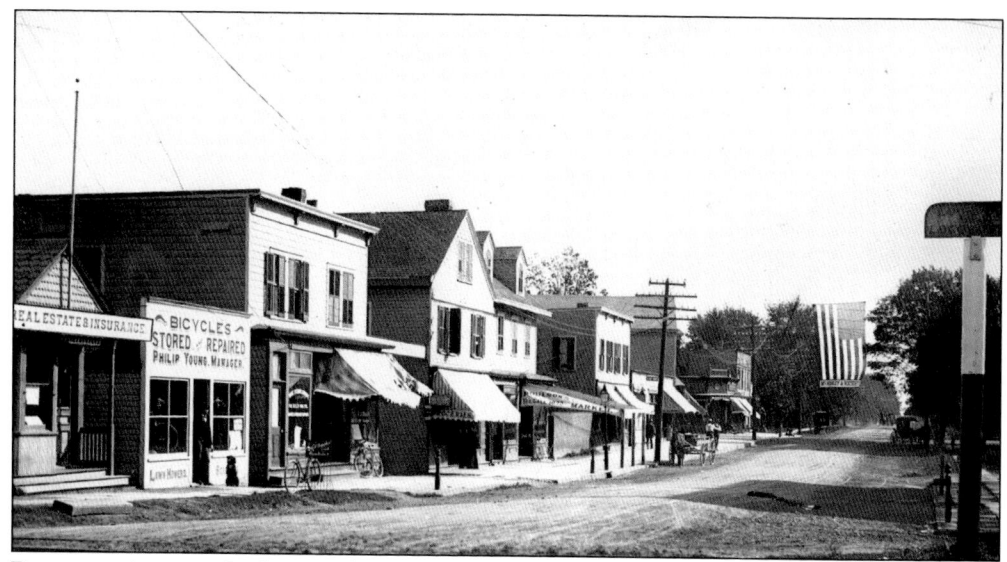

BELLEVUE AVENUE. In this view looking east from the railroad tracks, Laubenheimer's drugstore stands in the distance. The names under the flag draped over the avenue are McKinley and Roosevelt (William McKinley and Theodore Roosevelt), who took office in 1901. The unpaved street would have been muddy in late winter, thus contributing to the annual ritual of spring cleaning. In summer the streets were watered to keep the dust down.

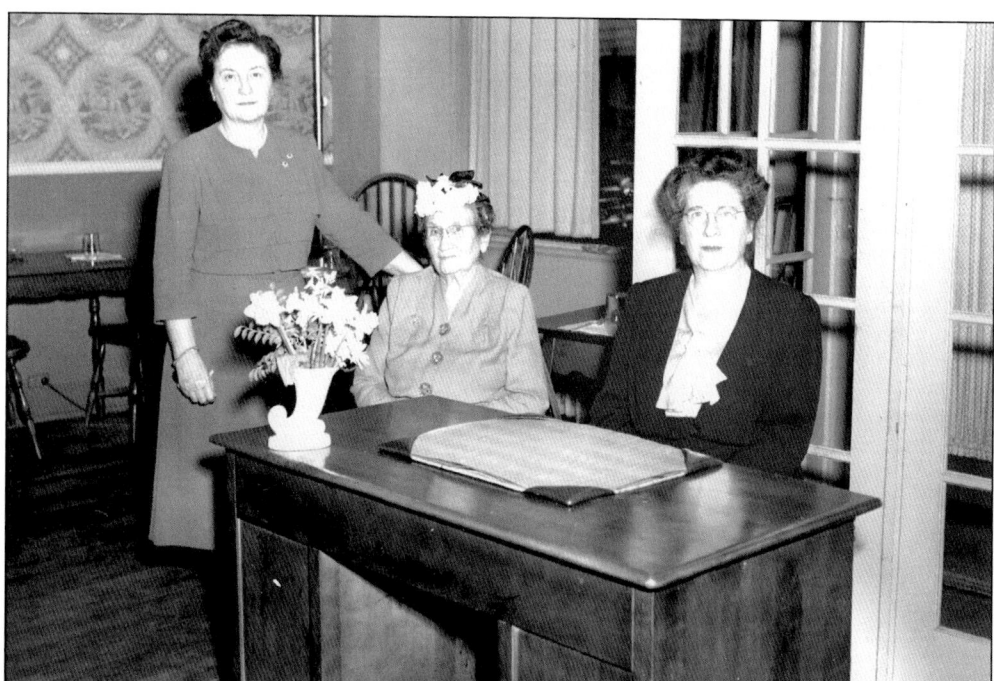

THE OLD ROAD COFFEE HOUSE. In 1927, Irma and Eva Rose, graduates of Wellesley College, opened a restaurant at 80 Church Street, once part of the old road to Newark. Later, their restaurant moved to 32 Church Street, where their mother, Dora Rose (center), remained part of the team. The luncheon spot was listed in the Duncan Hines book *Adventures in Good Eating*. (Courtesy the *Montclair Times*.)

Nine
ORGANIZATIONS

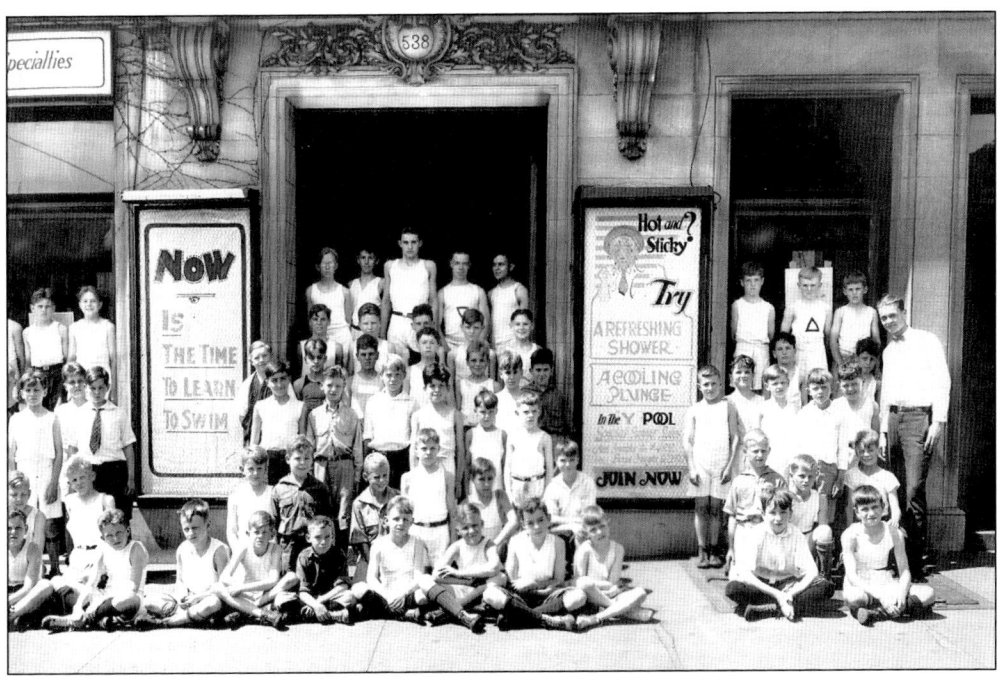

THE YMCA. First organized in October 1867, the original YMCA lasted 10 years. The present YMCA reorganized in 1891. For the first six years, it operated above a store at 510 Bloomfield Avenue. In 1899, the YMCA opened at 538 Bloomfield Avenue and, in 1926, moved to its current Park Street location. This photograph shows a 1920s scene of children in front of the 538 Bloomfield Avenue location. (Photograph by F.W. Kupper.)

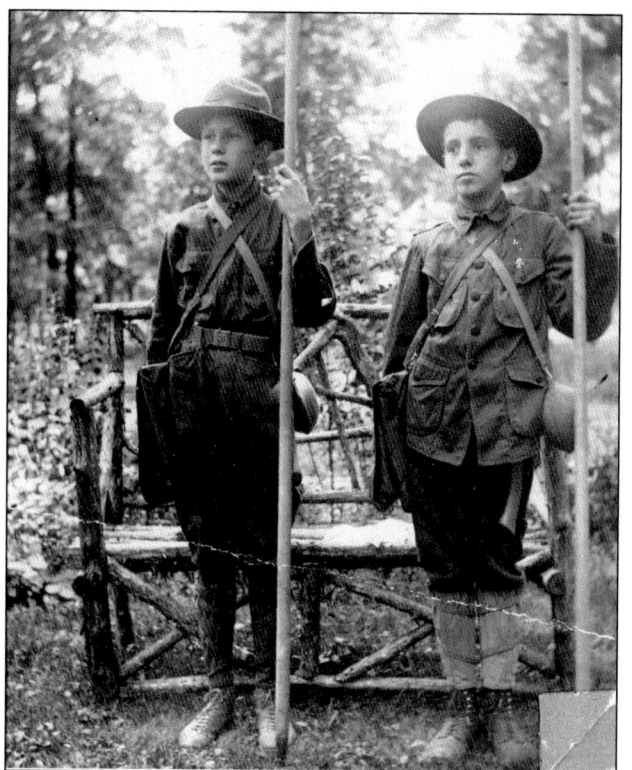

BOY SCOUTS, C. 1914. Frank Fellows Gray founded the Eagle Rock Council of Boy Scouts, the first in America, in March 1909, using the Lord Baden-Powell's pattern for training boys that was developed during the Boer War to supplement military work in England. The Eagle Rock troop was taught stalking, trailing, and woodcraft. The national organization was started in 1910. In 1911, Gray organized the first Boy Scout camp in America at Dudley Island in Sussex County.

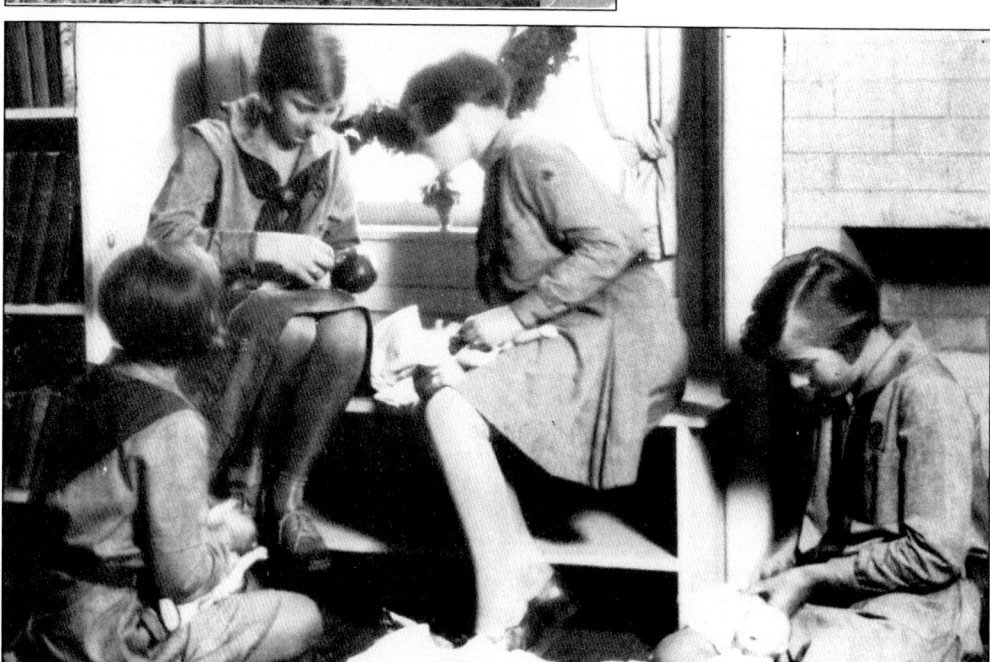

GIRL SCOUTS. In 1920, the Montclair-Glen Ridge Girl Scout Council received a charter. The office was located on 22 South Park Street. The first Brownie troop in Montclair was formed in 1924, and the first day camp in 1930. The Montclair-Glen Ridge Council still serves scouting in Verona, Essex Fells, Cedar Grove, Montclair, and the Caldwells.

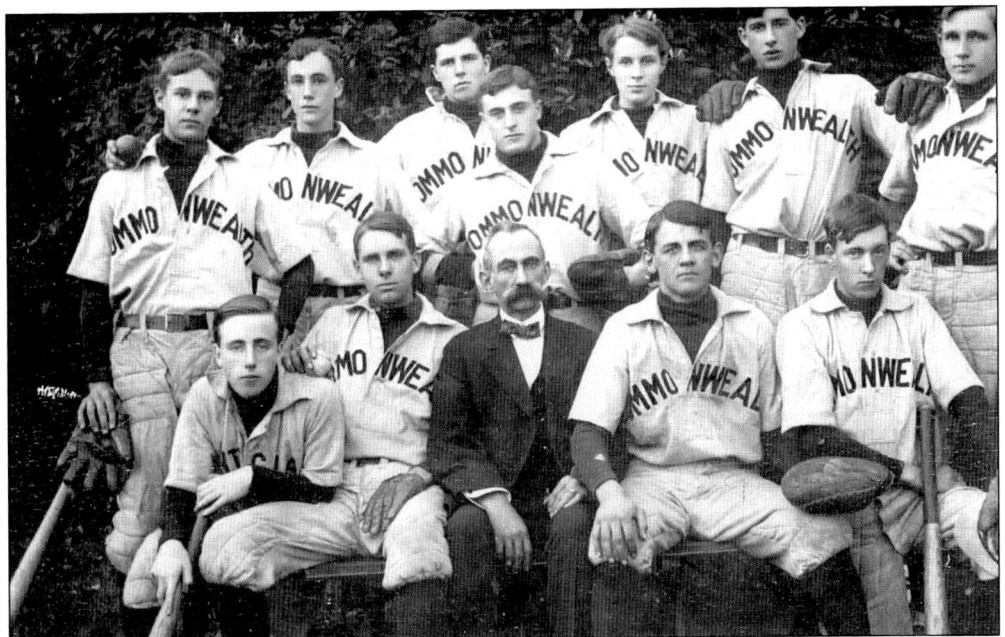

THE COMMONWEALTH CLUB BASEBALL TEAM, 1906. The oldest men's club in New Jersey, the Commonwealth Club was a social organization formed in 1904 for men and boys. It moved into the original Union Congregational Church building on Valley Road. It offered a variety of entertainment and athletic programs. From left to right are the following: (seated) George Murnane, Herbert Connelly, William Pearson, Cullis Young, and Fred Metz; (standing) Arthur Coates, Douglas McBurney, Bennet Fishler, Charles Bettinson, Warren Ayres, Clare Kobler, and Bancroft Gould.

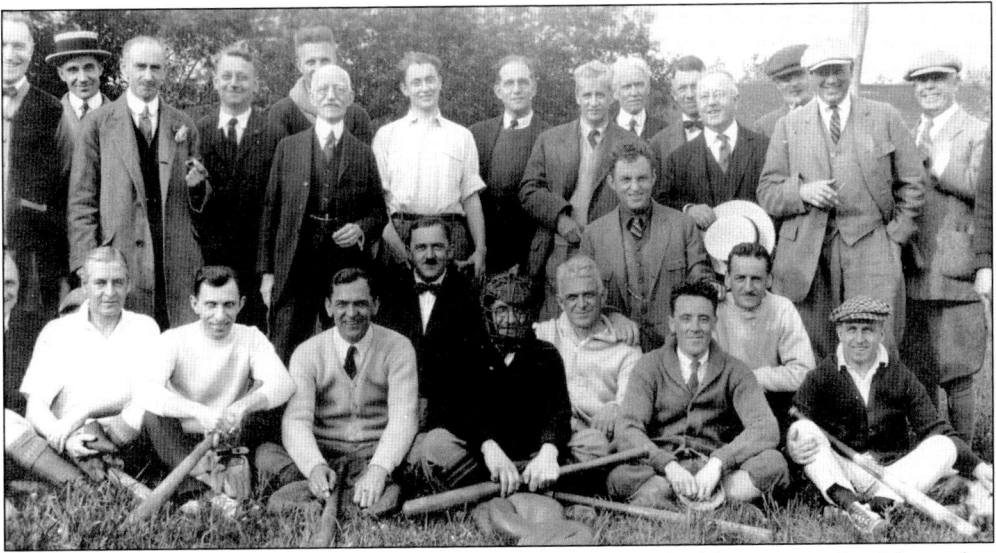

A MONTCLAIR GLEE CLUB OUTING. Formed in 1885 as a double quartet, the 36-member men's choir was directed by E.J. Fitzhugh. The first concert was performed at Cliffside Chapel in 1886. The subscription concert series was held twice a year. Well-known artists sang with the group. Choir director Mark Andrews, who was a renowned composer, organist, and conductor, is at the far right.

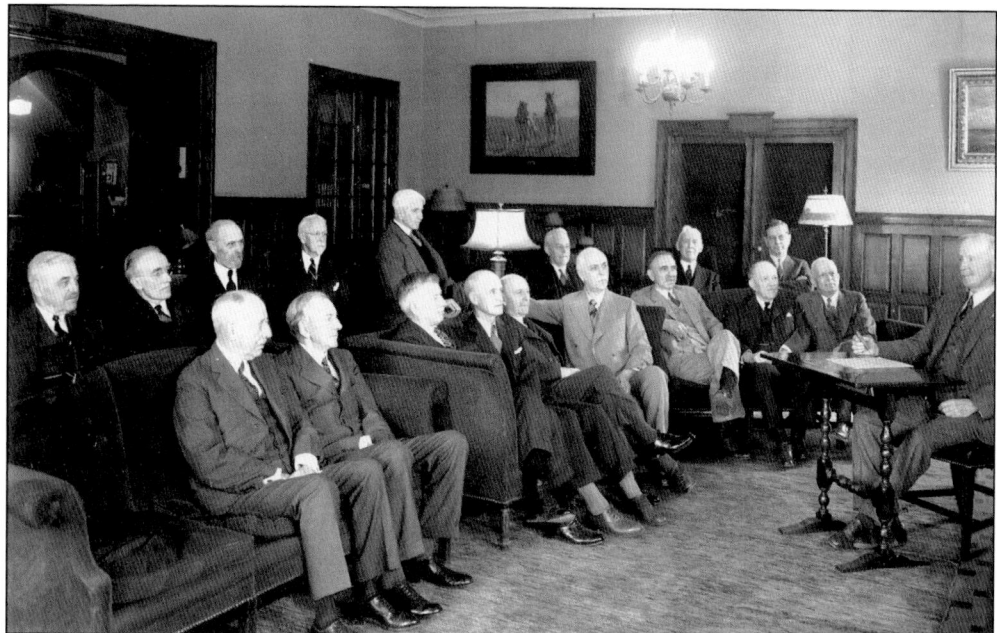

THE DUNWORKIN CLUB, MARCH 1937. Merton L. Beebe, general secretary of the YMCA, proposed the formation of a club of retired and semiretired business and professional men, the Dunworkin Club, at a meeting held on November 14, 1934. Edward McBrier was elected president of the club in December.

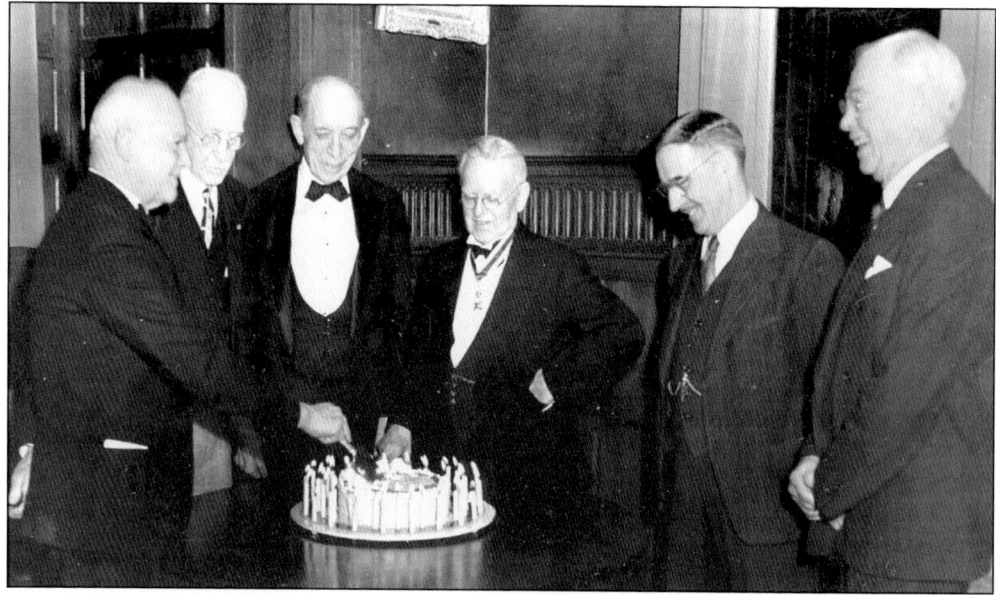

THE SONS OF THE AMERICAN REVOLUTION. Founded on January 4, 1910, the Montclair Chapter, New Jersey Society, Sons of the American Revolution, was a civic and patriotic club for men who were descended from Revolutionary War soldiers. Early leaders were W.I. Lincoln Adams and Rev. Harry Emerson Fosdick. The chapter conducted charitable work at the Baldwin Street Community Center and wrote a history of Montclair. The Daughters of the American Revolution, Eagle Rock Chapter, organized c. 1908.

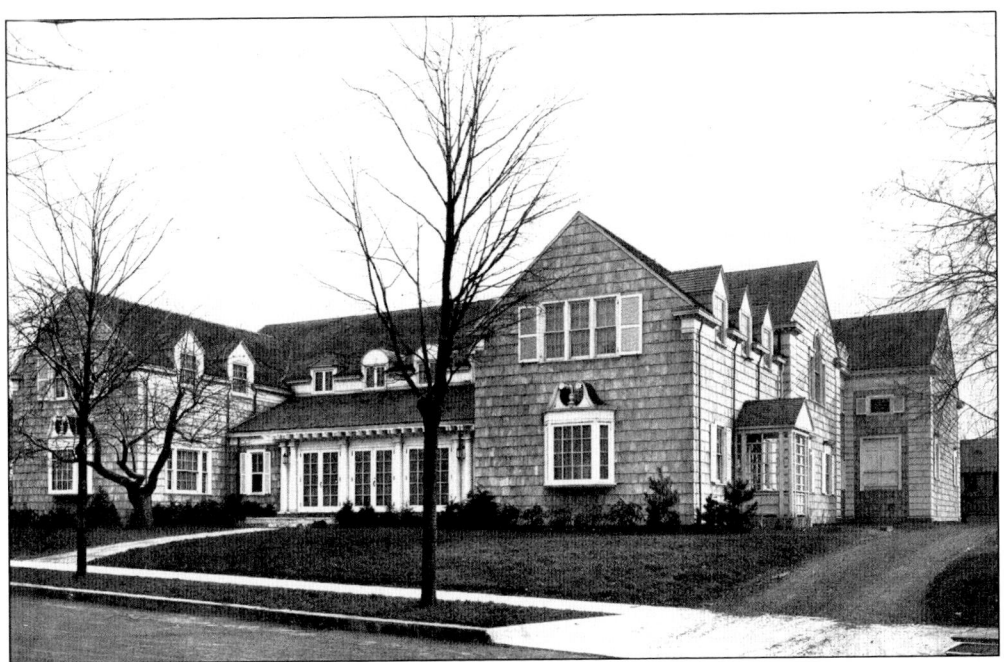

THE WOMAN'S CLUB OF UPPER MONTCLAIR. In October 1900, Mrs. Robert Hoe Dodd and eight other women founded the Woman's Club of Upper Montclair. In 1924, a clubhouse designed by Francis H. Nelson was built on Cooper Avenue. Speakers of world renown addressed the club. The clubhouse was also the scene of dances and other community social events.

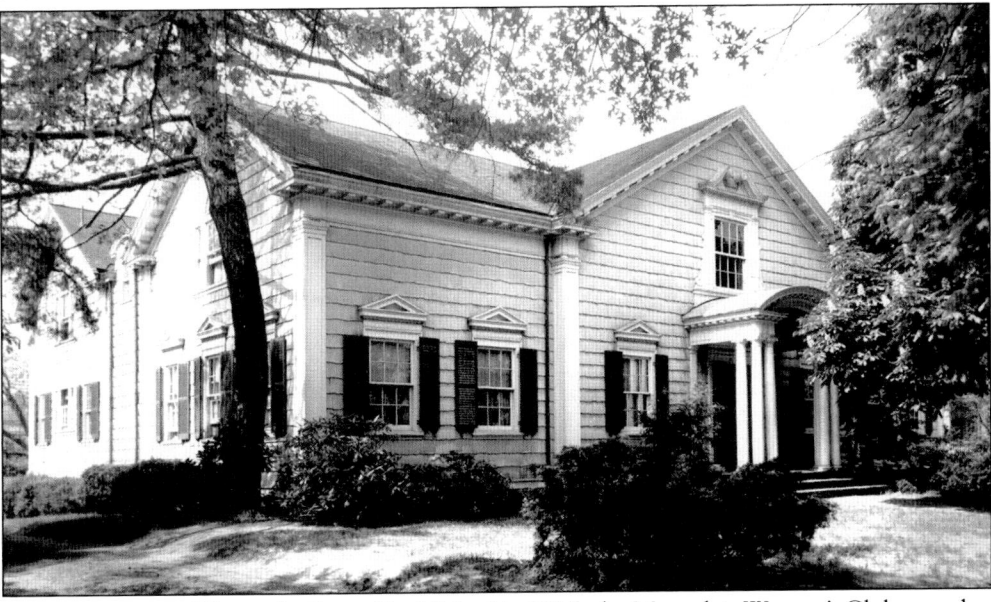

THE MONTCLAIR WOMEN'S CLUB. Established in 1915, the Montclair Women's Club served as a social gathering place for women in Montclair, hosting lectures, concerts, plays, and dances. In 1922, the club featured departments in literature, music and fine arts, civics, legislation, education, and home economics. Later, the club engaged in service work. In 1928, the clubhouse on Union Street was built. Other clubs rented the building for their activities.

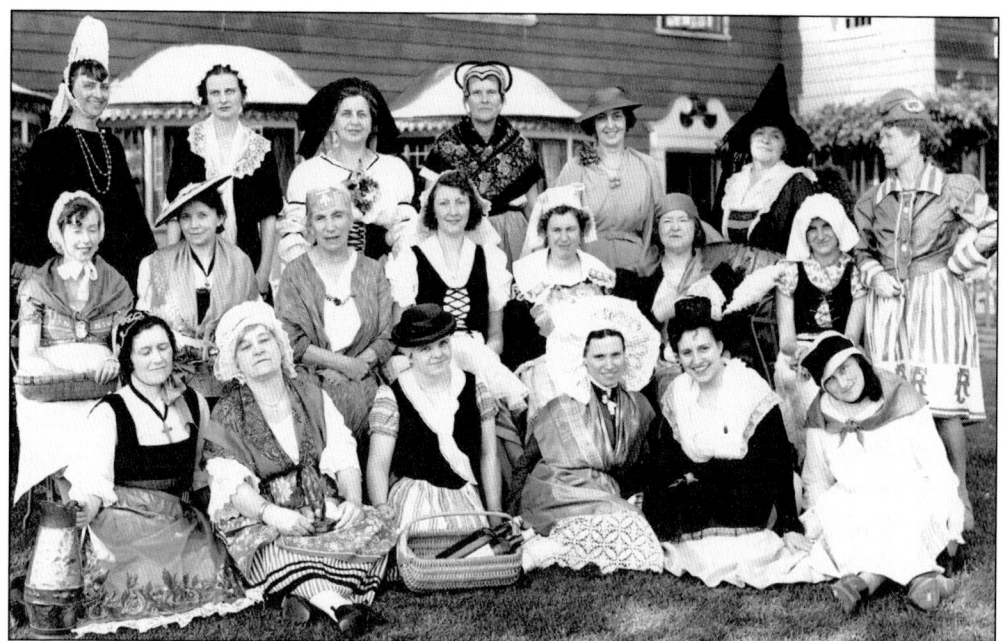

ALLIANCE FRANÇOIS, APRIL 18, 1941. Founded in 1913, the members of the Alliance François studied French culture and worked toward developing good relations with the French people. This scene shows a benefit for the Montclair High School Scholarship Fund at the Upper Montclair Country Club. Each member is wearing a costume representing a French province.

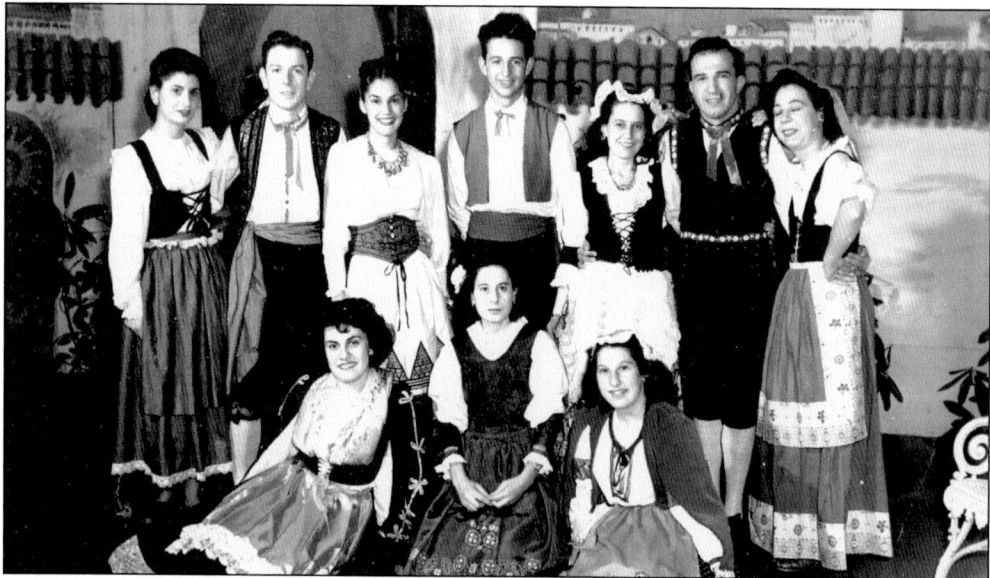

THE COSMOPOLITAN CLUB, ITALIAN FOLKLORE GROUP. In 1927, Elvira Fradkin, of the international relations department of the Montclair Women's Club, formed the Cosmopolitan Club of Montclair. The club was interested in promoting international goodwill and bringing people of various nationalities together. It remained a women's club until 1930, when men were elected to official positions. The Italian Folklore Group, founded in 1948 by Rose Greico, was one the club's activities.

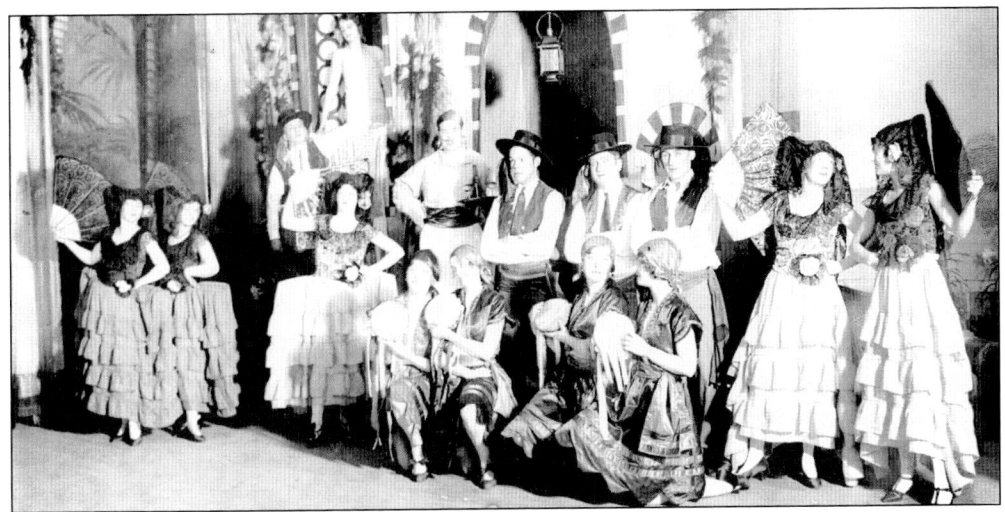

THE JUNIOR LEAGUE OF MONTCLAIR FOLLIES, SPANISH MOON, 1928. For women under 45 interested in service work, the Junior League of Montclair was formed in 1921. The national organization started in 1901. Early league activities included the Junior League Shop (1923), Junior League Neighborhood Community House (1926), and Children's Theater (1930). The Follies was an annual fund-raising event. In 1974, the Montclair and Newark chapters merged to form the Junior League of Montclair-Newark Inc. (Photograph by Drew Peters Studio; courtesy the Junior League.)

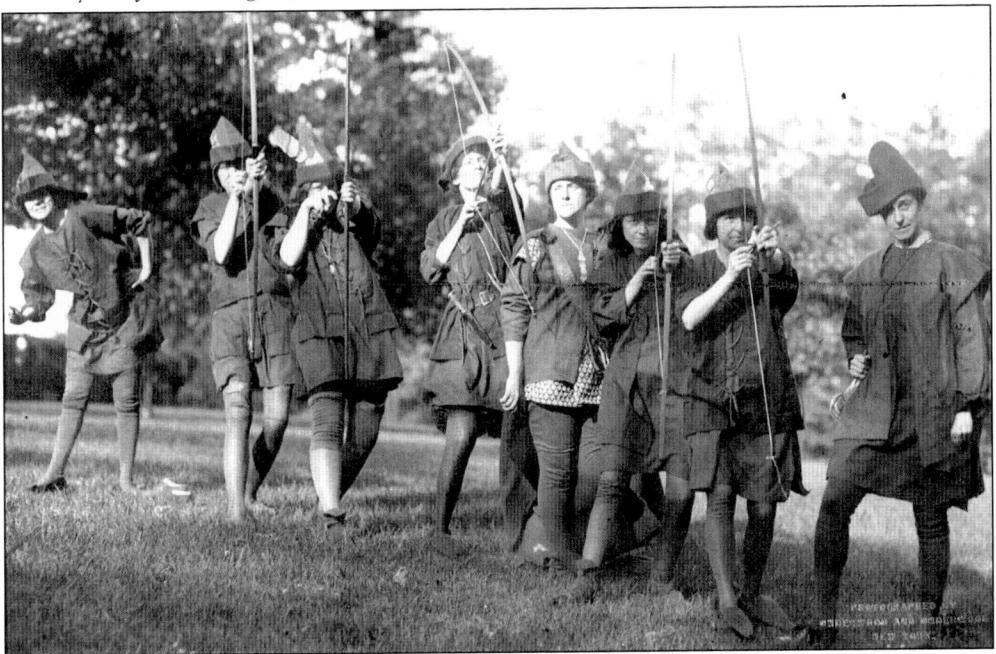

THE COLLEGE WOMEN'S CLUB, SHERWOOD, JUNE 1913. The College Women's Club was established on May 25, 1911, by Mrs. Walter Lloyd and Mrs. Gurry Huggins. Later, the club focused on raising educational scholarships for college-bound high school students through plays, musicals, lectures, garden tours, movies, bridge parties, and book sales. After women won the right to vote, the club became interested in public affairs. It became a branch of the American Association of University Women on June 18, 1928.

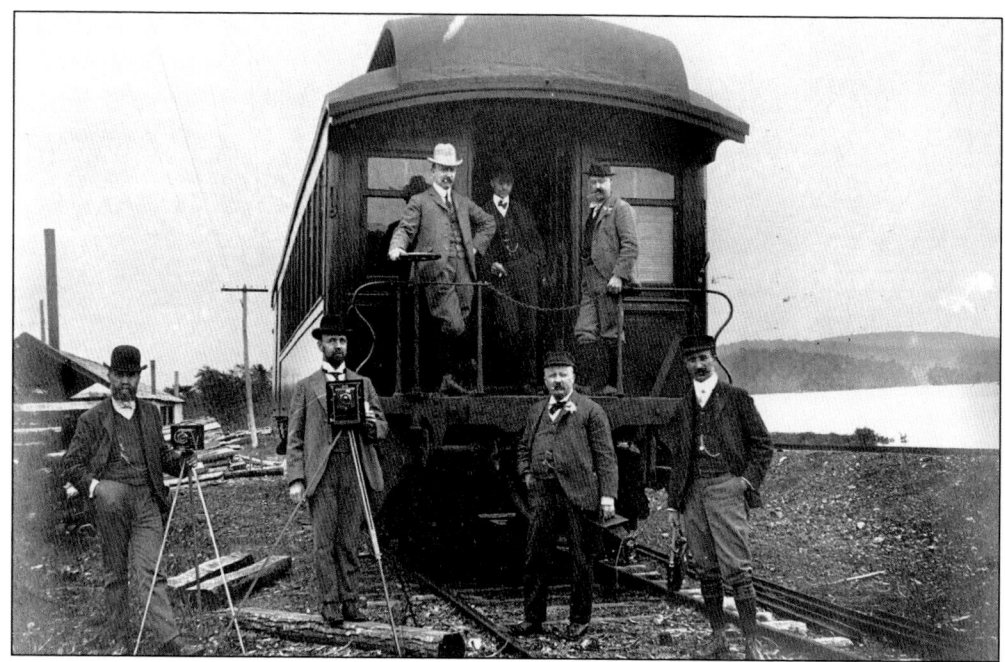

A MONTCLAIR CAMERA CLUB OUTING. On an outing at the head of the Erie Railroad at Greenwood Lake c. 1900 are, from left to right, Dr. Levi Halsey, I. Seymour Crane, and Charles Pratt. Among the prominent members of the amateur camera club were Randall Spaulding, William Crocker, Walter Greenough, and other members of the Montclair Art Colony.

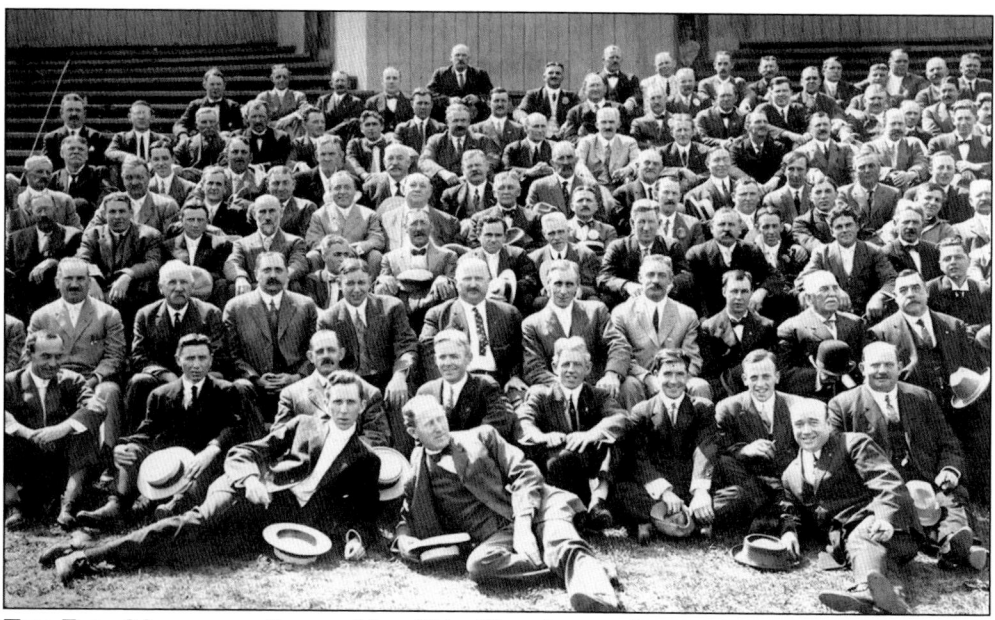

THE ELKS MONTCLAIR LODGE NO. 891, NEW JERSEY SHORE OUTING. This lodge was organized on January 18, 1904. The national organization had been established in February 1868. The Elks also had two African American branches in Montclair: Phyllis Wheatley Lodge for women and Henry Garnet Lodge for men. Fraternal organizations representing ethnic, business, and religious groups were numerous in Montclair.

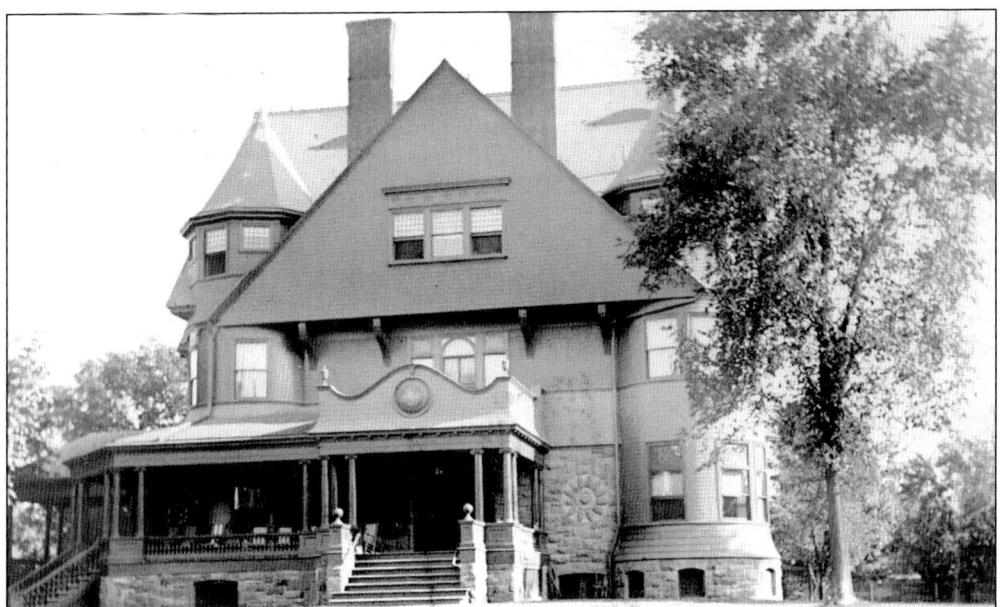

THE MONTCLAIR CLUB. Organized on October 15, 1887, the club for men purchased Dr. John J.H. Love's property on Church Street, and a clubhouse was built there in 1888. On Mondays, the families of the men could use the facilities, which included bowling, billiards, reading, and card rooms. The large hall was used for community theater productions, lectures, musical events, and art exhibits featuring the Montclair Art Colony. Members started the Montclair Athletic, Montclair Dramatic, and Outlook Clubs. The club closed in 1924.

THE OUTLOOK CLUB OF MONTCLAIR. The club, which was organized in 1889 to provide different points of view on current and vital themes by prominent thinkers in various fields, grew out of a lecture program offered from 1883 to 1887 at the First Congregational Church. Lectures offered a main speaker, who lectured for 30 minutes, and then one or two other speakers giving opposing viewpoints. The club also hosted other entertainments, which were held at the Montclair Club.

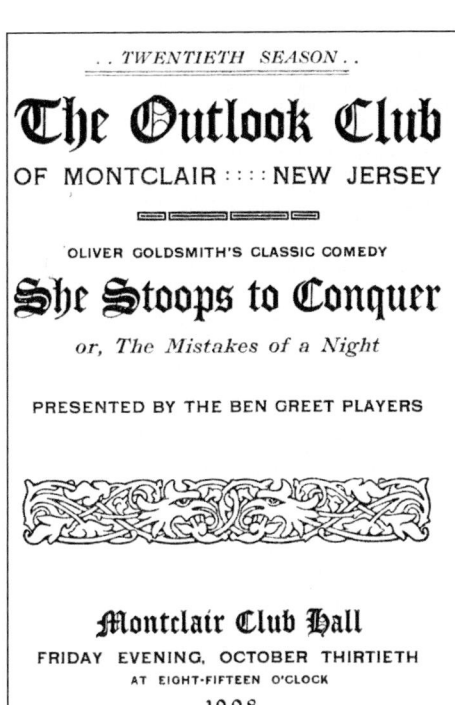

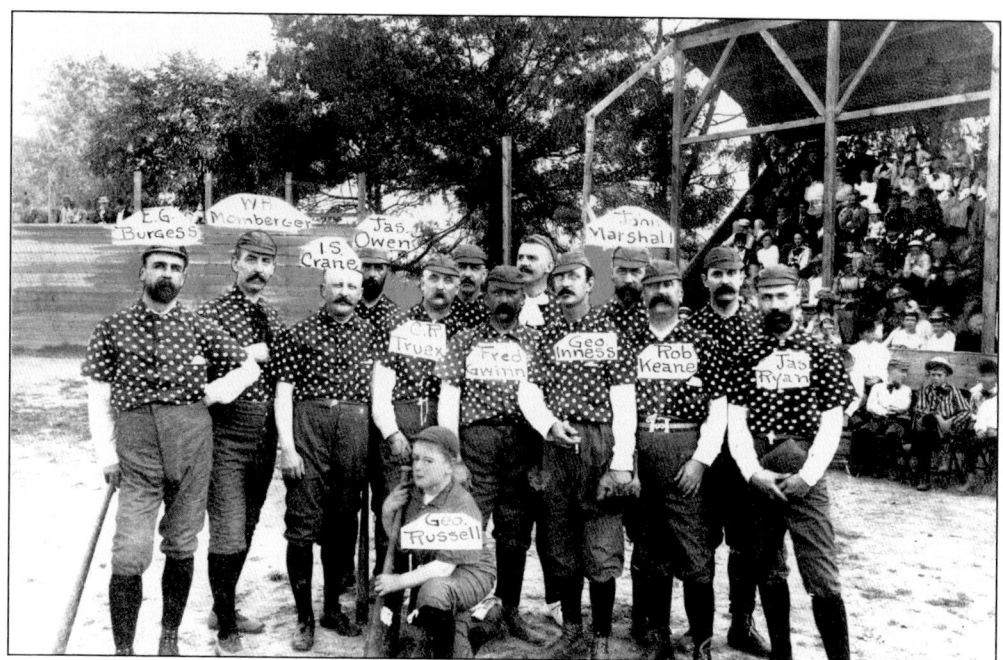

THE MONTCLAIR ATHLETIC CLUB, FAT MEN'S BASEBALL TEAM, 1891. Forerunner of the Montclair Athletic Club, the Montclair Baseball Club played baseball around town from 1883 to 1890. In 1889, the Montclair Athletic Association was formed to promote physical and social activities. George Inness Jr. (pictured) was the first president. There was also a Lean Men's Baseball Team.

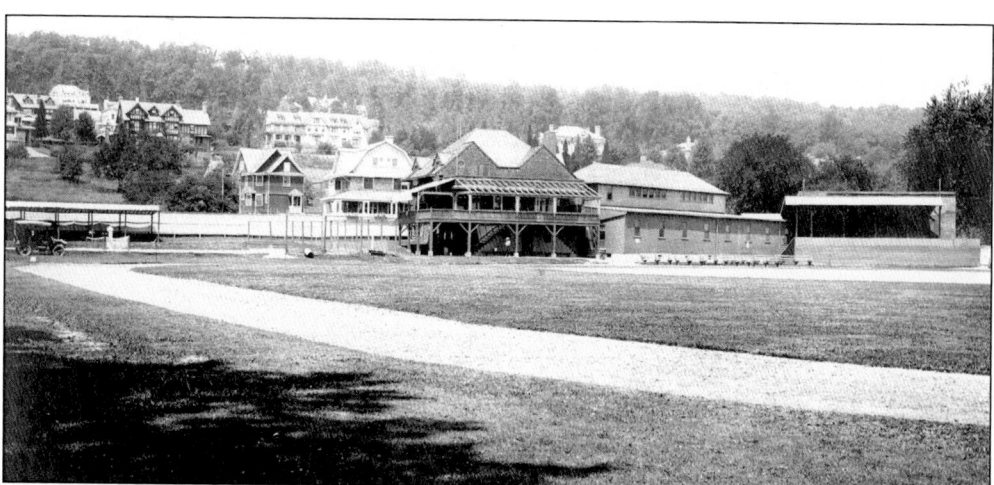

THE MONTCLAIR ATHLETIC CLUB. In 1891, the club built a small clubhouse and baseball diamond, shown here at 201 Valley Road. In 1914, a larger clubhouse was built, featuring facilities for baseball, football, tennis, badminton, squash, bowling, and swimming. Social functions included dances, banquets, bridge, and bingo tournaments. Although at its peak the club claimed 1,600 members, declining membership led to its dissolution in 1949. The club sold its property to Kimberly School in 1950.

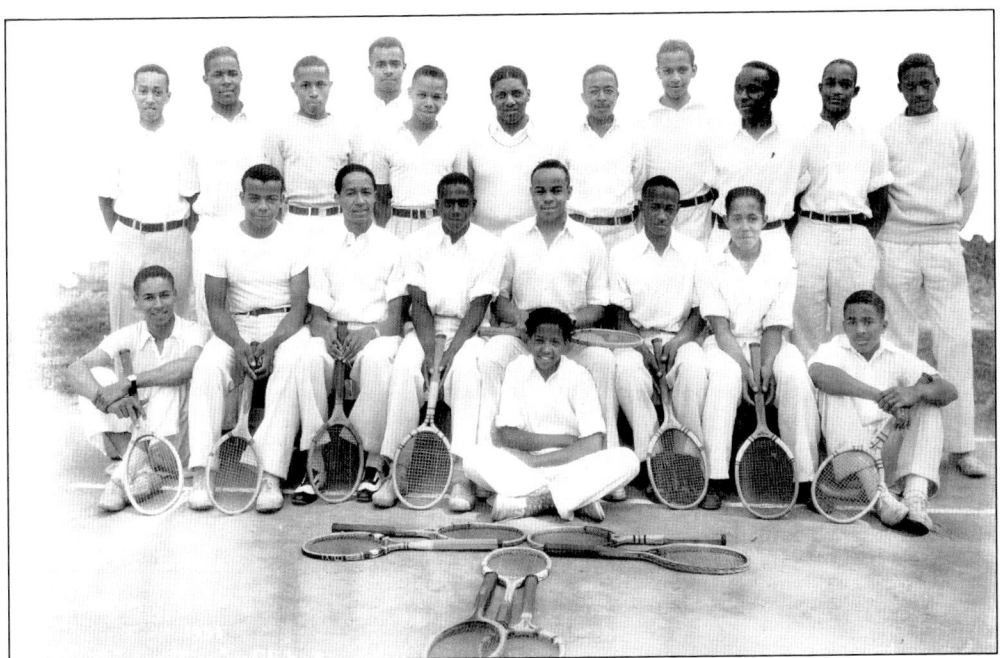

THE TRIUNE TENNIS CLUB, 1933. In the 1920s, a group of boys belonged to an African American Boy Scout troop. Later, as young adults, they started the Triune Tennis Club at an old tennis court on Elmwood Avenue. In 1947, these old friends along with other men decided to start the North Jersey Men's Club, which began as a hunting and fishing club and later evolved into a social club for professional African American men. (Courtesy Daisy Douglas.)

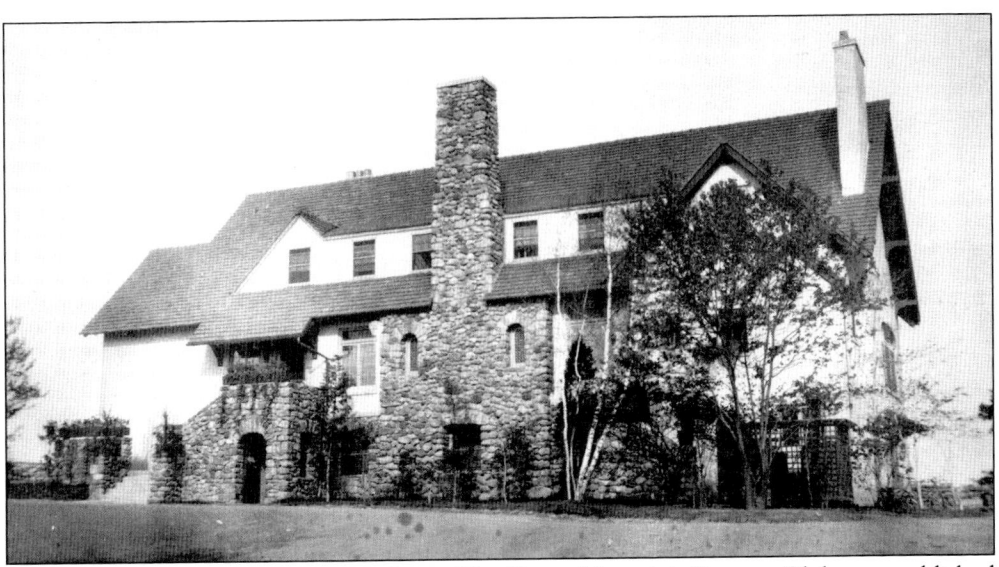

THE UPPER MONTCLAIR COUNTRY CLUB. The Upper Montclair Country Club was established in 1901, when the Upper Ten Club and others set up a nine-hole golf course north of Bellevue on Grove Street. The Cliffside Hose Company firehouse was moved down Bellevue Avenue to the golf course and served as the first clubhouse. Tennis and shooting were added. More Grove Street property was purchased in 1903. In 1912, the Elmbrook Clubhouse was built. The club moved to its present location in 1926.

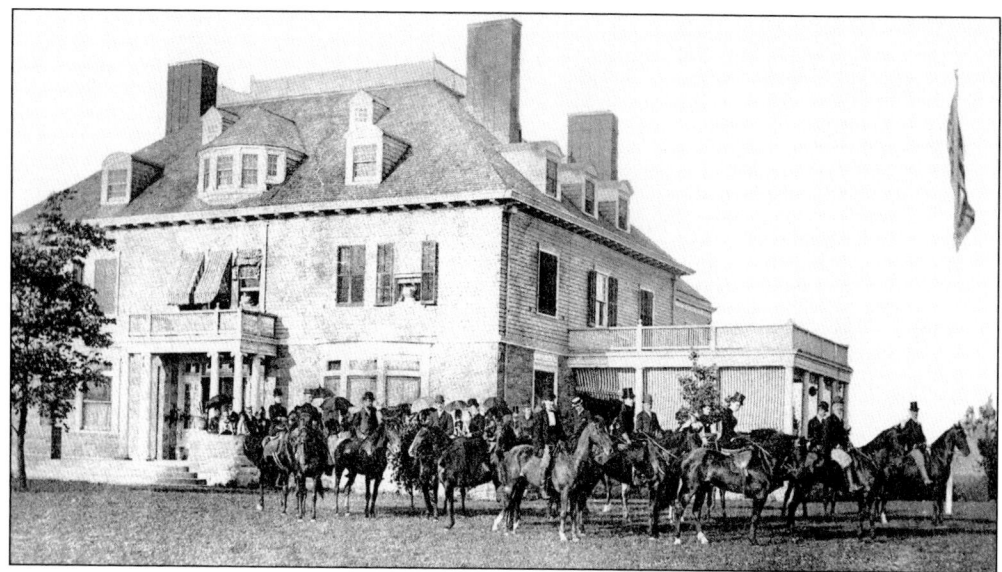

THE MONTCLAIR EQUESTRIAN CLUB. Founded in 1876, the Montclair Equestrian Club promoted riding and horsemanship. Since the members became more interested in fox hunting, the club became the Montclair Hunt in 1878 and was later called the Essex County Hunt. Beagles were purchased from England and foxes were at first purchased from Queens and later Montreal. In 1887, the Equestrian Club continued as a horseback riding club. This view shows a fox hunt meeting at Roswell Manor, the home of George Inness Jr.

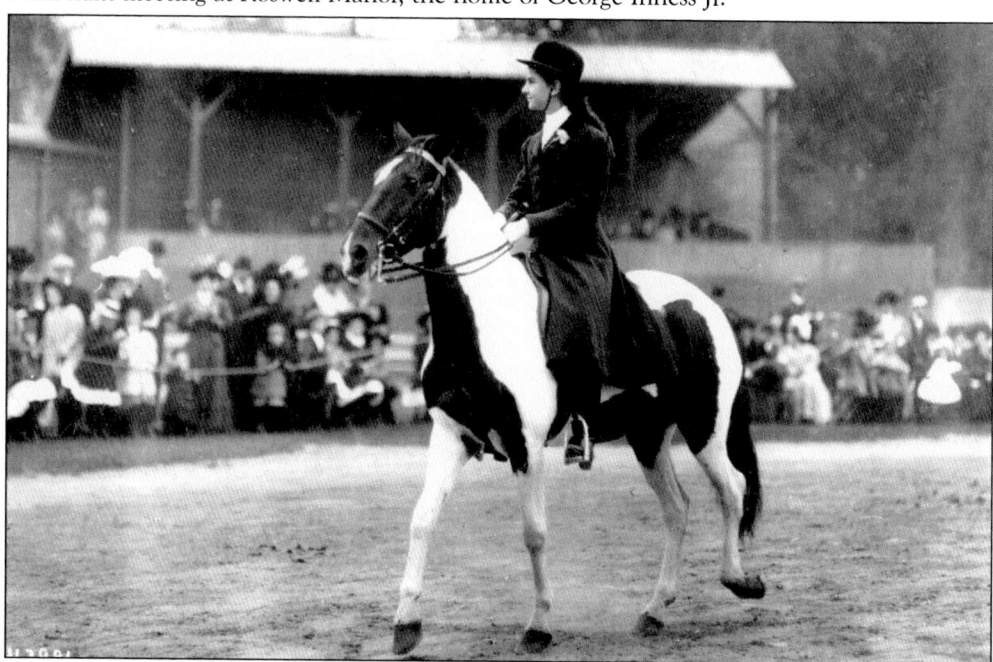

THE MONTCLAIR HORSE SHOW, OCTOBER 10, 1908. The first annual Montclair Horse Show was sponsored by the Montclair Riding, Driving, and Automobile Club at the Montclair Athletic Club on September 29, 1906. It was held annually until World War I. Revived in 1926 by the Montclair Federation of War Veterans as a benefit, it became incorporated in 1927. Scamp and Mrs. E.A. Sparks are shown here winning the Class V prize.

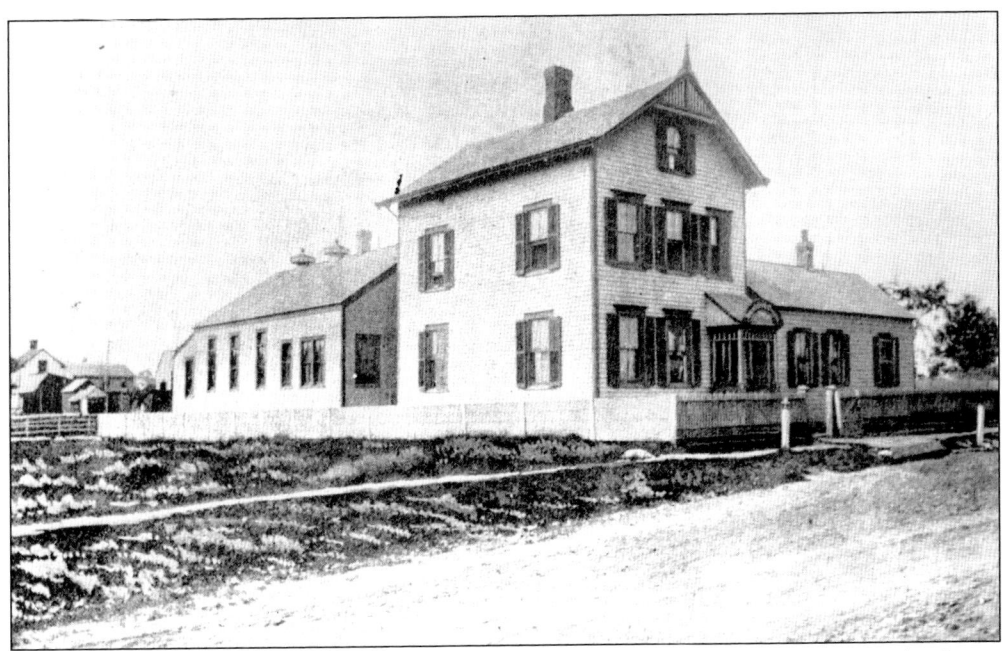

MOUNTAINSIDE HOSPITAL. Founded in 1890, this house on Highland Avenue in the future Glen Ridge served as the first 10-bed hospital in 1891. In 1892–1893, a new 34-bed hospital was erected. In 1904, a new surgical building, powerhouse, and laundry were built. In 1906, William Evans, then owner of Roswell Manor, gave land for the hospital and his house as the nurse's home. The central part of the current Mountainside Hospital was erected in 1915.

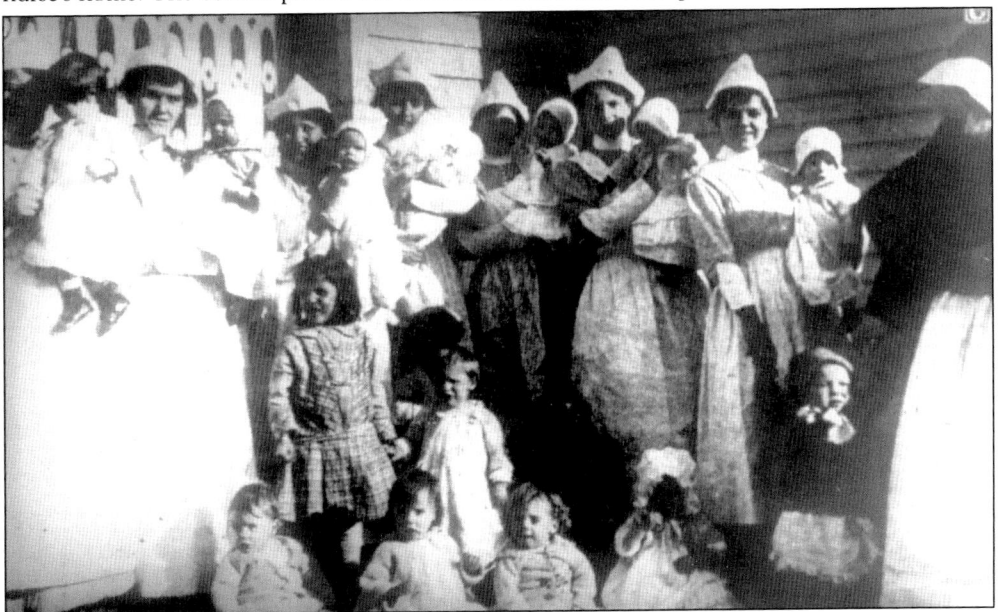

ST. VINCENT'S NURSERY AND BABIES HOSPITAL. A hospital was founded in August 1899 by the Sisters of Charity of St. Elizabeth to care for sick and abandoned infants and children. The first baby wards were in the old Immaculate Conception Church and a house on Elm Street. In 1926, the hospital cared for both women and children and, by 1930, became a general hospital called St. Vincent's. It closed in 1965.

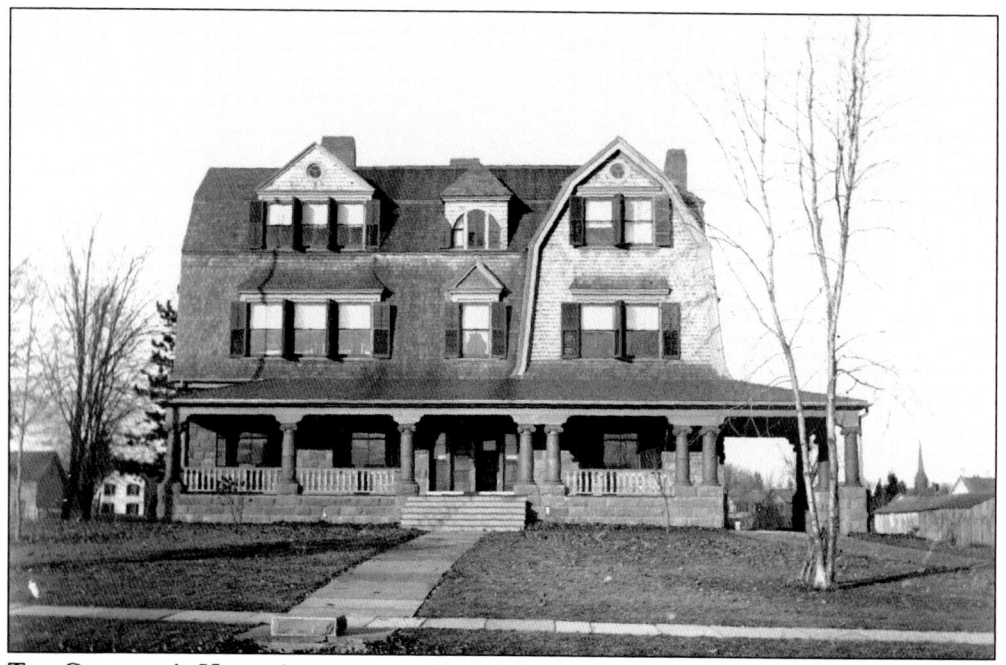

THE CHILDREN'S HOME ASSOCIATION. Founded in 1881 by Rev. Amory Bradford, Elizabeth Habberton, and Sarah Churchill of the First Congregational Church, the Children's Home rented a home on Plymouth Street and cared for 24 children. In 1886, the association bought the home shown here on Gates Avenue. The organization merged with the Child Welfare Committee to become the Children's Home and Welfare Society in 1931.

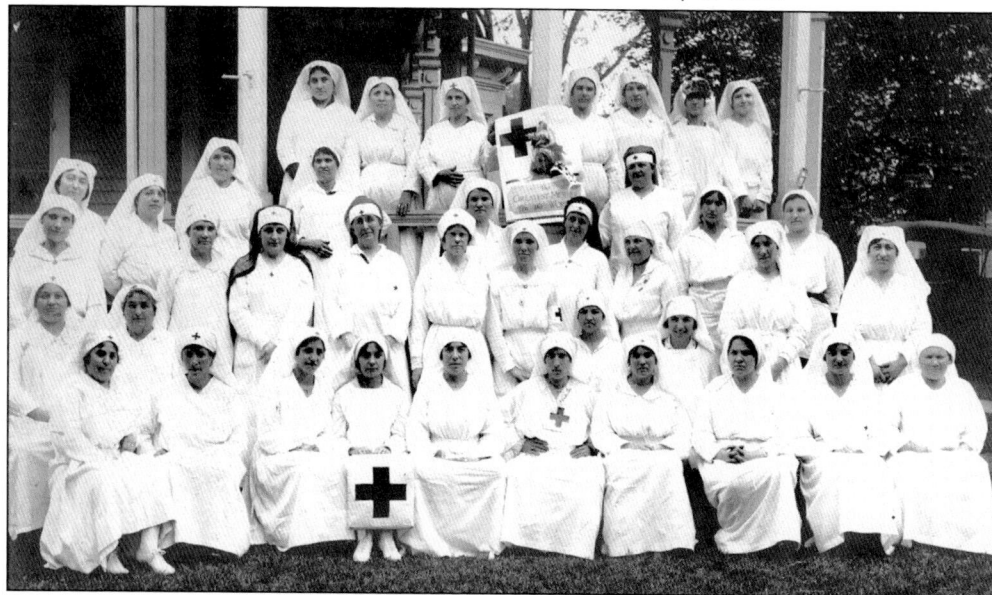

THE AMERICAN RED CROSS, C. 1917. The Montclair Chapter of the American Red Cross was established in February 1917. It supported the national Red Cross wartime activities and opened an office in the Madison Building. In 1922, the Red Cross established the first public health nursing service in Montclair. Since 1942, the Red Cross has been headquartered in a house at 63 Park Street.

Ten
MONTCLAIR VIEWS

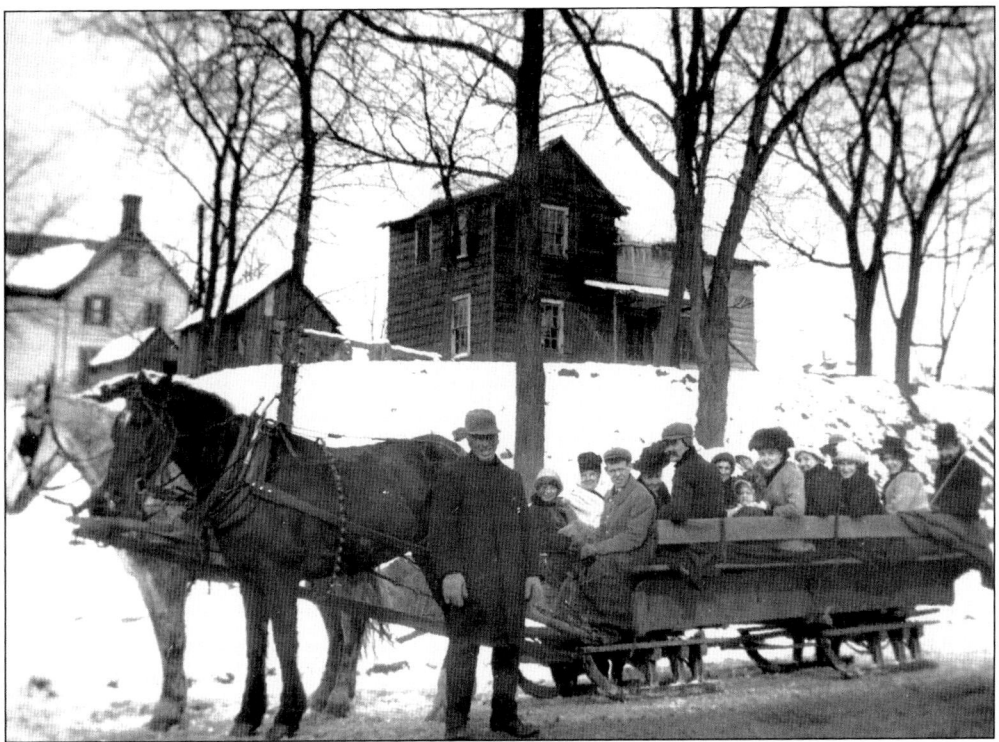

A SLEIGH RIDE. Edward Harrison is the driver for this multigenerational outing. Julius Wheeler wrote of taking a young lady on an all-night sleigh ride after promises to her mother. A sleigh was Dr. Sam Watkins's preferred method of making New Year's Day social visits. Sleigh travel was facilitated by dragging heavy boards over the roads to compact the snow.

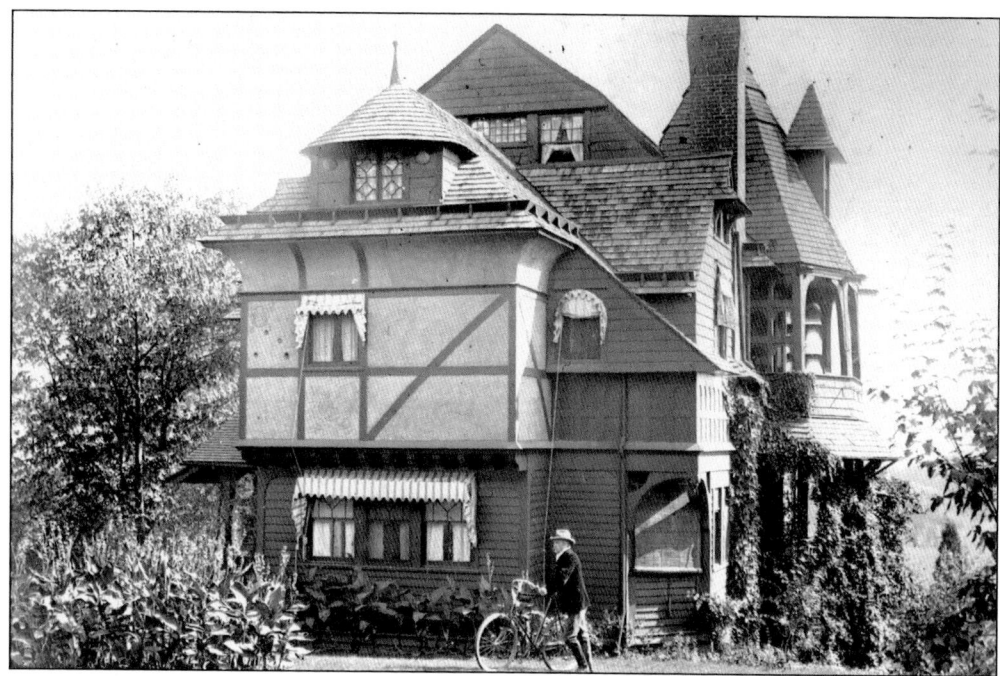

THE CEDARS. The home of illustrator Harry Fenn is reported to have been moved down the hill from Upper Mountain Avenue to become 208 North Mountain Avenue once the latter street was completed. Active in Union Congregational Church, Fenn made a sketch from memory of the parish church in his native England to guide architects for the church that stands on Cooper Avenue. The tall cedars in front of his home were removed in recent years.

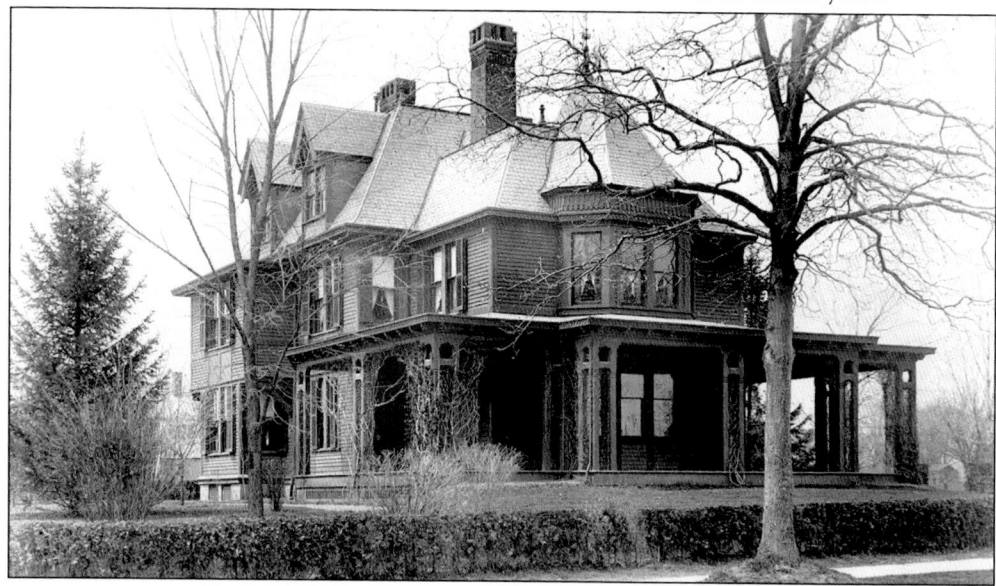

THE LIVERMORE HOUSE. Built in 1875, this home was designed by Charles F. McKim. Ship broker John Livermore was described by Edwin Goodell as "an energetic, public spirited and forceful citizen." Instrumental in starting a fire department, he served on the first Montclair Board of Education and championed the Children's Home. He opposed the trolleys. His home at 83 Union Street has been converted to condominiums.

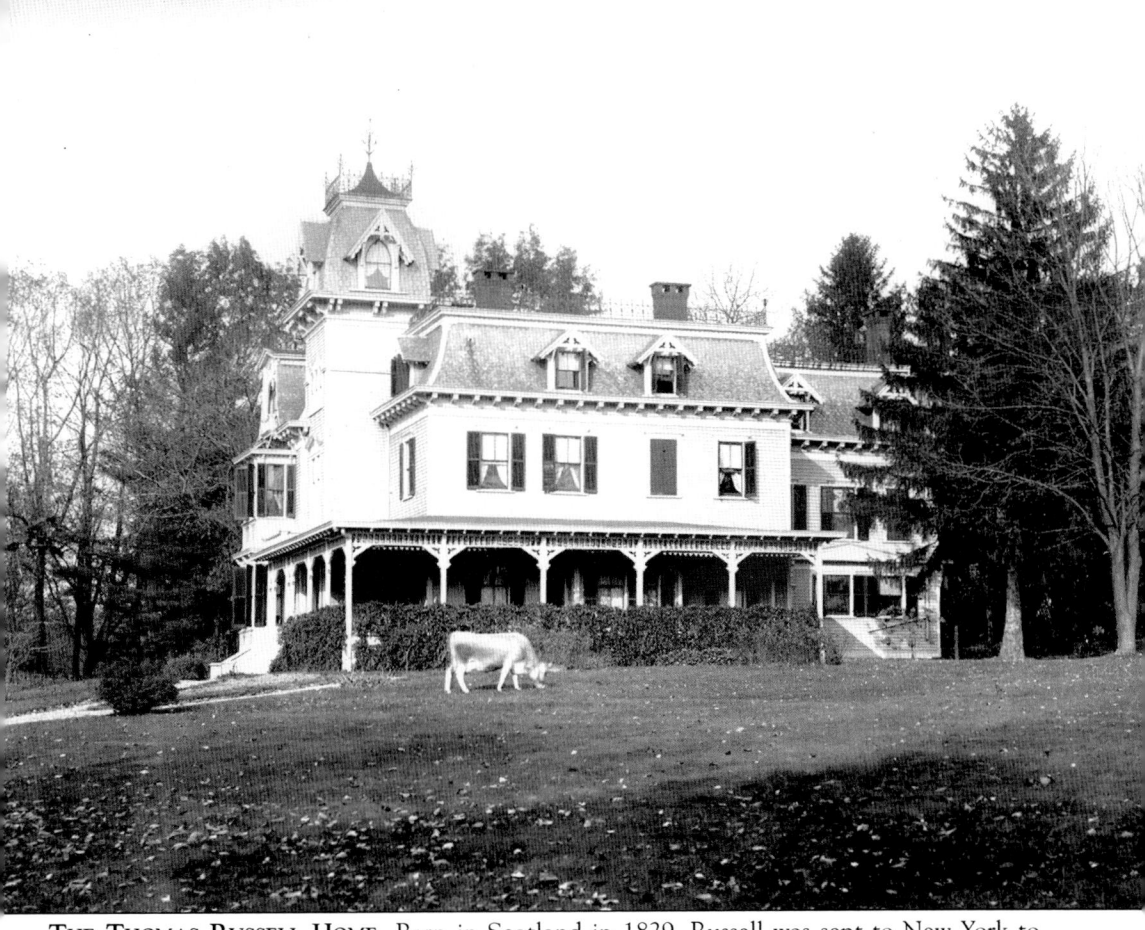

THE THOMAS RUSSELL HOME. Born in Scotland in 1829, Russell was sent to New York to manage the business of Mile-End Spool Cotton. After visiting Montclair, he acquired the former home of Samuel Wilde and remodeled it to the form shown here. The cow is a reminder of quieter ways of maintaining a lawn.

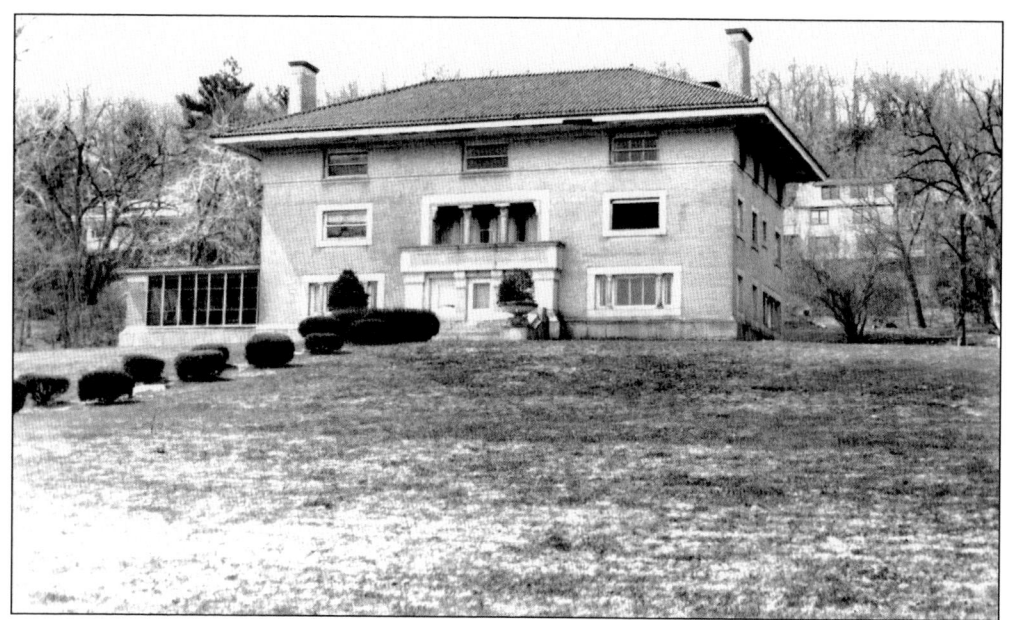

THE GATES MANSION. Frederick T. Gates, a Baptist minister who managed John D. Rockefeller Sr.'s philanthropies, built this home on South Mountain Avenue in 1902–1904. Raymond B. Fosdick, who succeeded Gates as head of the Rockefeller Foundation, described Gates as having "fire and drive and a mind that galloped to wide horizons." George Maher of Chicago was the architect. (Photograph by Sutters, Siravo, Santucci; courtesy the Junior League.)

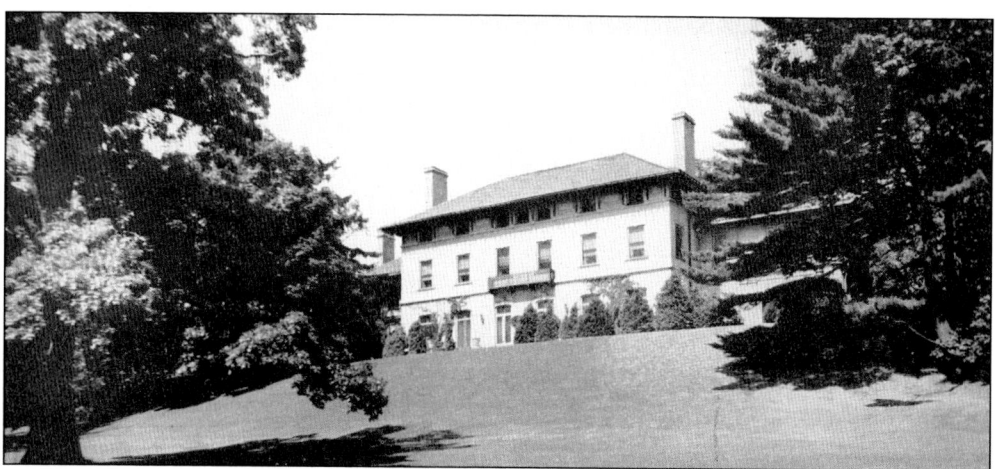

THE VINCENT MULFORD HOME. Resembling the Gates Mansion, the home of Vincent Mulford stood at 130 South Mountain Avenue. Mulford moved to Montclair in 1886 and attended Montclair High School. In 1924, he became co-owner of the *Montclair Times*. The first president of the local Red Cross, he owned a hotel in Palm Beach, where he died in 1960. Later the property was divided. Mulford Lane was cut through, and a new house came to stand between Mulford's home and South Mountain Avenue.

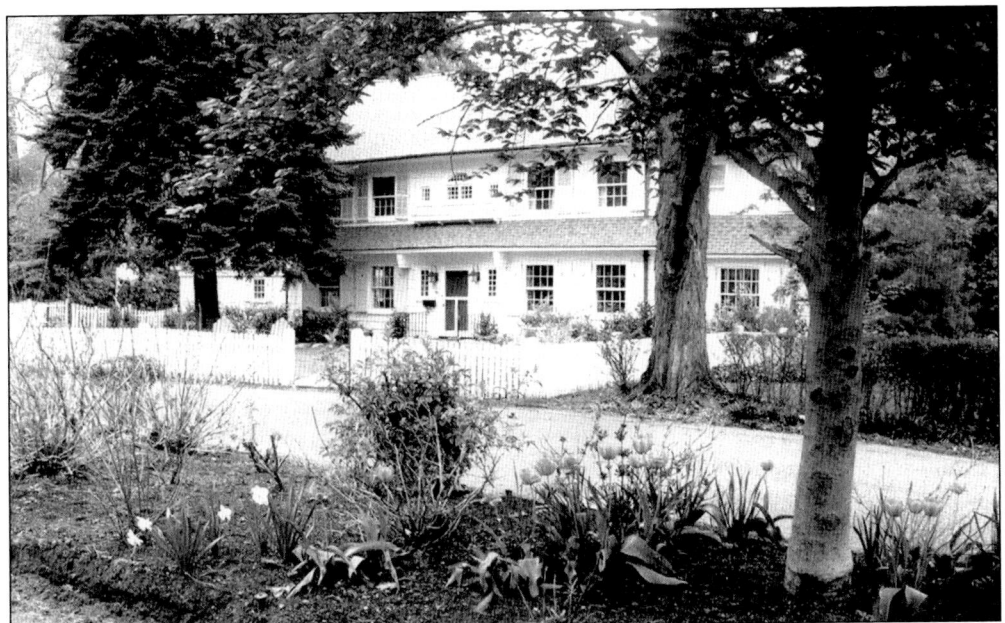

ERWIN PARK. With Toney's Brook running through and its century-old homes and giant trees, Erwin Park retains the graceful ambiance of the old Montclair. Named for Jared Erwin Harrison, the area was developed from his farm.

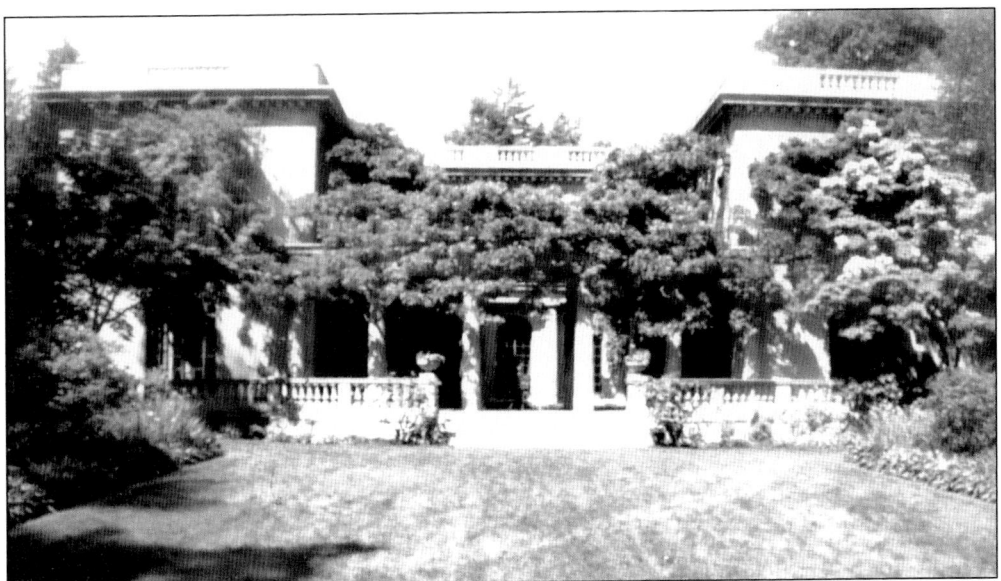

THE VAN VLECK ESTATE. In 1916, Joseph Van Vleck Jr. designed the home at 21 Van Vleck Street for his brother, William Van Vleck. In 1939, the property passed to Howard Van Vleck, who was chiefly responsible for developing the gardens on the nearly six-acre site. Howard Van Vleck died in 1992, and in 1993, the Montclair Foundation acquired the estate from his heirs. The gardens are open to the public from May 1 to October 31. The house is shown from the rear.

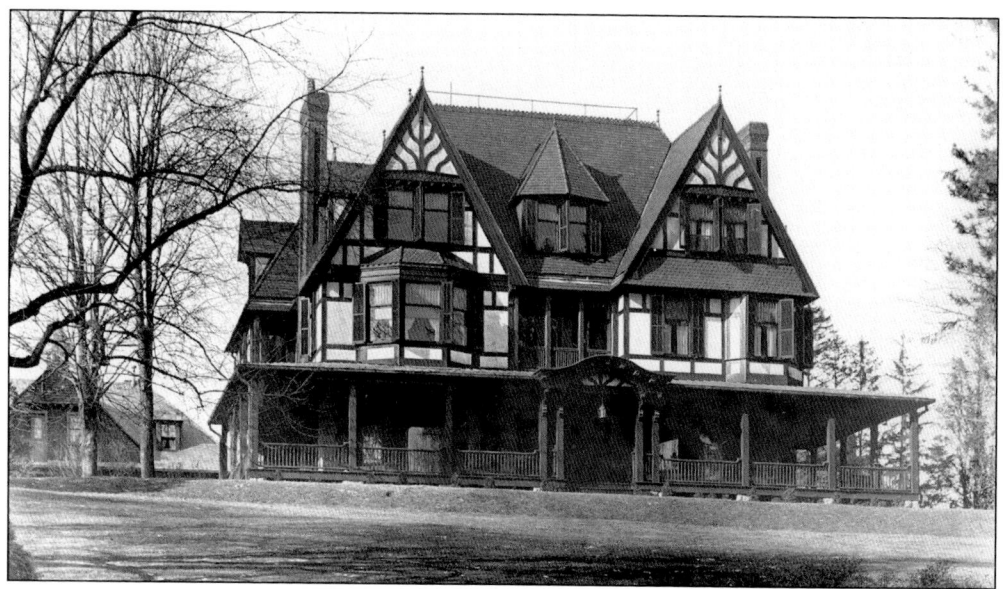

EVERGREENS. This home on North Mountain Avenue was built in 1896 for Charles S. Shultz, whose parents came from Germany and Bohemia. The architect was his friend Michel LeBrun of the firm Napoleon LeBrun and Sons, who designed the Metropolitan Life Insurance Tower in New York. The house was bequeathed to the Montclair Historical Society by Shultz's grand-daughter, Marian. Its interior contains many of the original furnishings and artifacts reflecting Charles Shultz's varied interests.

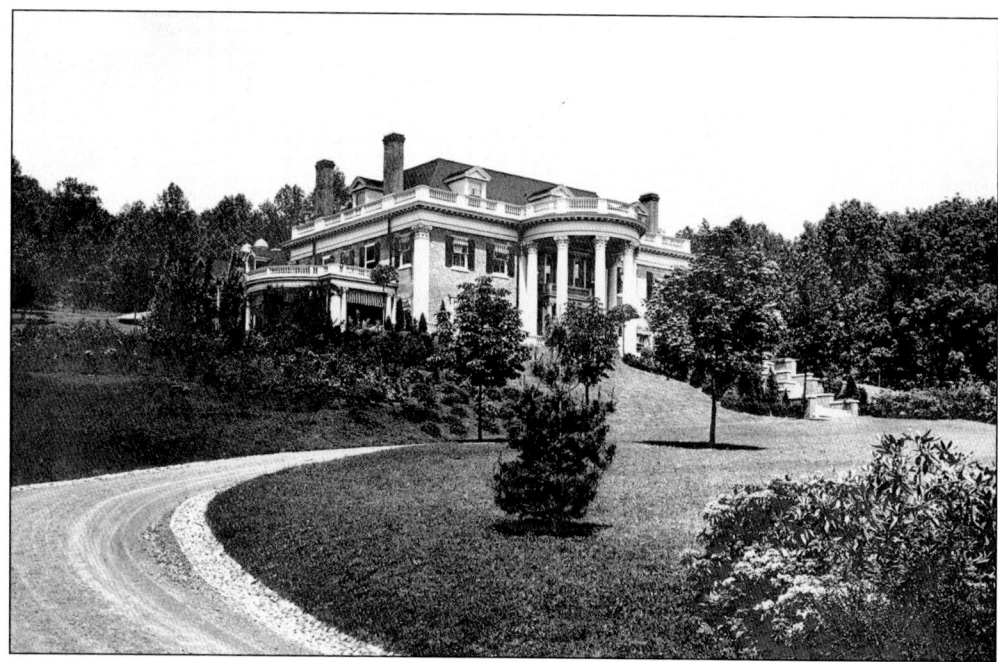

THE HENDERSON GREENE RESIDENCE. Representative of the elegant homes built on the upper side of Mountain Avenue (now, South Mountain), this one was designed by the firm of Joseph Van Vleck and located at No. 208. After serving for a time as the Southwest School, it was destroyed by fire in 1957.

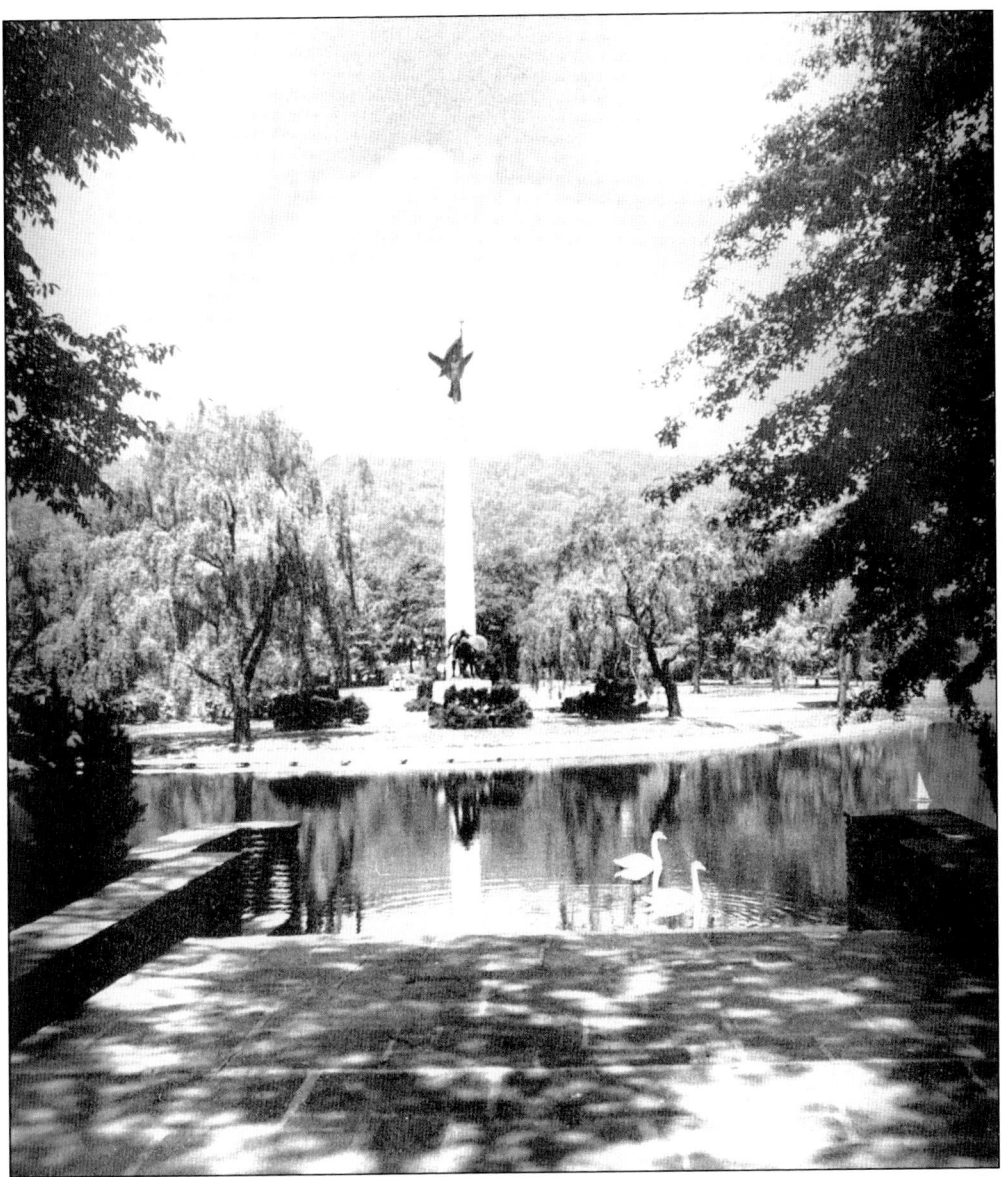

EDGEMONT MEMORIAL PARK. Farmed by the Egberts and Harrisons, this tract served briefly as the nine-hole course of the Montclair Golf Club. In 1906, it became a public park and, on November 11, 1925, home to a memorial to those from Montclair who gave their lives in World War I. Some 100,000 people were said to have witnessed the unveiling ceremony, and 5,000 men marched from Lackawanna Station accompanied by the West Point Band. The swans were a fixture for many years. (Courtesy the *Montclair Times*.)

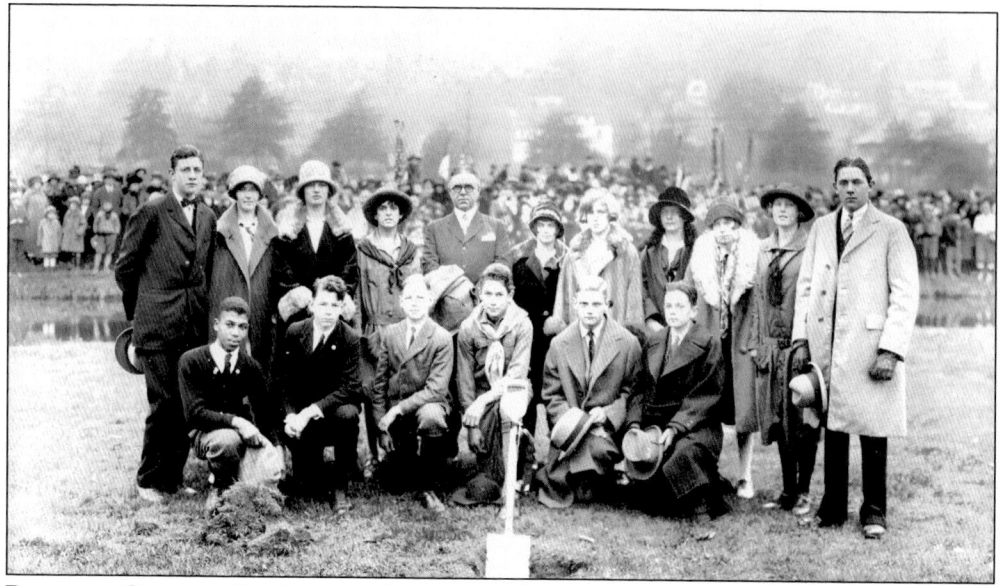

BREAKING GROUND. On Armistice Day 1924, a child from every school in Montclair removed a spadeful of earth at the future site of the World War I memorial in Edgemont Park. On Veterans Day 1992, tablets at the base of the monument bearing the names of those from Montclair who lost their lives in later wars were dedicated.

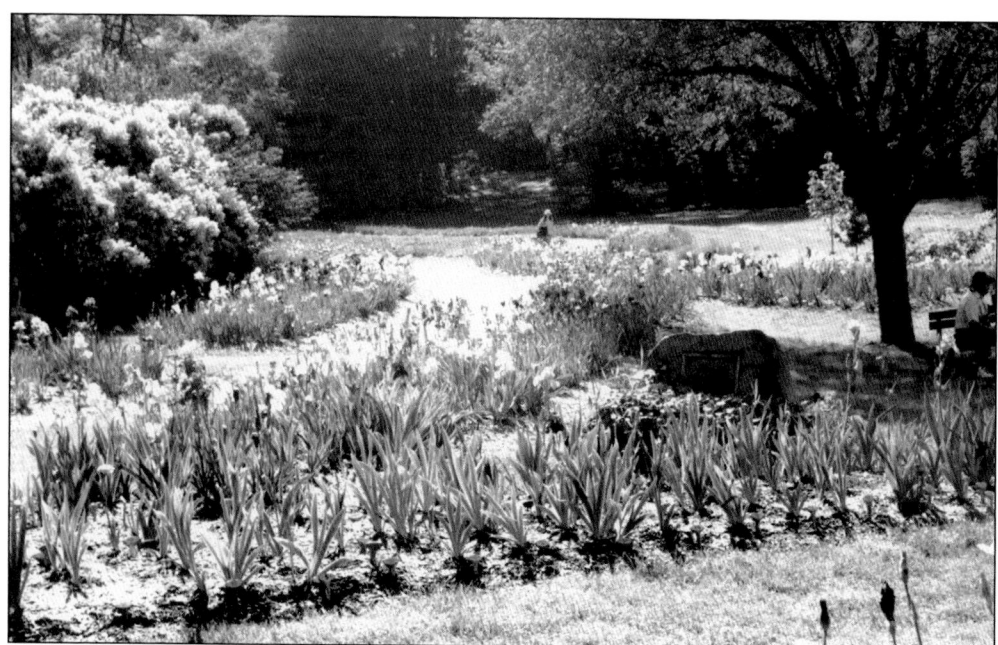

THE PRESBY IRIS GARDENS. In 1918, Frederick and Barbara Walther purchased a large house with a mansard roof at 474 Upper Mountain Avenue and soon persuaded the town to acquire land to the north and create there Mountainside Park. In 1927, iris gardens were planted in the park as a memorial to Frank Presby, one of the founders of the American Iris Society. Barbara Walther headed the first Citizens Committee named to care for the gardens.

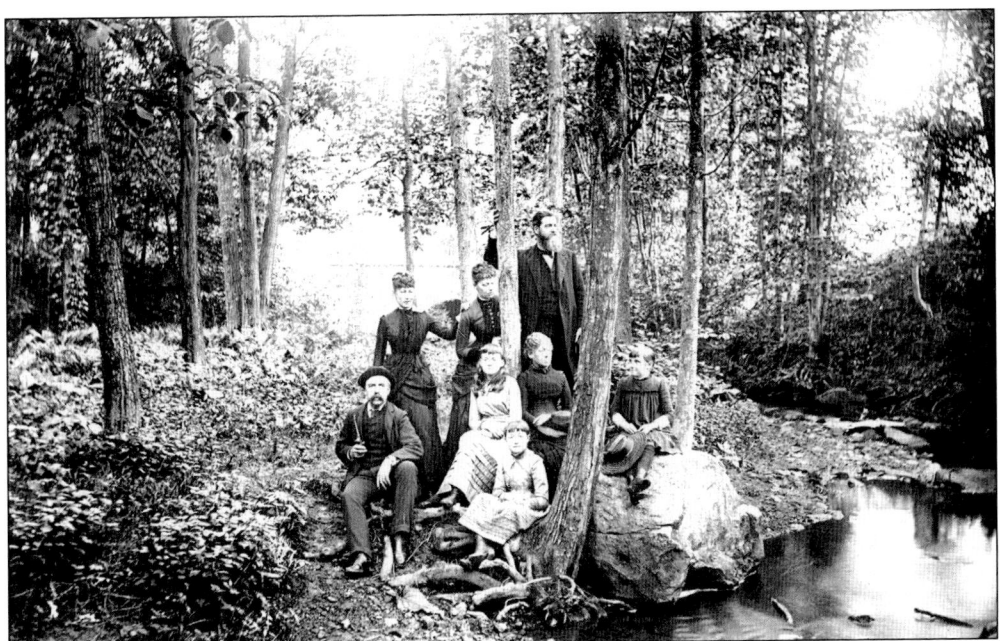

A FAMILY GATHERING. The bearded J.H. Ogilvie stands at the shore of Toney's Brook in what later became Rand Park. Mrs. Ogilvie sits below him, and to his left stand Ogilvie daughters, Mrs. Barker and Mrs. Atkins, who lived nearby at 137 Park Street, the future site of George Inness School. Other family members are seated on the ground. In 1882, when the Ogilvie house on South Mountain Avenue nearly burned down, J.H. Ogilvie campaigned for a fire department.

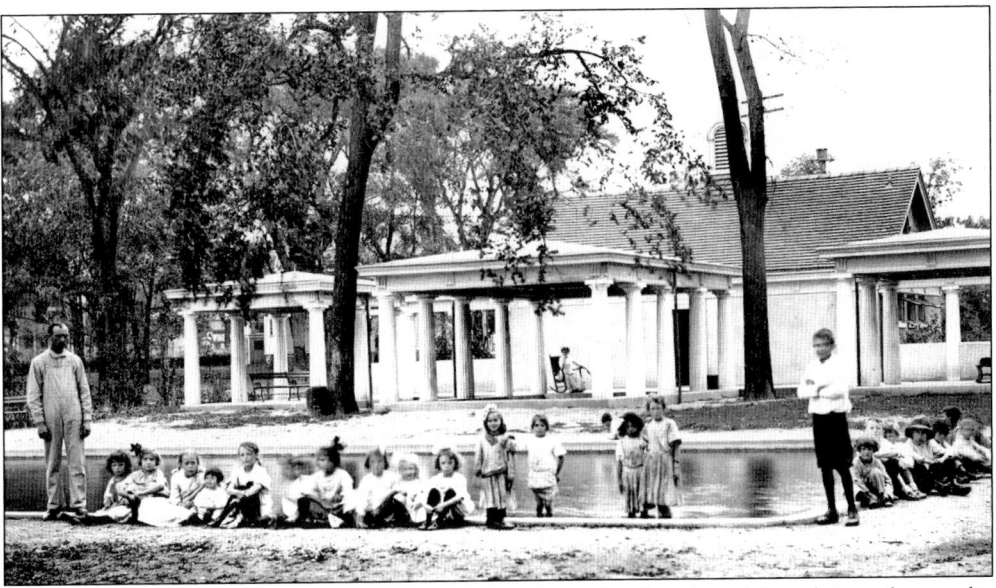

GLENFIELD PARK. Of the five Essex County parks to be found in Montclair, only two lie entirely within Montclair's borders. One is Glenfield, located south of Bloomfield Avenue along the Glen Ridge border. Consisting of 19 acres, the park has been host to a variety of recreational programs. The dress of the woman in the pavilion suggests the photograph may date as far back as the 1920s.

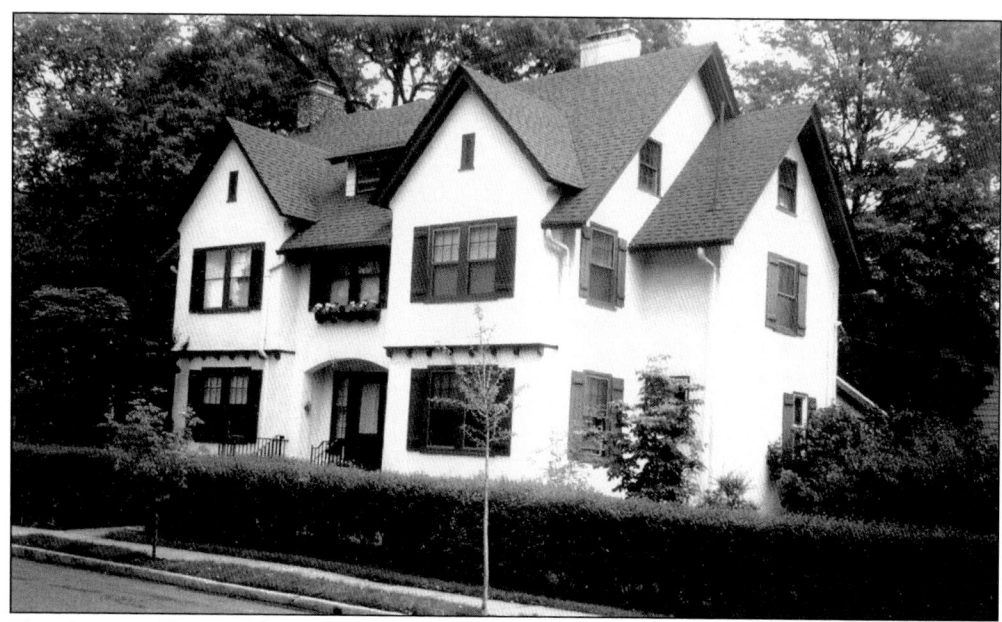

THE ALDRIN HOME. Edwin "Buzz" Aldrin Jr. went high as a pole-vaulter on Montclair High School's track team. He went far higher when he stepped onto the moon during the first moon landing on July 20, 1969. On September 6 of that year, he returned to his hometown for Buzz Aldrin Day. A stone provided by the Montclair Rotary Club marks "the original home of . . . Montclair's Man on the Moon."

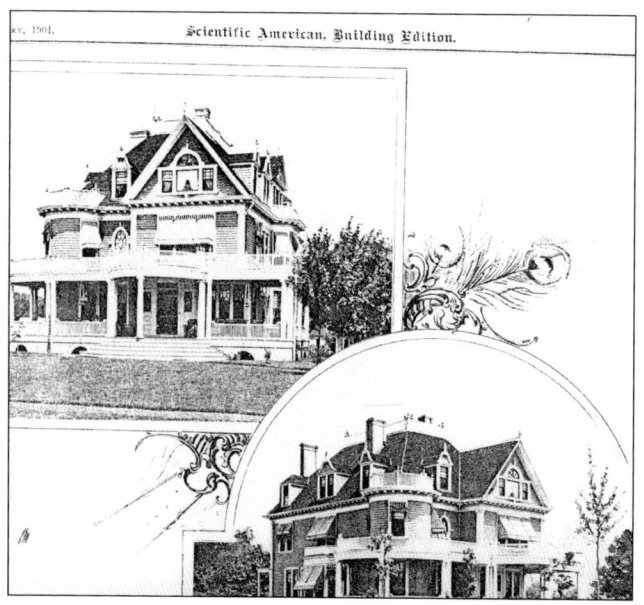

ARCHITECTURAL FEATURE. Over the years, several Montclair homes were featured in the building edition of *Scientific American*. This one in the February 1901 issue was built for Charles S. Phillips, who later became Montclair's mayor. The house stood on Cooper Avenue across from Union Congregational Church, where the Charles Phillips Memorial Window may be seen.

MONTCLAIR'S "SKYSCRAPER." Haddon Hall was built at 57 Union Street in 1908. Its apartments were elegantly appointed, and some offered spectacular views of the New York City skyline. Many residents were concerned that such high-rise apartment buildings would radically alter the character of the town. Reading between the lines, that concern appears in the plan John Nolen prepared for the Montclair Art Commission in 1909 and in the first report of the Montclair Planning Board in 1931.

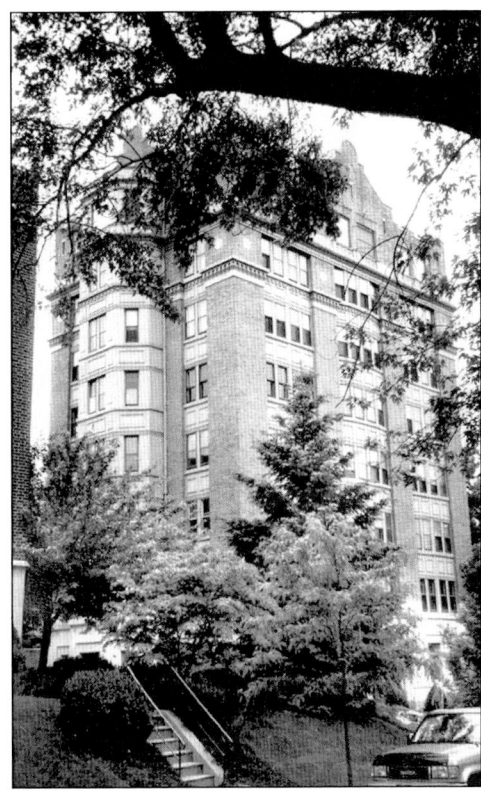

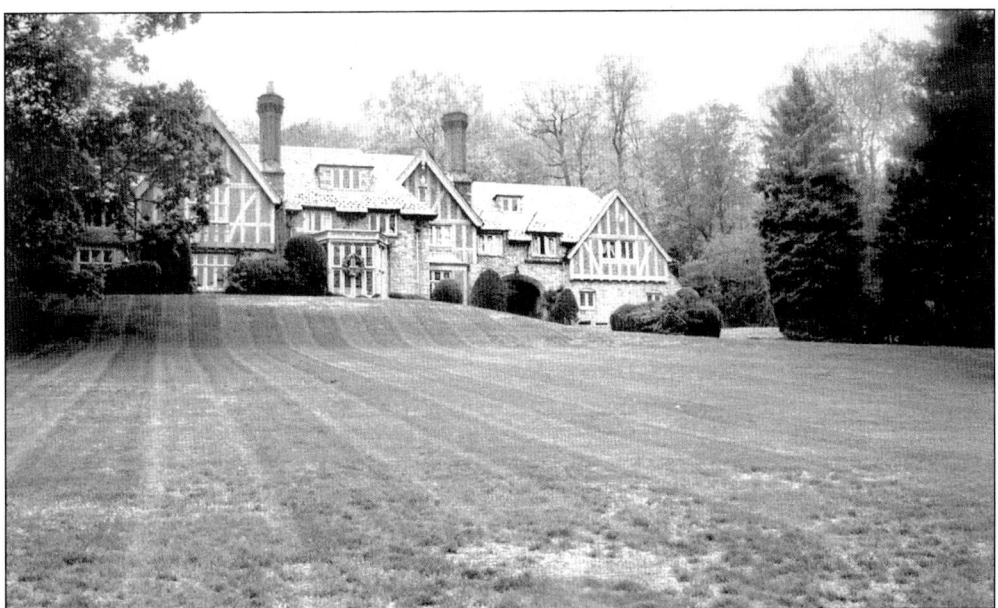

COBBLE COURT. By the 1930s, Upper Mountain Avenue could boast two miles of splendid houses. One was built in 1930 for Julius Forstmann, head of the Forstmann Woolen Company, a firm that had remained in the same family for seven generations. Two years later, a home was built next-door for Forstmann's son Curtiss, president of the company. The architects were H. Stevenson and Eastman Studs, who envisioned an English manor house.

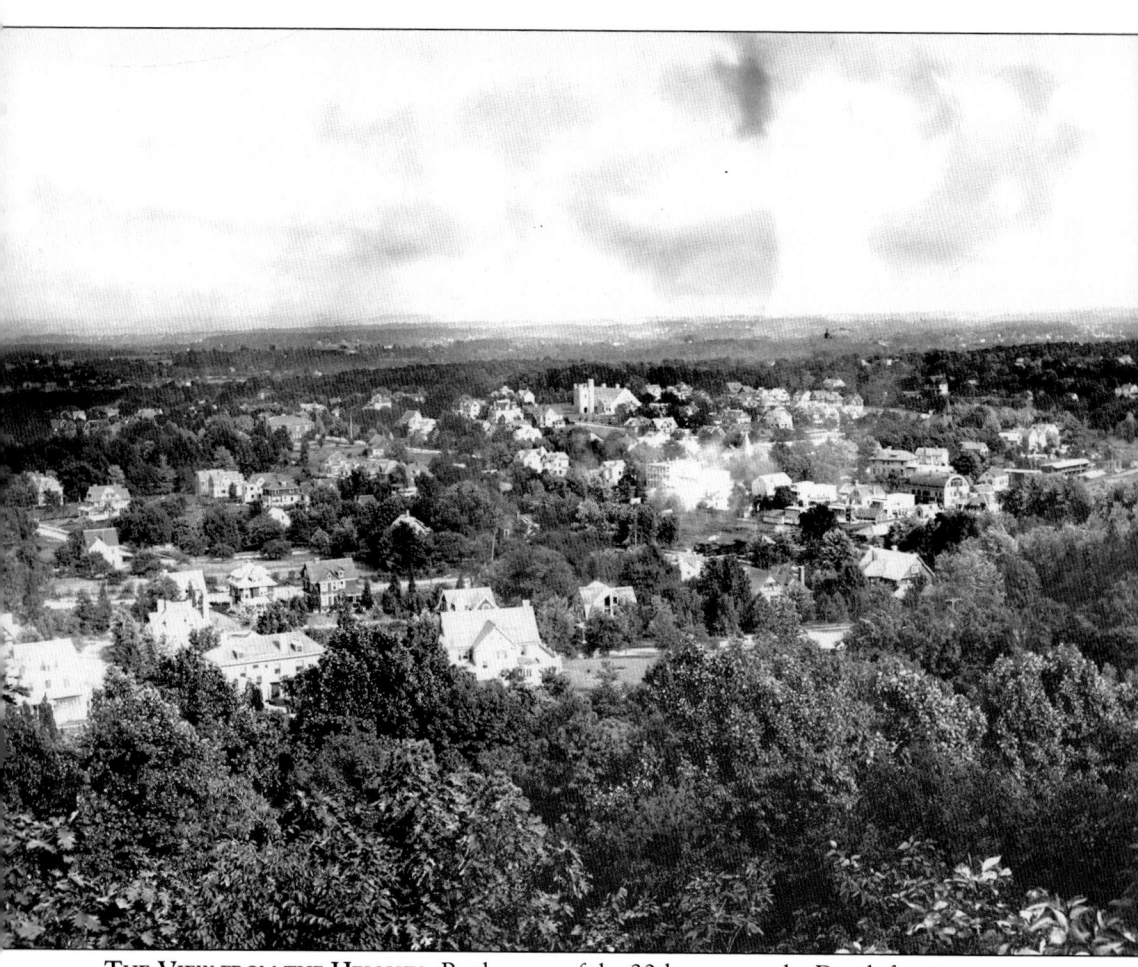

THE VIEW FROM THE HEIGHTS. By the turn of the 20th century, the Dutch farming community of Speertown had become Upper Montclair. A careful search will identify the recently built Union Congregational Church, Mount Hebron School, St. James Episcopal Church (still with a steeple), the Trunk Building (named for its shape), and the roof of the railroad station. Climb up to Mills Reservation a century later and look out. Some old landmarks will be gone. New buildings will have appeared. However, homes still predominate. As Harry Trippett, town clerk, said long ago, Montclair "is essentially a home town."